"For I am persuaded that neither death, nor life, nor angels, nor principalities, nor powers, nor things present, nor things to come, nor height, nor depth, nor any other creature, shall be able to separate us from the love of God, which is in Christ Jesus our Lord."

Romans 8.38-39

...NOTHING CAN SEPARATE US...

...NOTHING CAN SEPARATE US...

CONNIE JACKSON

GREEN KEY BOOKS
Holiday, Florida

NOTHING CAN SEPARATE US
Connie Jackson
Published by Green Key Books

©2002 by Connie Jackson. All Rights Reserved.
International Standard Book Number: 0-9705996-3-3

Cover Art: Michael Molinet

For information:
GREEN KEY BOOKS
2514 ALOHA PLACE
HOLIDAY, FLORIDA 34691

Library of Congress Cataloging-in-Publication Data available upon request.

Printed in the United States of America

Writing *Nothing Can Separate Us* and talking about it have built a bridge of understanding between my three children and me. I dedicate this book to Miriam, Rick, and Cathy for their courageous spirits and their honest contributions to the story.

ACKNOWLEDGEMENTS

For several years, the challenge of writing my children's story had rumbled in the back of my mind. I would read my journals, look at photos, and wonder where to begin. "You can do it, Mom!" Rick, Mim, and Cathy encouraged me.

I am grateful to them for support as I took the plunge and began to write. Each had memories of their siblings, which they allowed me to weave into the story. I thank them, too, for their taped interviews that became "Life After Loss."

Steve Castor, the children's father, graciously offered his memoirs of Karen, Jon, and David. His words gave insight into a dad's love under the duress of Batten disease.

A "thank you" goes to my pastor, Jeff McDowell, whose affirming notes after reading parts of the manuscript spurred me on. His prayers helped bring healing to my spirit.

Shirley Chapman faithfully typed, edited, and provided computer disks of the completed book. She deciphered my ragged handwritten manuscript and returned it in excellent order. Shirl was my cheerleader. "Keep going, Connie," she assured me, "It's a good book!"

The editors and staff at Green Key Books were delightful to work with as we fine-tuned the final copy. Their patience, guidance, and belief in the story inspired me to keep plugging. I'm grateful to them for working through the myriad details that made *Nothing Can Separate Us* possible.

Above all, I thank God for His unfolding grace throughout the children's lives and in helping me to capture their essence.

Connie Jackson
May 2002

...Nothing can Separate us...

This world is not conclusion;
a sequel stands beyond,
invisible as music,
yet positive as sound.

– Emily Dickenson

But in all these things we overwhelmingly conquer through Him who loved us. For I am convinced that neither death, nor life, nor angels, nor principalities, nor things present, nor things to come, nor powers, nor height, nor depth, nor any other created thing, shall be able to separate us from the love of God, which is in Christ Jesus our Lord."

PART I

KAREN

ONE
SECURITY THREATENED

In 1963, a cold March wind rattled the windowpanes of my small gray bungalow on Ridge Road in Webster, New York. I wrapped my housecoat around me, stepping over the boots, scarves, and mittens piled at the bottom of the hall stairs.

Only a few minutes before, Steve had issued an ultimatum. "If you don't hurry up, we'll be late to Sunday School. Come on, kids!" Following their dad, jackets unzipped, two little boys and their eight-year-old sister, Miriam, had tramped down the cellar stairs. I breathed a sigh of relief as I heard the station wagon pull out of the garage.

A cup of coffee and the Sunday comics—I needed an oasis after the flurry of finding a lost shoe, a missing Bible, and Ricky's frayed blanky. Settling into the old settee with the wooden arms, I leaned back and surveyed my little home. The living room sofa and two matching chairs were upholstered in black flowered twill—hand-me-downs from my parents. In the dining room, a cherry hutch was a comforting reminder of my childhood. A brick fireplace with a gas log was flanked by two built-in bookcases. I noticed that Rick and Jon, inseparable three and four-year old brothers, had parked their matchbox cars in rows on the bottom shelf.

I sipped my steaming coffee and chuckled, remembering how only yesterday two sturdy little bodies were standing on chairs pulled up to the kitchen sink. The boys were half-naked and sported crewcut heads, blond and chestnut, capped with suds. Piles of iridescent bubbles flew as they tossed them high into the air. The dish detergent bottle was empty. "Hey, you two! What are you up to?" I yelled.

"Me have good idea," Jon grinned, piling mounds of suds on his brother.

"Yeah, fun!" Ricky agreed.

Miriam's pert smile, in a photo on the end table, brought to mind my next-to-the-oldest daughter. What a joy she was! Her real live baby was her eleven-month-old sister, Cathy. Miriam would dash in from the school bus, calling, "Where's my baby sister?" Fresh from her afternoon nap, bouncing up and down gleefully in her jumpseat, Cathy held her arms out. It was an after-school ritual—the two laughing and rolling on a big blanket, tossing stuffed animals helter-skelter.

Cathy, with her curly blond hair, ready smile, and sparkling blue eyes delighted all of us. A surprise after four other children, it hadn't taken me long to fall in love with her. Harder for Miriam was spending time with her older sister Karen, who often retreated into her own world "Mom, she doesn't even want to play school anymore," she complained. "I don't know what we can do together."

Ah, Karen. Hazel eyes, a smattering of freckles on her up-turned nose. At ten, she was the oldest child. Those beautiful eyes were blind now. Over four years, a mysterious web of scar tissue on the macula had gradually taken her vision. Learning was difficult for her, especially arithmetic. A resident at New York State School for the Blind in Batavia, she enjoyed her weekends at home.

This Sunday morning her face had been flushed. "You're coming down with something," I fretted. "You'd better stay home from church with Mom." When I tucked her into our big double bed, Karen had snuggled under the quilt, contented.

Baby Cathy was taking her morning nap; Karen, too, must have fallen asleep. Peace settled over me in the unaccustomed quiet. Suddenly, I heard a choked cry, "Mom, Mom, come quick!" I ran up the stairs to my bedroom.

Karen's shaking hand pointed upward. "I see, I see a star going 'round and 'round," her voice trailed off. I watched in horror as her back arched and her body convulsed, arms and legs jerking. What was happening to my daughter?

I grabbed a spoon, remembering the danger of swallowing the tongue. I pressed it into her mouth. Not good! Her face was blue from lack of oxygen. I had never seen a seizure like this. "Oh, God, she's going to die!" I cried helplessly. "Breathe, Karen, breathe!"

Slowly, the spasms decreased. In great gulps, Karen gasped for air, making sounds that frightened me. Where was that trickle of blood coming from? Had she bitten her tongue?

I called the pediatrician. No answer. "Sunday, and of course, nobody's available," I muttered. Frantically, I dialed other numbers, and finally, a doctor's wife answered. "My daughter, she's had a seizure, a bad one. She's very pale and won't respond. She's in a deep sleep," I stammered.

"Get her to an emergency room as soon as possible," returned the terse voice.

With trembling fingers, I dialed the church. Steve asked, alarmed, "What's happened?" I explained the situation incoherently. "Calm down, Connie. I'll be right home."

A friend made lunch and cared for the rest of the children while Steve and I bundled up Karen. She was awake now, looking surprisingly alert. "Where are we going?" she asked her dad.

"To Rochester General Hospital," he explained. "The doctor's going to give you a check up."

"What's the matter with me?"

Tears came to my eyes. I was still trembling from the shock of the seizure. "You've had a problem, honey, and medicine might help you." I tried to keep the fear out of my voice.

The young intern took Karen's vital signs and shone a light into her eyes. He stepped back, rubbing his chin thoughtfully. "I think the seizure has something to do with her blindness," he ventured. "Get her right in to see her pediatrician. In the meantime, I'll write you a prescription for phenobarbital from the hospital pharmacy."

Monday, Karen woke up, eager to go back to School for the Blind. "I'm okay, Mom," she insisted, "I don't want to go to the doctor's again." I sighed, relieved. She was her old spunky self. Nevertheless, we insisted that she be examined.

Dr. McGuire, our children's cherub-faced pediatrician with kind brown eyes, was perplexed after he had thoroughly examined Karen. "Perhaps your daughter was spiking a fever. That can trigger a seizure," he suggested. "But to play it safe, I'm calling Dr. Smith at Strong Memorial. He's Chief of Children's Neurology at the hospital."

My mother's heart pounced on Dr. McGuire's explanation. Yes, Karen had been flushed and warm. The fever—that's what did it, I concluded.

Back home, I sipped a comforting cup of raspberry tea in the living room. Karen slept on the sofa as the afternoon sun touched her hair, a nimbus of gold. A little smile played on her lips. Long lashes against her freckled cheeks spoke to me of unplumbed beauty and innocence. Her face, cupped in her hand, was peaceful and free of the strain of squinting to see.

"Oh, Lord Jesus," I breathed a prayer, "take care of my little Karen." Tears welled up. "She's so vulnerable. Protect her from evil. Let her know how much You love her." Karen stirred in her sleep. The sun was covered by a cloud, shadowing her face.

The jarring ring of the kitchen phone broke my reverie. "Hello, Mrs. Castor? This is Doctor Smith, head of Children's Neurology here at Strong." The voice sounded cold and efficient. My stomach knotted.

"Did Dr. McGuire talk to you about our daughter, Karen?" I asked.

"Yes, he did. He informed me of her blindness and about the recent seizure." There was a pause as he cleared his throat. "Mrs. Castor?"

"Yes, I'm listening."

"I've cared for one other child with a similar syndrome." Another pause. My chest felt tight.

"The combination of severe visual problems and a grand mal seizure most likely indicate a rare genetic disease, juvenile lipidosis," he continued.

"What, what does that mean?" I spoke in a hoarse whisper. "What will happen to Karen?"

"This is a storage disease caused by a malfunctioning enzyme. Instead of being broken down and absorbed into the bloodstream, a lipid residue gradually clogs the cells. The dead cells first appear as lesions in the macula of the eye. Later, the brain is affected." I was trembling, sensing the seriousness of the disease.

"What will happen to my daughter?" There was an edge of anger as I repeated the question.

The impersonal voice continued. "As nerve cells in the brain are destroyed, there will be personality changes. She will be severely brain-impaired to the point of being unable to do anything for herself."

I was barely able to voice the final question. "Will this disease kill Karen?"

"She may have from five to ten years before her death." I slumped into a kitchen chair. "Of course, I want to have her admitted to Strong to do the necessary blood work," Dr. Smith concluded. "There is an accurate test for juvenile lipidosis."

I hung up the phone, numb with shock. My dear little Karen! How could this be? Where had this insidious disorder come from? I wished I'd asked the doctor more questions. "Who do you think you are, Dr. Smith?" I spat out the words in fury, "What right do you have to destroy my world with your cold, impersonal diagnosis? Over the phone? Why, you haven't even seen my daughter!"

Then came the tears. My nose was running, and my eyes were streaming when Miriam came home from school. "Mom, what's the matter?" She wore her compassionate heart in the concern on her face.

"It's Karen," I replied, wiping my eyes. "She has to go into the hospital for tests."

"Is it something bad?" her voice quavered.

"I don't know, honey, 'til after the tests. Let's not say anything that might upset Karen and the boys."

Wise beyond her years, Miriam nodded. "I'll help with dinner, Mom."

That evening, the steamy kitchen was fragrant with bubbling spaghetti sauce. It was a cozy place. The freshly painted old white cupboards looked straight out of *Good Housekeeping* with wrought iron strap hinges. Newly hung wallpaper brightened the walls with geraniums and daisies. Just last week, I'd proudly put up my home stitched cottage curtains, trimmed in red rickrack. The bungalow, our first house, we'd purchased in 1956 for $14,000. Home for our growing family, it was our center of love and security.

Steve had just come in from an after-school session with the debate club. He was chairman of the English department at Webster High. "Time for supper, Jon and Rick," he called, tossing his youngest son into the air. He carried both boys, squirming, one under each arm, into the kitchen. I helped a drowsy Karen to her chair and then tied a bib under Cathy's chin. Her first birthday was only three weeks away.

As I dished out spaghetti and tossed salad, Steve stood beside me, an arm around my shoulders. "What's the matter, Connie?" he asked quietly. "You've been crying."

"We'll talk after supper," I answered abruptly.

"Mom's worried about Karen," Miriam whispered to her dad.

"Any news?" His face clouded with worry.

"We'll talk after the children are in bed," I answered.

We held hands around the table. "Stop pinching me," Jon accused Ricky.

"I'm not holding Cathy's hand—boogers on it," Ricky changed the subject.

"Sh-h-h, time for grace," Miriam reminded us. Together, we prayed our family blessing:

"Be present at our table, Lord.

Be here and everywhere adored.

These mercies bless, and grant that we

May feast in fellowship with Thee. Amen."

It was all so normal, so reassuringly routine: Rick, the clown, stuffing a meatball into his mouth with his fingers; Jon, helping himself to his third slice of Italian bread; Miriam helping Cathy grab a piece of slippery spaghetti; Karen laughing when her dad teased her. I was the silent one. There was nothing familiar about my thoughts. An alien, sinister disease threatened one of my own. The foundation of this dear familiar world was crumbling. I poked my food and couldn't manage a bite.

Later that evening after the children's baths, Jon and Rick listened to a well-worn record, *The Three Billy Goat Gruffs*. Jon was the troll under the sofa, his voice deep and menacing. "Who's that walking on my bridge?"

Rick replied in a squeaky falsetto, tramping on the cushions, "It's me, little billy goat gruff." The troll grabbed a leg, trying to capture a howling billy goat.

Miriam rocked Cathy, who was sucking her thumb and rubbing the worn ribbon of her blanky under her nose.

I sat next to Karen, who was reading aloud from her Braille Bible storybook. Her slender right hand fingered the raised dots as she slowly pronounced the words. It was the story of the beggar, blind Bartimaeus, pleading with Jesus to have mercy on him.

"What is it you want me to do for you?" Jesus asked the man.

"Lord, that I might receive my sight."

Jesus heard him. "'Go,' said Jesus, 'your faith has healed you.' Immediately he received his sight and followed Jesus along the road." (Mark 10.52)

Karen made no connection between herself and the blind man. I did. As she turned to me, her eyes were focused upward, straining to catch a glimpse of my face in peripheral vision. Feeling like a beggar, I prayed, *Lord, have mercy on my daughter. Stop this terrible disease. Heal Karen, I ask You.*

After the children were all tucked in for the night, Steve and I were alone in the living room. The silence was palpable. I wished for the buffer of children's voices that had held at bay my surging emotions. "Tell me what you found out about Karen," Steve demanded. I recounted the conversation with Dr. Smith.

"I'm so afraid, Steve. This disease will strip her of everything," I cried.

Steve was angry. "How can Dr. Smith be so sure, before even seeing Karen?" he stormed. "At least he could wait for a diagnosis until after the test results are back!" Now, Steve's eyes were brimming over with tears. We held each other in mutual misery. Our anger masked fears for Karen's future and for us, her mother and father. Only God knew the depth of our pain.

TWO
JOURNEY TO EVANSTON

Certain naïve assumptions under gird young couples as they begin married life. One of mine was that our children would automatically be healthy and bright. I captured, in the beginning of a poem I wrote about Karen, that magic moment, so full of hope, when a mother holds her newborn for the first time:

> She slept
>> eyes tightly closed as infants do,
>
> One small hand
>> lightly held in mine,
>>
>> fragile fingers
>>
>> miraculously fine,
>
> Her face solemn in sleep for one so new.
>
> I counted toes,
>> I checked our first newborn
>>
>> and wondered that this one
>>
>> tucked warmly in my arm,
>
> (We two locked in meditative calm)
>
> Was mine to love and nurture,
>> mine to form.

Karen was delightfully normal, her early years chronicled in telling photos. There's a picture of a one-year-old Karen grinning mischievously, one goopy hand in her mouth, the other in a jar of baby cream. Another, at age two, catches her in an Easter bonnet and fluffy-skirted, violet-flowered dress, ready for church. At three, the family Christmas shot featured Karen smiling down at her baby sister Miriam. The next year, the two were sitting at a little table, having tea with their dolls.

In her fifth year, encouraged by her dad, Karen developed a surprising talent. Fascinated by every kind of car, she knew each make by name. As traffic whizzed by on Ridge Road, her sharp eyes noted details, and she would call out gleefully, "It's a Ford!" or "That's a Chevy!" The snub-nosed Volkswagen was her favorite: "Oh, boy, it's a Beetle!" In an area that eluded me, my daughter was an expert. She beamed proudly while her dad praised her, "Hey, girl, you really know your cars!"

The last thing I looked for was a visual problem in my oldest. In the spring of 1959, six-year-old Karen enjoyed a visit from my parents, Grammy and Grampy Jackson. Darkness had descended as our little family sat around a campfire in the back yard and roasted marshmallows. Grammy took her granddaughter's hand and walked with her to a nearby field. It was one of those clear May nights with just a sliver of a moon; peepers sang in the marsh, and the scent of lilacs made the air sweet. "Look, Karen, aren't the stars beautiful?" my mother asked. The little girl opened her eyes wide, gazing up into the night sky. "Do you see the evening star?" her grandmother queried, pointing west. "It's like a bright diamond, right up there."

Straining, turning her face from side to side, Karen mumbled, "I don't see anything but darkness." She hung her head, almost in shame. Her grammy pulled her close, holding her.

Later, Mother took me aside. "Connie, there's something the matter with that child's eyes." My mother's face mirrored my anxiety. "You'd better have her checked."

Denial was my response as I rationalized, "There's nothing wrong with our car expert." Come to think of it, though, it had been a long time since she called out the names of passing automobiles.

It wasn't long afterward that the school nurse called me at home. "Mrs. Castor, I've had a request from your daughter's kindergarten teacher to check her vision. Karen can't even see the big E. She may need special glasses."

Her father took her to the optometrist. "Whatever the problem is with her eyes can't be helped by glasses," he concluded.

Next step was the ophthalmologist who carefully examined the back of Karen's eyes with his slit-lamp and indirect light. His face expressed concern as he explained his findings. "The examination has revealed scars on the macula in both eyes."

"What could be the cause?" Steve inquired.

"Probably her mother had rubella or perhaps another prenatal disease that caused abnormalities like this," the doctor replied.

"Will she lose the rest of her sight?"

"Probably not. I predict the scars will remain stationary. Karen will need specialized help in school," he explained. "At 20/200 she is legally blind."

I was shocked when Steve brought back the result of the eye exam. "Good vision! I've just taken it for granted," I thought. "Now I have a handicapped child who will have the barrier of legal blindness to overcome." My heart was heavy. Pride was involved here; my assumption of mothering perfectly healthy children was smashed. God had let me down. In a back room of my emotional being, I buried the hurt and disappointment. Gargantuan tasks lay ahead for the burgeoning family, so there was no time for self-pity.

Around the end of May, Steve announced that he had been honored to be a recipient of a John Haye Fellowship to Northwestern University, all expenses paid. At this point, I was seven months pregnant with child number four, only fifteen months between babies. I sighed. It was great news for Steve who would be pursuing a graduate degree in English, but I dreaded the ordeal of renting our home and packing up the children. It would mean loading up a trailer and heading west in August for Evanston, Illinois.

Norman Richard Castor II arrived, all 9 lbs. 3 oz. of him, on July 19, 1959. I held this surprise of a baby boy who peered up at me from slitty eyes and had the distinction of a cry an octave lower than any other infant in the nursery. "I hope you're a tough one, Ricky," I whispered to him. Two weeks off to recuperate gave me time to enjoy this naturally happy little guy.

I look back amazed at my energy level as we left behind a scrubbed house clean to the bone and rented to three teachers. The station wagon was loaded with suitcases tied on top and pulled a trailer bristling with highchair and cribs. Leaning back against the front seat as we began the long trip to Evanston, I knew my morale was at a low ebb. I felt utterly depleted.

Twelve hours later, we arrived at Oak Park, Illinois. My sister, Marti, and her husband, Bill, welcomed the bedraggled Castor clan to their apartment for an overnight stay. After supper, I found a quiet nook to nurse baby Ricky. With every pull on my breast, pain throbbed in my temples. Trying to hide my aching head behind forced civility was impossible. Finally, I yanked the cover over my eyes early that night, exhausted.

The next morning, Marti led the way to our new home for the next nine months. Steve followed close behind. She described the challenge of furnishing a large apartment for us, from sheets, pots, and pans to beds and sofa. I had been so wrapped up in my own world of moving the Castor tribe that I had neglected to appreciate Marti's backbreaking care for us. Now we were in Evanston, turning up a shaded street lined with arching elms. A tall gray Victorian house on Library Place was our final stop.

After Marti unlocked the brown paneled front door, we crowded into the entry. I walked up the creaking stairway. Stale cigarette smoke and Italian cooking had seeped into the yellowed walls and brown woodwork. My stomach turned.

Steve opened the door at the top of the stairs. A small room off the hall would be the nursery for baby Rick and toddler Jon. Soon, the cribs were hauled out of the trailer, trundled up to the second story, and set up for the boys.

A backroom behind the kitchen had two windows that filled the girls' quarters with sunlight. Karen and Miriam bounced on their twin beds with red striped spreads.

In the front of the apartment was the master bedroom. Gray light filtered through lace curtains. The double bed was clean and inviting with its white chenille spread. A limed oak dresser and aging office desk completed the furnishing. The air was tinged with a combination of pine air freshener and tobacco.

At the end of the long living room, two narrow crusted windows on either side of the shallow marble coal-burning fireplace cast a dull light. The ceiling was ten feet high. A new charcoal gray sofa with aqua flowers and two easy chairs on plush maroon carpeting made the room decidedly livable. How had Marti and Bill managed to bring in all the furniture? "Bill's family store and crew have been a big help," Marti explained.

The bathroom was huge, big enough for a hamper and changing table. It began to dawn on me that Marti had scoured the countryside to make ready this apartment for her scruffy northern relatives. "How can I thank you?" I grabbed Marti's hands and looked into her tired eyes. I could see she was exhausted from preparations.

"Just let Bill and me borrow little Jon for a weekend," she requested. She picked up her nephew who nestled against her shoulder. "Now, wait until you see the dining room, Connie!" Marti led the way into a room where double windows flooded the place with sunlight. In it were a bleached blond table and chairs with a matching sideboard on a beige rug. "I'll make this my headquarters," I announced.

We moved toward the kitchen with its one dusty window. "I'm sorry about the stove," Marti apologized. "It was the best I could do." I creaked open the oven door. Cockroaches dropped to the floor and scampered under the cracked linoleum. "Guess I didn't get 'em all!" Marti exclaimed, chagrined. I'd never seen a roach before. It was the beginning of a long battle against the dreaded insects that I never quite won.

The Castor crew settled into a new routine in Evanston. Mornings, Steve was off to studies at Northwestern. Intellectually stimulating classes, tennis matches, and the camaraderie of other John Haye fellows for him were a refreshing change for him from the routine of high school teaching.

Karen was attending sight-saving classes, struggling to learn to read. Her dad devised flash cards with pictures and a phonic approach to words that helped her understand the process of reading. Four-year-old Miriam listened and watched, learning along with her sister. The two sisters set up school in their backroom with chalkboard and student dolls, reinforcing their evening lessons.

There was a strange dichotomy in my life during that year in Evanston. Gatherings with John Haye families found me outwardly the party girl, laughing, effervescent, and friendly. Sitting high up in the bleachers for football games in the gigantic Northwestern stadium sent my morale soaring. The marching band, the pompom waving cheerleaders, the roar of the crowd—what a contrast to Webster High!

However, daytimes, caring for a baby, a toddler, and a four-year-old, I experienced deep-seated feelings and questions that frightened me. I felt emotionally abandoned by Steve as he became more involved with academic life. There were evening hours alone with the children that left me isolated from adult companionship. Where did I fit in with his whirlwind life? I longed for a sign of affection. The naïve assumption with which I had entered married life was that our relationship would grow in strength and caring. This tenet eroded as the distance grew between us.

Karen's diminishing eyesight was a constant reminder of the unreality of my healthy children belief. I knew the scars on her retina were not stationary but growing in size. Why had God allowed her eyes to be damaged?

My childhood faith as a Baptist minister's daughter was being sorely tested. I remembered as an eight-year-old the first time I discovered that Jesus loved me. The highlight of summer was our month-long vacation in an old farmhouse on a coastal hamlet called Corea, Maine. For $25.00 rent (a sizeable chunk from Papa's $34.00 weekly salary), this weathered clapboard home became our August vacation paradise. The distinctive musty smell of oilcloth, wood smoke, and kerosene before Mama opened all the windows spoke to my childish heart of thirty-one days of bliss.

Climbing rocks, hearing the murmur of surf, pulling in flounder off the wharf with Papa, swimming with my brother Buddy in the cove—all against the backdrop of blue skies and sun diamonds sparkling on the ocean—what more could a child ask for?

But one particular night in August, I, an eight-year-old girl, lay on the lumpy mattress of my brass bed feeling acutely uncomfortable. It hadn't been a good day. I had snitched a couple of thin mints from the cupboard. When discovered, I had blamed Buddy. I was also thinking of the pennies I had taken from Mama's dresser drawer to buy PayDay bars. Then there was the time I had thrown a shoe at my brother, and it crashed through the window and fell to the ground. I realized that I was selfish and that I had sinned.

As I lay there crying, a picture of Pilgrim at the foot of the cross flickered on the screen of my mind. In the spring, my father had presented John Bunyan's *Pilgrim's Progress* during the Sunday night services in the Baptist church at Brewer, Maine. Vivid stereopticon slides depicted Pilgrim on his journey, carrying on his back a big burden of sin and guilt. Through the Slough of Despond, up the hill he struggled. Looking into the light, his face wreathed in joy, Pilgrim now re-named Christian, knelt at the foot of the cross, letting his burden roll down the hill.

"Dear Jesus," I prayed. "Please take the big lump of sin away from me. I ask you to forgive me. I want to be like Christian. I want you in my heart."

A presence of warmth and light surrounded my bed and held that little girl in unconditional love. Peace seeped into my troubled soul. "Jesus really loves me!" I exulted. "Thank you, Lord! I want to tell Mama and Papa!"

I jumped out of bed, charged down the narrow rickety steps, and burst into the living room. "I've been converted!" I announced. My parents looked at each other, smiling. They sat me between them on the horsehair sofa, each holding a hand. They listened intently as I told my story. We shared Scripture from the third chapter of John and prayed together. I sensed the joy Mama and Papa were feeling.

It wasn't long after that I, a child in a white robe, stood with my father in the baptistery of our church. Its ethereal background of misty blue hills and lilies linked me with Heaven. "I baptize you, Connie, my daughter, in the name of the Father, the Son, and the Holy Spirit." Those strong arms lowered me beneath the water and up again into the light.

THREE
PANIC ATTACK

For years, my simple childhood faith had served me well. Insulated by the protective love of my family, I lived a life with few struggles. Academics came naturally to me. I graduated from Hope High School in Providence, Rhode Island, as valedictorian in a class of five hundred. Later at Houghton College, there were signs of rebellion. I backed away from church and called on God mostly to help me through exams. Full of myself, I had relegated God to the role of celestial bellhop.

Now ten years later, with four children to care for, I felt inadequate as a mother and bereft of hope. Fear of again becoming pregnant plagued me. I made an appointment with a doctor when Ricky was five months old. After an examination, he offered an opinion. "Mrs. Castor, there's an indication of a somewhat enlarged uterus. But you're still nursing, so it's hard to tell."

Even a hint of another child sent my spirits plummeting. "I bet I'm pregnant again," I thought morosely. "That would explain the dizziness and queasy feelings."

When at last my period arrived, Steve and I celebrated in a quiet restaurant. I had expected the grayness of my days to lift, knowing number five was not en route. Instead, the tentacles of despair only tightened around my being. Nervously, I waited to broach the subject of how I was feeling. "Steve, I've really been down since we've been living in Evanston," I said hesitantly.

"I find that hard to believe, Connie," he responded. "Look at the way you enjoy socializing. What's bothering you?"

"When we go out, I put on a mask, the party girl, you know." I noticed his fingers drumming on the table; his eyes looked off into the distance. "You're not around much, and when I'm alone with the kids all day, I feel so isolated." I began to cry.

Steve reached out and patted my hand. "It's hard to adjust, but you'll be all right." He hadn't heard me.

"Well, I'm not all right. I'm really depressed!" The door was shut on personal communication between us.

Nights were difficult. I would awaken startled, breathing hard, my heart racing. In the early morning hours, around three, I would sit on the hamper in the bathroom, my teeth chattering and my entire body shaking. A panic attack! Why was I so afraid?

I was afraid of dying. I didn't know how to pray anymore. God seemed far away. He had let me down by giving me a daughter going blind and a dead marriage! I didn't deserve that! Yet life without connection to God was meaningless and frightening.

Church didn't help. The pastor preached a strongly Calvinistic message. All my dreary life was predestined. Where was the Jesus who had loved me as a child? I was a mess, so how could God care about me when I doubted His very nature? I gave up any attempts at communicating with Him. The Bible was an alien book to me.

One morning, I was tying Jon's little white high-topped shoes. Looping the shoelace into a bow, I had the strangest feeling of being one of thousands of mothers all over the world lacing shoes or buckling sandals for their toddlers. All of life was pinpointed to this one moment which had absolutely no meaning for me! I wanted to let out an existential scream!

Lynne, my neighbor, shared some of my feelings. She lived in the downstairs apartment with her professor husband, Jerry, and her toddler son, Tony. Occasionally, we talked over coffee as the children played with blocks and little cars. Her concern was for Jerry who was clinically depressed. "He's going through the manic stage now, staying up all night, writing his thesis," she revealed one morning. "I don't even exist in his thinking. What frightens me is when he plunges into a low. He's mentioned suicide before."

"Is Jerry seeing a counselor?" I asked.

"Yes, a psychiatrist who told him to call any time, day or night." I shivered as I caught a glimpse of his frenetic, empty world. It echoed the void in my own life. How far into the depths would depression take me?

One morning in February, I loaded wet laundry into a basket and started on my way to the basement to dry the clothes on lines. As I entered the dark stairway, I heard voices. "What's going on down here?" I called.

A burly police officer stopped me. "Better not come in," he warned. "We're taking out a body."

"A body! What happened?"

"A man hung himself, a young professor at the university."

It was Jerry. What was it like to find living so excruciatingly painful that killing oneself was the only alternative?

After the funeral, Lynne and I met upstairs at my dining room table for a final cup of coffee. She was reliving the night before her husband's death. "Jerry called his psychiatrist in a state of panic," she recounted. "I still can't believe the doctor's response. 'Take a sleeping pill and come see me at the office in the morning.'" Anger and grief darkened Lynne's tired brown eyes. "It was a cry for help that went unheeded!" I wept with my friend for her lost husband and the indifference that blocked a desperate plea.

The next day, I watched a rented moving van, driven by Lynne's brother, slowly move down Library Place with her and Tony following in their Plymouth. It was the last time I ever saw them. Never again did I go down to the basement to line-dry my laundry.

Jerry's death intensified my inner tumult. I felt alone, abandoned, not only by God but by my husband and the church. Who really cared about me anyway?

It was Marti, my sister, who helped me begin to see the good things in my life. Because depression had diminished my appetite, I, one who had continually struggled with weight, was now a size nine. One day, my sister dropped by with a box from Marshall Fields under her arm. "Surprise for you, Connie!" She hugged me. "Open it now!"

I eagerly unwrapped tissue paper and lifted out an exquisite blue summer dress, embroidered with flowers. "Marti, it's beautiful! I can't remember the last time I've had something pretty just for me!" I was moved to tears by her thoughtfulness.

"Try it on, Connie," Marti urged. I shed grubby shorts and slipped the dress on while Marti zipped up the back. It fit perfectly.

"You're looking great, kiddo!" she exclaimed. I twirled and preened, feeling cherished and feminine.

Two-year-old Jon's occasional weekend visits were bright spots in Marti and Bill's life. "He's the cutest little guy!" Marti raved. "When we go out to eat, he sits right up in the highchair, gobbling up everything on the tray. And that smile and dimples! People think he's ours." She and Bill showered him with gifts, a little grey suit and play outfits.

I appreciated the sweet funny nature of my toddler, especially when Marti joined the children and me for an afternoon on the shores of Lake Michigan. Jon chased the waves, squealing when the water tickled his toes. Ricky clapped his hands, occasionally escaping from his playpen to crawl off toward the lake. Karen and Miriam piled buckets of sand high into castles. Marti and I soaked in the warm sunshine, companionably chatting. I never told her about my struggle with depression. Splashing waves, the cry of gulls, the children's glee, and blanket picnics temporarily restored my spirit.

One spring morning, Jon gave us a scare. Steve had rigged a childproof catch on the other side of the gate in our fenced-in, scraggly back yard. Grass and dirt were Jon's domain where he could "brum-m-m" his trucks. Often Miriam and Karen joined their little brother, building an elaborate road system around weedy tufts.

On this clear sunny day, Jon contentedly played by himself. I hung out the wash and then climbed the stairs to tackle the breakfast dishes. Later, when I checked on Jon, he was gone, nowhere to be seen. Frantically, I looked up and down Library Place. Judy, my next door neighbor, joined me. No sign of my little son.

I tracked down Steve in the university library by phone; he came right home. "Those little legs of his couldn't have taken him too far," Steve tried to calm me.

"But what if he's out in the middle of Main Street?" my voice shook. Just then, striding down the shady sidewalk came a linebacker of a young man with Jon on his shoulders.

"Anybody belong to this little guy?" he boomed. Our son was grinning from ear-to-ear, crying, "Mama, Daddy," as we ran toward him. "I found him toddling along the sidewalk, just around the corner," the Northwestern graduate student explained. "He was calling for his mama."

To hold Jon's warm chubby self and to see the dimples as he smiled gave me a sense of gratitude and comfort. No more solo play times for our son who later showed us how he'd climbed up, using a truck for a footstool, and had unlocked the gate.

Ah, to be back in our Webster bungalow! The end of June found us dismantling the cribs, stuffing toys in boxes, and packing our suitcases. Before Marti and Bill arrived to repossess the furniture and return it to McCartney's store, Karen and Miriam took one last jump on their backroom beds. "We're going home! We're going home!" the girls chanted.

"Me too, me too!" Jon chimed in. How could I ever thank Marti and Bill for their steady support and generosity to their northern family? They waved goodbye after we shut the rear door. Steve turned the key, and we moved slowly down Library Place.

As the weathered Dodge station wagon, top-heavy with suitcases, chugged along Main Street in Evanston, I sensed a chapter had closed in my life. The despair that had haunted me in the apartment, I left behind in that old Victorian house. I pictured our home on Ridge Road in Webster awaiting us. To open windows to fresh air, to see the pear tree's silvered leaves tossing in the summer breeze—what joy to be in familiar territory again! But deep inside me, assuaged for the time being by the beauty of summer and the anticipation of homecoming, lay unanswered questions.

FOUR
A PLACE FOR KAREN

"First one to spot our house gets fifteen M&Ms," Steve challenged as the station wagon pulled onto Route 104 in Rochester. Baby Ricky in his car seat rocked and bellowed while Miriam and Jon elbowed each other to get a better view. Karen tilted her head, trying to see with her side vision. "Mom, everything is blurry," she cried.

I tried to comfort her. "Honey, pretty soon we'll be there, and you'll see your bunk bed. Remember how you love to climb the ladder to the top bunk?"

"I see it! There's our house!" Miriam yelled. In front of the porch, dahlias luxuriantly bloomed in bright yellow, red, orange, and pink. Our tenants had taken the tubers in for the winter and had replanted them. A patch of pansies bloomed in the back yard where the lawn was neatly mowed and the bushes clipped. "Bless those three teachers," I breathed a prayer of thanks. Sure enough, the pear tree's silvered leaves danced in the breeze, lifting limbs to welcome us.

Inside, the kitchen sink and stove were polished, the floor shining. Upstairs and downstairs were immaculately clean. My folks' old sofa and chairs and the cherry hutch reassured the child in me that I was safely home. We opened sparkling windows as light and fresh air flooded our bungalow on Ridge Road. "It's so good to be back!" I sighed as Steve and I hugged each other. A new beginning for us? For me? I longed for the wind and light to sweep away every remnant of darkness that had cobwebbed my spirit in Evanston.

Karen had climbed up the ladder to her bunk bed and was napping. The boys were brum-m-ming their cars in the living room. Miriam had found Karen's bike in the garage and was teaching herself to pedal down the driveway, and Steve and I began unpacking.

At last, I sat down on the sun porch with a glass of lemonade. (Yes, a frosty pitcher was awaiting us in the refrigerator.) Three red geraniums atop the bookshelves caught the afternoon sun. My heart overflowed with gratitude for the thoughtfulness of three women who had lived in our home and cared for it so lovingly. A big "WELCOME" sign in the kitchen and now these plants in full bloom spoke to me of kindness and hope.

What about school for Karen? She'd be in second grade, Miriam starting kindergarten. It would have to be mainstreaming for our oldest daughter with the Association for the Blind supplying a magnifier and large print books.

Before school opened, we met Mrs. Brooks, the second grade teacher. She expressed concern, "You know, I've never had a student like Karen with severe vision problems." I sensed a tinge of resentment in her voice. "Do you think the School for the Blind in Batavia might be a more appropriate place for her?"

"School for the Blind! Her sight's not that bad!" I bristled. "Let's give her a chance!" I wished sight-saving classes had been available.

Karen was miserably unhappy in elementary school. Mrs. Brooks, with a class of twenty-five students, didn't have extra time for the handicapped child. Bewildered, Karen tried to tag along after the other children, but she often lost her way. Large print books and the magnifier were inadequate for her failing vision. My heart ached when, after getting off the bus, she'd sit beside me on the sofa. "I don't have any friends," she cried. "Nobody likes me."

"I do, Karen," Miriam comforted her, "let's play dolls." How thankful I was for the friendship between the two sisters and for five-year-old Miriam's compassion!

Early spring, Steve and I visited the New York State School for the Blind in Batavia. As we approached the old brick building set back in stately aloofness from the street, I thought grimly, "Typical institution! I don't want to put Karen in a cold, regimented place like this!"

The principal met us in the front office. With graying hair, kind eyes, and a warm smile, he shook hands with us. Sensing my discomfort, Mr. Sanborn reassured me, "It's difficult to think of sending your daughter away from home, isn't it, Mrs. Castor?"

Tears filled my eyes. "She's only eight years old," I replied hesitantly. "How will Karen fit into a big old place like School for the Blind?"

"That's why I'm taking you to Knight Hall first," he countered. "I want you to meet Selma White, our head housemother."

Walking through the long halls of Severne Hall and noting the brown-stained woodwork, we were aware of the building's antiquity. Doors were open in classrooms, so we stopped for a moment to observe third grade. Braille writers clicked as the teacher gave a spelling quiz. We mentioned the smallness of the classes. "Lots of individual attention," Mr. Sanborn explained.

Knight Hall, tucked behind Severne Hall, was a one-story modern structure. Mrs. White met us at the main entrance with a warm welcome. We followed the housemother to cheerful quarters for primary school girls. "Here's where Karen would be staying," she explained. "She'd have a roommate, but you can see there's plenty of space for her belongings." Designs in primary colors brightened the halls and rooms. "Many of our students are partially sighted," Mrs. White continued.

Down the hall came a bevy of chattering little girls. "Classes are over for the day. I want to introduce you to our girls. Come meet Mr. and Mrs. Castor," the housemother invited them. "Their daughter, Karen, may be living here at Knight Hall soon."

Some of the older students used a white cane; others, who could partially see, held the hands of little ones. Now surrounded, we experienced what it was like to be a sighted minority. Hands reached out to touch us; faces with the sliver of sight remaining came close to see us. "What's your girl's name? How old is she? When is she coming?" Questions bombarded us. Curiosity quenched, the children were soon on their way to the playground.

Our next stop was the empty classroom for second and third grades. Mrs. Peruzzin showed us the Braille alphabet and Braille writer, the abacus for math, the fat Braille textbooks, and raised maps and globe. The classroom was rich in color and texture. Pictures and designs by the students decorated the ample bulletin board. Mrs. Peruzzin was encouraging as we raised our concerns about Karen. "I know it hurts to place your daughter in our care. But we do all we can to make learning fun and encourage each child to use their individual skills."

Returning to Knight Hall, we said goodbye to Mrs. White, the house-mother. "Would someone tuck Karen in at night and say prayers with her?" I asked tremulously.

"Oh, yes, Mrs. Blake is on nights. She loves the girls and respects their faith in the Lord," she comforted me. "Leave us a copy of Karen's bedtime prayer."

My fears subsided. On the way home, Steve and I agreed that the New York State School for the Blind would be the right place for our daughter. "We'll see her on weekends," we reminded each other.

Karen had a passion for lavender and purple. It was a deluge of gifts in her favorite color that stoked her excitement about her new school. We picked out a life-sized baby doll. I made her a long lavender dress, trimmed in lace. "O-o-oh, she's so beautiful!" Karen exclaimed. "Her name is Baby Mary! But, Mom, she needs a nighty and some diapers." I dug out from attic boxes some of Miriam's baby clothes. We packed a little suit-case for Baby Mary.

"What about me? Don't I get a present?" Miriam asked plaintively. A friend dropped by with a pigtailed doll for little sister. *She's going to miss Karen*, I thought, *especially with that empty bunk*.

When we left for Batavia a week later, the station wagon was full. Included in the load were a crib and stroller for Baby Mary. Karen was excited when we arrived at Knight Hall.

Mrs. White chuckled as she watched us tuck in lavender sheets, toss a violet-sprinkled spread on the bed, and hang up purple and lavender play outfits and dresses in the closet. "Karen, let me guess what your favorite color is!" she challenged her newest resident. "Lavender," they both exclaimed.

We left her with Mrs. Peruzzin in the classroom. "She'll be fine," her teacher affirmed. "Right now, we're taking a snack break so that everyone can meet her. With only eight students, Karen will be right at home."

On the way home, grief surged over me, followed by a tidal wave of guilt. "I'm the one who is supposed to take care of my little girl. I hate sending her away to an ...an institution." My complaints were laced with tears. "Who's going to read to her at night? Who's going to sit on the edge of the bed and really listen to how her day went? I'm her mother!"

Steve was struggling with sadness too. He quietly listened to my torrent of emotions. "I think we have to trust her to God," he said.

God! I thought, not daring to voice my inner doubts. Where was God in all this? Why was this child afflicted with increasing blindness? *You could stop it. You could heal her.* My silent prayer was more like an accusation. I felt myself slipping into the darkness again. God and I had unfinished business.

· · · · · · · · · · · · · · · ·

The empty bunk and place at the table, Miriam's moping for her sister, and worries about Karen's well-being brought back that old feeling of life being out of control, of purposelessness. I was talking to God more than I had for a long time, pouring out a barrage of feelings and questions, followed by a plea for Karen's healing.

A small bus from the School for the Blind delivered my daughter safely home Friday afternoon. The bus driver handed her Baby Mary and a bag full of papers. "'Bye Karen! Have a great weekend!"

Her face lit up with a grin, "'Bye, Mr. Bill." She then ran into my arms for a hug. "Mom, see what I have? I'm learning Braille. I'm gonna practice writing the alphabet this weekend!" It had been a long time since I'd seen her so happy. What a contrast to the bewildered child who had been lost in elementary school! We sat at the kitchen table as she munched a cookie and sipped milk, telling me about her first week at School for the Blind.

Her younger sister Miriam noticed the change. "Karen's different. She wants to ride her bike again, and now I don't have a bike of my own," she complained.

"Hey, how come you're so good at peddling now?" I asked Karen.

"Oh, we go out and ride on the road in back of school. No cars allowed," she explained. We began taking the girls over to a school parking lot where they furiously biked in circles. Miriam was happy with a hand-me-down model donated by a friend.

It was gratifying to see Karen blossoming as she learned Braille. Her fingers sped over the bumps that spelled words of familiar stories. Miriam, the kindergartner, was reading on her own, too. Playing school took on a new dimension with a blind teddy bear.

A visit two months later at Batavia revealed what a healthy adjustment our daughter had made to her new surroundings. Her modicum of sight and happy spirit had made her a leader among the other girls. "She enjoys helping, especially dusting the shelves and dresser," Mrs. White reported. "We're teaching the students homemaking skills." Her classroom teacher, Mrs. Peruzzin, also assured us that Karen was an eager student limited in math ability but doing well in reading"

My prayer that night was one of gratitude. *Thank you, Lord, for providing a place for my handicapped little girl where she's accepted just the way she is.*

FIVE
ARIDITY TO ABUNDANCE

Slowly, subtly, the gray mists of depression again began infiltrating my thinking and affecting my mothering. Awaking with a knot of anxiety, I felt a strange sense of dread. Lately, during her weekends at home, Karen had been sullen and uncooperative. "Time to dry the dishes," I'd remind her, giving her a towel. She'd throw it on the floor.

"I don't want to!" She'd stamp her foot, turn to leave, and knock over a chair.

"Listen, young lady, you can do your share of the work around here! Your sister isn't complaining about scrubbing the counters." Comparisons are odious; my mother's axiom rang in my ears. *What's going on with Karen?* I wondered. She's always enjoyed helping.

Her third grade teacher, Mrs. Peruzzin, noted that she was failing in arithmetic, unable to apply reasoning to numbers, and a note from the dorm mother stated that she was having trouble keeping her room neat and making her bed. She resented correction and was often withdrawn.

Unwittingly, I expected Miriam to help carry the responsibility of making Karen happy. "Mom, can I go over to Sue's house," Miriam asked after clearing the table of Saturday's lunch dishes. "Just for a little while to play dolls?"

"No, you stay home and play with your sister," I cut her off. "Just think what it's like to be blind." She turned away, tears of disappointment in her eyes. Later, I heard the girls in the sunroom, pretending school. Miriam was scolding Karen for not being able to add simple numbers.

In counterpoint to concerns about my oldest was the boys' sheer delight in being alive. Jon and Rick helped me bracket my gloom and laugh. Only fifteen months apart, they were partners in mischief now that little brother Rick was walking all over the place. One morning, I was defrosting the freezer, prying loose layers of ice and frost when I heard,

"Brum-m-m, Brum-m-m," as the boys backed two dump trucks into the melting mess. "Fill 'er up, Joe," ordered Jon, alias Roy, the truck driver.

"Okay, Roy," Rick, alias Joe, his cohort, returned.

"I need mittens, Mom," Roy requested.

"Me, too," echoed Joe. The trucks were soon piled high with ice, chugging out the side door down the driveway into the yard and brum-m-ming their way to an old dump out back. I was so busy chipping frosty shelves that I hadn't noticed the strange collection of items piled by the side door. By now, the boys' knees were grubby with grass stains and dirt as they returned from their fifth dumping trip. The smell of something decidedly unsavory wafted my way.

"Hey, you guys," I looked down at two innocent smiling faces, blue eyes dancing, each nose sun-touched pink, and two pairs of sticking-out ears on crew-cut heads, one brown and one blond. "What's that I smell?"

"Not me!" Rick exclaimed, not potty trained at two.

"Surprise, Mom!" Jon pointed to a dead frog atop the pile. I was beginning to get the picture! Each trip brought back from the dump a return of earthy treasures: a beer can, soup can, clump of dirt containing a wiggling earthworm, acorns, and an old spoon. "For my town," Jon informed me.

"My town, too," Rick copied his brother.

"The frog has to go," I commanded, "it stinks!"

"We want to put the frog and the worm in our zoo," Jon objected.

"Yeah, zoo," Rick repeated. We made a deal to heave the frog and wash whatever was safe to keep. An old plastic dishpan full of warm water and suds kept the boys busy in the back yard.

After I returned the last package of frozen peas to a clean freezer, I stretched out in a lawn chair, watching Roy and Joe create their town. Along the roads, they placed their treasures from the dump. At the end, in my pansy patch was a stick cage, housing the earthworm that had burrowed to safety. Dump trucks were replaced by little cars chugging along the dirt highway. I listened to the funny dialogue between Roy and Joe in their make-believe world. What a gift these little brothers were, so close in age and so open to immediate joy!

Savoring the moment was rare. What was the matter with me that I was unable to relax and take in the goodness in my life? I continued to question the meaning of who I was and my purpose for living. Every Sunday, the whole family was in church and Sunday school, yet there remained an inner barrier that blocked the connection to knowing Jesus personally.

The pear tree shed its silver leaves, and fall winds whistled around the bungalow. Karen was back at School for the Blind, happy to be with her friends again. The latest eye exam revealed that the macula was severely damaged, clogged with dead cells. She was almost totally blind. "There must be an explanation for the deterioration for our daughter's vision," Steve and I queried the ophthalmologist.

"In all my experience, I have never seen anything like this." The doctor was as baffled as we were by the growing scars.

Dismaying to us as parents were the low marks on Karen's first report card. She continued to fail arithmetic with Ds in both social studies and English. In contrast, Miriam brought home straight As. A conference with Mrs. Horner discouraged us. "Karen is not able to recognize the key facts," her teacher explained. Why was her cognitive ability declining?

There were other unanswered questions that kept me awake early in the morning. Why was there such distance between Steve and me? He was often away, arriving late for supper and preoccupied when he was home. It was tiresome to replay the same old thoughts and feelings. I looked in the mirror, "You aren't any prize, Connie Castor," I said to myself. "You're a partner in a hum-drum marriage; your oldest daughter is blind and limited intellectually; your world is this little home."

Deep down, I knew that the cause of my quiet desperation lay in the realm of the spirit. How could a good God create a child with the seed of blindness in her? How could a loving heavenly Father bring two people together only to live emotionally separated from each other? My true self was wizened and depleted because I could not believe in the goodness of God. I longed for my childhood faith when I felt secure and loved. Was there an answer to these recurrent questions?

Unobtrusively, direction came on a Sunday afternoon in the winter of 1962. It was a bone-chilling day in early January. Snow flew in flurries by the kitchen window as a bare limb of the gnarled pear tree tapped on the windowpane. In the living room, Karen and Miriam played quietly with their dolls, Chatty Cathy and Baby Mary. Rick and Jon were tucked in for their afternoon nap. Steve was working on lesson plans, spread out on the dining room table.

In the kitchen, I sat at the table, absorbed in a book. It was a slim volume by Roz Rinker called *Prayer Conversing With God*.[1] For the past two years, I had been unable to pray genuinely, but now I was weary of the load of anger and fear I was carrying. The chronic dullness of spirit and lack of zest had worn me down.

The author focused on prayer as a conversation with God, both privately and in groups. The one idea that gripped my attention: I could talk to God gut-level—simply let it all hang out, nothing held back because God already knew what I was thinking and feeling.

The other concept that pierced my unbelief was the possibility that God really loved me. Rinker powerfully portrayed divine Love that gave His dearest Son to carry my black load of depression on the cross.

Something pulled me up the stairs to my bedroom. I knelt down beside the four-poster bed, buried my face in my hands, and began to cry. Wordless grief spilled out, then angry questions. "How could you allow Karen to go blind? Look at her last report card, mostly Ds and Fs. What about her mind?" I pounded the mattress. "And look at my dead marriage! Why did you permit Steve and me to marry in the first place?" Then came the fears. "I'm scared to die, Lord. I feel lost, like a little child in the dark." It felt as if the dike had broken and all my pent-up doubts, emotions, and accusations were tumbling out in a mighty flood. Finally, repentance. "I'm sorry, Lord, I'm sorry. Please forgive me. It's not your fault. It's me." Exhausted, I ended the long prayer with a whispered request. "If you're anywhere out there, just let me know you love me."

Words are inadequate to describe what happened next. I was a child in the brass bed in Corea once again. A gentle presence was there in the room almost tangibly warming my body. Now, the presence enveloped my whole being in wave after wave of sheer love. From the top of my head to the tips of my toes, all the darkness was absorbed in the light that flowed through me. I felt clean, forgiven, loved, and new-born.

One niggling critical part of me stood back asking, "What's this, Connie? An emotional orgy?" I knew where that was coming from! "Leave, dark one!" I retorted. Then, I praised God. "Thank you, thank you, Lord God Almighty." The questions didn't matter anymore. God was here, present, alive, and loving me.

The next morning, it was as if I saw everything with new eyes. The children looked different to me, each one a precious unique creation. Waiting for the seven-thirty bus from Batavia, I held Karen close, looking beyond her sightless eyes into her sweet spirit. "Oh, Lord, take Karen into your loving arms and give her a wonderful week," I prayed.

"Thanks, Mom." A big smile wreathed her face as she climbed up into the bus.

Miriam was now in first grade, reading far ahead of her grade level. I gave her a hug. "Thank you, honey, for taking time to play with your sister," I smiled at her pert and compassionate self who needed more time to nurture friendships with other girls. In my self-centered gloom, I had almost missed the treasure Miriam was.

Shortly thereafter, as I began preparing breakfast for the children, I asked, "Pancakes or scrambled eggs?"

"Eggs," yelled the boys.

"Pancakes," Miriam declared.

"Both then," I agreed. A surge of joy and gratitude welled up inside me as I looked around the breakfast table.

Steve responded to the change. "There's something different about you, Connie. You're happy!"

Outside the kitchen window, the bare limbs of the pear tree seemed to pulsate with hidden life. Jon's face shone with unmasked delight as he stabbed a chunk of pancake with his fork. A shaft of sunshine lit up Ricky's blond crew cut and set his ears aglow. Miriam pulled on her boots.

"Tonight the tooth fairy might come," she announced. She wiggled her front tooth, which was hanging by a thread.

"Hey, let me pull it out before you lose it in your peanut butter sandwich at lunch," I teased.

"If it's still there after school." We hugged.

"I love you, honey," I called as she dashed for the bus.

Later, I sorted laundry down in the basement and one-by-one dropped the boys' smelly socks into the churning washer. The last one, Jon's navy blue sock, I held for a moment in my hand. "I am a mother! Yes, God, I love being mom to this wild and wonderful crew!" I prayed. Something amazing was going on inside me when even dirty socks looked good!

• • • • • • • • • • • • • • • •

A hunger to rediscover Jesus Christ brought me downstairs at six in the morning for quiet time before the rest of the family awoke. With a cup of coffee and the Bible open to John's gospel, I sat at the table reading. "In the beginning was the Word, and the Word was with God, and the Word was God." (John 1.1, NIV) I realized that God's very nature is to express himself. What better way than through the eternal Word, His Son? "In him was life, and that life was the light of men. The light shines in the darkness, but the darkness has not understood it." (John 1.4-5, NIV) I continued to read. Strange thing, I thought, the darkness that had enveloped me when life caved in was rooted in my lack of comprehension of who God is. I blamed Him for Karen's blindness and my empty marriage. When at last I got down on my knees and honestly prayed, garbage and all, the light began to shine in my darkness.

After church on Sunday, I waited for a moment to talk with Pastor Crawford. "I feel like a new person, Pastor. I see things so differently now."

He laughed. "Sounds to me like you had an encounter with the Holy Spirit, Connie." He opened his New Testament and shared a verse from Romans 8: "But if Christ is in you, your body is dead because of sin, yet your spirit is alive because of righteousness." (Romans 8.10, NIV)

"That's it, all right. It's joy!" I agreed. "And I have a thirst to know Jesus. Where should I start?"

"Read the first three chapters of John's gospel, and come join our Sunday school class next week."

Now, as I ended my time with the Lord in prayer, I could only thank God for coming to me in unconditional love. I thanked Him for the living Word in Jesus, for the light that healed my despair.

The pivotal experience that turned my life around had occurred to a broken young woman crying out to God in abject misery and very little faith. The gift my Creator gave me that day was the unshakable deep-rooted knowledge that I am loved just as I am.

I began to realize that Pastor Crawford was right. Someone new was living in me—the Holy Spirit. Sunday school became important to me, and sharing insights with other believers helped me in my study of John's gospel. Jesus became alive!

In the third chapter of John, Jesus stood face-to-face with Nicodemus, a questioning Pharisee. On a rooftop at night, Jesus explained the mystery of being born again to this spiritually hungry teacher of the Law. The Spirit within me gave witness that I, too, was a child of God, drawn to the One who was lifted up on the cross and who carried my sin and the sins of the world. Every day, I marveled at the freedom I felt. The guilt and fear and unbelief were gone.

Jesus' encounter with the outcast Samaritan woman in John chapter four also spoke to me. There, He was sitting beside the well. He was weary and dusty from a long journey and thirsty for a drink of cold water. Along came a woman to lower her bucket into the well. "May I have a drink?" He asked her.

"I, a despised Samaritan woman, giving you, a Jewish rabbi, water?" Something about the light in His eyes must have caught her attention. What Jesus said next caught mine.

"'If you knew the gift of God and who it is that asks you for a drink, you would have asked him and he would have given you living water…the water I give him will become in him a spring of water welling up to eternal life.'" (John 4.10,14b; NIV)

I saw myself as that parched needy woman, both of us in darkness for different reasons. I saw Jesus, reaching out to me in infinite compassion and placing His hand of healing on my head. Now, I was drinking that living water. Inside flowed a perpetual spring, refreshing my soul with eternal life.

I wept tears of gratitude, tears of awe and wonder that Jesus Christ had lifted me out of an arid desert into overflowing abundance. Little did I know how important this relationship would be in the days that lay ahead.

SIX
HEALING MISSION

My relationship with God anchored me amidst the storm of grief following the diagnostic phone conversation with Dr. Smith. It had been two years since the Holy Spirit had broken my depression and bathed me in healing love. My faith had been strengthened as I daily studied God's Word, prayed, and read Christian classics. But nothing could have prepared me for the next discovery.

Karen was in Strong Memorial Hospital undergoing a series of tests. Conclusive results from the blood work were still pending. Surprisingly, she was content. A kind aide made sure Karen participated in the day program, an upbeat mixture of crafts and fun.

The normal routine of life at the Ridge Road bungalow continued. One particular evening, bath time for Rick and Jon had been boisterous. A regatta of fifteen boats and a tidal wave had left a puddle on the tiles. "Don't let go, Joe!"

"I'm holding on, Roy!" When I heard their alter ego voices and a huge splash, I came up to investigate.

"Okay, guys. Time to mop up!" After a quick drying with a big bath towel, two naked "ex-sailors" helped me soak up the mess. I thanked God for these two brothers, sturdy in body and joyful in spirit.

Now, Rick and Jon were in their Dr. Denton sleepers. They were still a little damp and smelling of Johnson's baby shampoo as they snuggled next to me on the sofa. "Shall it be a Henry Higgins story or Giant Grummer?" I asked.

"Giant Grummer!" they chorused. Actually, it was a Christmas tale, but they loved to hear about the antics of this monstrous creature that smashed children's toys and refused to hang a huge stocking. It was St. Nick who finally softened the giant's hard heart by leaving him an enormous odoriferous chunk of Limburger cheese.

I stopped reading while the boys looked at the vivid illustrations. Jon complained, "Ricky's hogging it. Let me see the picture of Giant Grummer!" He grabbed the book and held it close.

"It's not fair," his brother yelled. "He's got the picture right up to his nose."

"I just can't see that far away!" Jon cried.

A stab of fear made my heart skip a beat. Was Jon experiencing the beginning of juvenile lipidosis? Unthinkable! I was overly sensitive. After finishing the story, I had to know. I devised a simple chart for both boys. Circles, squares, and lines could be identified at various distances. It was obvious that Jon squinted as he tried to see, finally moving in close to the board while Rick easily recognized the shapes.

Intuitively, I knew the flaw was there in Jon. We said our evening prayer:

> "Jesus, tender shepherd hear me.
> Bless thy little lamb tonight.
> Through the darkness be there with me.
> Keep me safe 'til morning light."

As I tucked him in, I kissed his soft cheek and touched his sleepy lids. *Have mercy, O Lord, on my son Jonathan,* I prayed. *Deliver him from this terrible disease.* I couldn't hold back the tears.

Later, when Steve returned home from an administrative board meeting at church, I was waiting for him in the living room. "Steve, I think Jon's eyes are failing," I blurted out. "He had trouble seeing the pictures during story time."

"Connie, don't jump to conclusions!" Steve was angry. "Karen hasn't had an official diagnosis yet, and now you're saying Jon might have juvenile lipidosis!"

I started to cry. "See the circles and squares on the blackboard? He had to come close to see them. Rick had no problem at all!"

Steve looked stricken. "But Jon's so different from Karen, Connie!" he objected. "So bright and quick with numbers. So, so..." his voice trailed off as he collapsed on the sofa. We sat together in silence, unable to process the possibility of another child with this dreaded disorder.

The next morning, Steve took time off from school to take Jon to the ophthalmologist at Strong. As we waited for our appointment, Jon pushed a little car along the table, his eyes dancing with pleasure as he drove over mountains of magazines. "That little guy can be happy anywhere," his dad commented.

I agreed. "He's one adorable kid."

A unique booster chair was cranked into position as the eye doctor carefully examined Jon's eyes. Dr. Smith had prepared him beforehand with information about the beginning stages of lipidosis. Uneasily, we sat in the reception room as our little son endured a barrage of tests.

Now, an assistant beckoned to us. "Mr. and Mrs. Castor, the doctor would like to talk with you. I'll take care of your son."

His face was serious as we sat down in his office. "There's the beginning of a network of dead cells on Jon's macula," the doctor put it bluntly. "His sight measures 20/200 which means he'll need special assistance in school." It all had a sickeningly familiar ring to it.

"Is it the beginning of juvenile lipidosis?" I asked.

"You'd better question Dr. Smith about that," he replied uneasily.

The next afternoon, Dr. Smith met us in Karen's hospital room. He escorted us to an empty office where we bombarded him with questions. Yes, the blood tests came back positive for juvenile lipidosis. We could take Karen home now. Dilantin would be added to the phenobarbital to control seizures.

As for Jon, he was in the early stages of the disease. It was not uncommon for other children to be affected since it was a genetic disorder with both of us carrying a recessive gene.

The emotional impact of the dual diagnosis sent Steve, the father, and me, the mother, reeling in two very different directions. Steve immersed himself in church committees and extracurricular activities. He sought comfort in relationships. I withdrew from social outings and church meetings, except Sunday worship. Nights were restless. I'd sleep until three A.M. and then awaken with a jolt. Reality rushed at me like a pack of dogs. Two of my children were going to sicken and die, and there was nothing I could do to stop it.

I crept downstairs to wrestle with the unfairness of life. The first antagonist was guilt. Why had Steve and I married in the first place? There had been no prayer on my part. In the Christian college culture of the '50's, you found your man and tied the knot. The alternative? Spinsterhood.

Our wedding took place just before our senior year at Houghton. Karen was born sixteen months later before we really knew each other. During my nocturnal ruminating, I reverted to old patterns of perceiving God's nature. "Are you punishing me for being out of Your will in the choice of a husband?" I asked. No answer.

The second antagonist was fear. A frightening question haunted me: What would the disease do to Karen's and Jon's personalities? Dr. Smith had painted a picture of violent aggressive behavior that would require restraints. I couldn't communicate with Steve about my fears, but I surely could talk to Jesus.

Yes, Jesus the healer! Ravenously, I read every account in the Gospels of Jesus' healing. With infinite compassion, he drove out demons, made the blind to see, and raised a little girl from death. I lifted Karen and Jon to the Savior, imagining his loving hands touching their eyes, restoring perfect sight and health.

I collected books on healing. Agnes Sanford's principles in *The Healing Light* became a way of perceiving reality. Mrs. Sanford essentially believed that complete healing is God's will for His children, so we must align ourselves with His laws of love and faith in order to unleash His healing power in our lives.[2] She also claimed that we need to perceive God as a loving Father who desires the best for His children and that a lack of healing is primarily due to our unbelief and failure to walk closely enough to Him so that His healing can manifest itself in our lives.[3]

I was determined to discover these laws and tap into God's power to heal my children. I became convinced that God was going to heal Karen and Jon of juvenile lipidosis, so on Fridays, I did no housework. I spent the day fasting and praying, opening myself to the presence of God. At this time, I kept a journal called A *Diary of Private Prayer*. The following entry dated April 8, 1963 reveals my struggle between despair and expectant faith:

"Lord, I'm feeling discouraged, full of doubts that You will heal Karen and Jon. I am haunted by what lies ahead. It seems almost unbearable at times. Please help me to live one day at a time, glad that basically Jon is a happy normal five-year-old, that Karen is still herself, and that You are surrounding them with Your love and care. Help me to know that You have us all in Your almighty hand. You have never let us down before. I trust You for the future. In Jesus' name, Amen."

That spring Joe Bayly, a well-known speaker in Christian circles, came to our church as the main preacher for a missionary conference. At home, I was caring for Karen and Miriam who were recuperating from tonsillectomies. Steve returned from Sunday morning worship exuberant. "Connie, it was the most moving service I have ever attended," he reported. "Joe Bayly spoke on the lordship of Jesus Christ in such a personal way that it challenged me at a deep level. And the choir sang 'The Hallelujah Chorus' at the end. I wish you could have been there."

I was envious. Tied to the house with two sick girls, my anxious self in need of a boost, I had missed a powerful outpouring of the Holy Spirit.

Later that afternoon, the doorbell rang. There standing at the front door was Joe Bayly himself. "May I come in and talk with you?" he asked. There was a warmth about him, an aura of compassion that I liked. Pastor Crawford had shared our pain with Joe. "My wife and I have experienced the death of two children. Perhaps, I may be of help to you," he offered.

As we sat together in the living room, Joe Bayly's story unfolded. The first son had died as an infant during surgery. Another son, Danny, a beautiful sensitive five-year-old, had been diagnosed with leukemia. In anguish, Joe and his wife looked for God's direction. They took James' injunction seriously, "Is any one of you sick? He should call the elders of the church to pray over him and anoint him with oil in the name of the Lord. And the prayer offered in faith will make the sick person well; the Lord will raise him up." (James 5.14-15, NIV)

Therefore, elders of their church had gathered around Danny and anointed him. The disease went into remission, and the little boy enjoyed a period of normalcy. Suddenly, the symptoms of leukemia returned. It was not long after that Danny died at home in his father's arms.

I listened, appalled. So much hope, so much gratitude, only to be dashed as the disease ran its course! Joe went on to tell us that his two-year-old had cystic fibrosis and another son had hemophilia.

"Joe, how do you see God in all this?" Steve asked. "How could you preach such a powerful sermon on Jesus Christ as Lord when you are experiencing such tragedy in your own family?"

The humble man shared what he and his wife were learning through suffering. "You know, Steve and Connie, that there's only one relationship that ultimately counts," Joe said. "It's abiding in Christ. Our pain is like a refining fire, burning away the dross that keeps us from our Lord."

With empathy, Joe listened to Steve and me as we poured out our yearning for our children's healing. He gently put his arms around our shoulders. "Don't count on Karen and Jon being healed," he warned us. "Be prepared to walk with them through the valley of the shadow of death."

Inwardly, I rebelled at his words. *I don't want to hear this, Joe Bayly. Our situation is different. God is going to heal our children.*

In May, out-of-the-blue a check for fifty dollars arrived anonymously with a terse note, "Please use this toward a trip to Katherine Kuhlman's healing mission." Miss Kuhlman's book, I *Believe in Miracles*, had left a deep impression on me.[4] Secretly, I had been preparing for this journey. My hours of Bible study and prayer had become a kind of bargain with God. There was going to be nothing in me to block His healing power. It must have been difficult for Steve to live with such a "spiritual giant" because I had been trying to push him into the same devotional life I felt necessary for me.

It was in late April that we packed Karen and Jon into the station wagon for a visit to the healing mission in Pittsburgh. Jon clutched his box of little cars, and Karen held her doll, Baby Mary. "Where we going?" she asked.

"To Pittsburgh."

"For fun?" Jon queried.

"To hear Miss Kuhlman," I answered.

"Why?" Jon persisted.

It was Steve's turn. "She teaches us about Jesus, how He loves and heals people."

"Oh, like Sunday school," Karen observed.

"And after we hear Miss Kuhlman, I have plans for plenty of fun! You'll find out later," Steve promised.

Although it was an hour before the service on this humid Friday evening, the aisles were crowded with people in wheelchairs. An older couple approached as we found seats near the front. "Do you have special needs?" they asked. Steve took them aside and explained the reason for our visit. "We'll make sure Miss Kuhlman prays for your children. When the time comes, just follow us."

The informal, almost carnival atmosphere was alien to my conservative Baptist upbringing. People were emotional as they testified of personal healing. "Praise the Lord" and "Amens" resounded all over the auditorium. Katherine Kuhlman's sermon was folksy and simple, inviting listeners to accept Jesus as Savior and healer. Our usher friends led us forward. As Miss Kuhlman laid hands on Karen and Jon and prayed for them, I felt uneasy.

Steve felt none of my qualms. I cringed when he dropped a twenty dollar bill in the collection plate. *Why did we subject the children to this mass of pushing humanity?* I wondered. Not once had they complained. I was the only sour grape in the bunch.

Steve carried Jon, and I held onto Karen in the crush of people exiting. Near the door, the friendly couple stopped us. Bill needed to tell his story. In a straightforward witness, he told how he had come in a wheelchair five years ago, dying of cancer. God, through Miss Kuhlman's ministry, had completely restored his health. "I'm so grateful!" he exclaimed. "That's why I volunteer to usher every week!"

Ellen, his wife, added, "Not just Bill's body was healed. His whole attitude has changed now that he knows Jesus! We'll keep praying for your children!"

Saturday morning after a breakfast of pancakes, we piled into a cable car that creaked its way up a very steep hill. "Hold on, everybody," Jon chortled. Our reward at the top was a tropical aviary. Brilliantly plumed birds flew from tree to tree. Exotic flowers and plants bloomed and flourished luxuriantly. Birdcalls, fragrance, bubbling of waterfalls, and the feel of soft moss—the children's senses were satiated. Karen laughed when a parrot squawked, "Hello, cutie." Polly sat on Jon's shoulder.

Next, we drove to the planetarium. Entering the mysterious domed skies, the children listened intently as a voice took us back to Jesus' time.

The Easter story, with the stars and planets of Judea's heavens, was reverently narrated. "That was neat!" Karen smiled.

We ended the day in a lovely park by a lake, munching on take-out burgers and fries. After supper, we rented a rowboat. Jon, in the prow, trailed his fingers in the water, and Karen leaned against my shoulder. Steve rowed along the shoreline of weeping willows and grassy slopes. The splash of oars and the rhythmic creak of the locks soothed my spirit after the crush of the previous day.

In the car on the way home to Webster, I remained quiet, trying to sort out my thoughts about our trip to the healing mission. I had a feeling Joe Bayly was right. We had to be prepared to walk through the valley of the shadow of death with Karen and Jon. I reflected on the simple pleasure of being together. I couldn't stand to see these two dear ones deteriorate and die. Why hadn't God healed them as he had Bill of cancer? Why had he sent us to the mission?

The next morning, I began the dreary routine of housework with a sense of futility. All day long angry questions continued to race through my mind. I recalled a sentiment from Sanford's *The Healing Light*, reminding me that after the struggle, at the end of myself, I must surrender myself, both flesh and spirit, to God's purpose.[5] I was probably the one blocking healing with my need to control. How could I let go with the specter of lipidosis shadowing the future?

As I swept the kitchen floor after tucking the children into bed that night, I began to think back on what I'd seen in Pittsburgh. I had to admit there was something undeniably genuine in the witness of those who'd been healed, especially Bill. And something, too, that Karen could understand in Katherine Kuhlman's message. On the trip home, she talked about Jesus her friend. I hadn't paid attention. There was power whether I could accept it or not.

The word *power* echoed in my mind. Slower and slower, I swept the kitchen floor. Finally, I chucked the broom in the closet and sat down in the living room. I opened my New Testament to Paul's prayer for the Ephesians. "I keep asking," I read, "that the God of our Lord Jesus Christ, the glorious Father, may give you the Spirit of wisdom and revelation, so that you may know him better. I pray also that the eyes of your heart may be enlightened in order that you may know the hope to which he has called you, the riches of his glorious inheritance in the saints, and his incomparably great power for us who believe. That power is like the working of his mighty strength, which he exerted in Christ when he raised him from the dead and seated him at his right hand in the heavenly realms." (Ephesians 1.17-20, NIV) Suddenly, as I read, that "power" was no longer safely locked into printed words. I realized it was flowing through me like a strong electric current.

The skeptic in me thought, "This can't be happening to inhibited Connie!" But the power pulsing through me swept away doubts and angry questions that had been plaguing me. Instead, I found myself experiencing the presence of Jesus Christ. Knowing He was there through the Holy Spirit, I was free to praise Him. "Thank you, thank you, Jesus, for being with me and Karen and Jon and all of us each step of the way," I prayed.

I went upstairs to be with Karen. Touching her lightly, I asked, "Honey, are you still awake?"

"Mom, I feel something warm and tingling coming from your hand." So, she felt it, too.

"Karen, when you listened to Miss Kuhlman, what did you hear?" I asked her.

"That Jesus loved me and I could ask Him to live in my heart."

"Did you ask Him?"

"Yes, I did. I just know He's here now, Mom."

As I prayed with her that night, the power diminished until all that was left was a sense of peace and well-being. I knew from then on that whatever happened to our children the living Christ was with us.

SEVEN
BURNOUT

"Jesus, heal me some day whole." Each night Karen would pray these words as I knelt beside her bed. With all the love that was in our family, we continued to yearn for her physical healing.

I began to notice a change in Karen, a way she had of talking about her friend Jesus. Inviting Him into her heart in Pittsburgh was making a practical difference. It dawned on me that the Lord had given us an answer to our prayers in her wholeness of spirit. Karen's simple faith in Jesus as her Savior was transforming her moodiness into a joy for being alive.

Big changes were rumbling on the home front during the summer of '65. Our bungalow on Ridge Road, inhabited by a family of seven, was bursting its seams. The boys had moved down to the 12' x 7' sunroom, spilling trucks and blocks out into the dining room.

Steve's casual invitation at dinner one evening raised my hopes. "How about looking at a house with me over on Woodard Road, Connie?"

"What's it like? How many bedrooms? How about the yard?" I peppered him with questions.

Steve's knowing smile intrigued me. "Wait until you see it. I'll pick you up tomorrow during the lunch hour."

The next day, all I could say was "WOW!" as we parked in front of a brand-new saltbox colonial on a prime location bordering the golf course. Five over four windows, the double garage with a cupola, and the paneled front door left me breathless. The builder, John Martin, a friend of Steve's conducted the tour. An elegant entryway with one wall of brick and a graceful stairway led to a spacious living room and chandeliered dining room. Windows flooded the house with light. Cherry cupboards in the kitchen and sliding doors in the adjacent family room gave me a sense of visiting the Taj Mahal. "How could we ever afford this gorgeous home?" I asked incredulously.

"I'll tell you later. Let's just say that the Castor estate has been settled," Steve replied.

I suppressed questions and eagerly noted details as we moved to the paneled den, laundry area with a chute, and a powder room. Loads of closet space would hold our junk. Upstairs a 21' master bedroom with its own bathroom and three other bedrooms with double-sink bath completed the picture of the ideal home for a growing family.

Both of Steve's parents had died unexpectedly, his father in 1958 and his mother in 1962. "Mom and Dad would have been happy to see us settled into the Woodard Road house." Steve was pensive as we talked later that evening. "It feels right to use my inheritance for a place that reminds me of the Castor homestead."

The Pennsylvania homestead had recently been sold, so now we could bring back Steve's share of the antiques. "With grandfather clock gonging the hours in the living room and the old pine corner cupboard gracing the dining room," I predicted, "there'll be memories of Castorville."

Our old trailer was called into action, toting thirty loads of furniture and boxes across town. One of Steve's students worked with me to scrub and polish the bungalow until it shone. Its location on Ridge Road made it an ideal place for a dentist's office. Before the final farewell, I stood beside the gnarled pear tree outside the kitchen window. It had been the totem for our family, lifting its limbs in welcome, tapping the panes in sadness. Buffeted by storms, warmed by sunshine, it had faithfully blossomed in May and produced pears in September. It was a metaphor of my life. I would miss the connection.

It didn't take us long to settle in at Woodard Road. Somehow, I found time to sew new slipcovers for the sofa and chairs and create curtains for the windows. The grandfather clock ticked in the living room; the pine corner hutch displayed family glassware, and around the old cherry drop-leaf table were the familiar arrowback chairs. I was moved to see the generations spanned in our new home.

Karen was bewildered by the move. How difficult it was to be blind and dislocated! I prayed for understanding in helping her to adjust. She unpacked her Braille books and placed them in a new bookcase. She tucked Baby Mary into her crib. Almost twelve now, faltering as she walked, Karen was slender and showing signs of puberty. Her I.Q. had dropped into the 70's. Since she now required more one-to-one care, I wondered how I could manage her needs with four other children demanding attention.

Karen was sleeping more, comfortable to be tucked in bed with Baby Mary for an afternoon nap. Several times, I heard a sound that frightened me—a loud thump on the floor and the pounding of her arms and legs. A seizure! Always my heart leapt to my throat as I rushed upstairs to turn her on her side until it was over. I never got used to them.

I noticed I was more irritable with Karen, sometimes giving her a swat. She asked questions over and over again. At night, she would cry out with bad dreams. Steve slept through it all while I got up with her. Dr. Smith described the nightmares as seizure activity.

A lack of connection with God fed into that short fuse when it came to patience with Karen. Her slowness to obey when I asked her to fold laundry or dry the dishes ended with a lecture that confused her. *Shame on you, Connie,* I later berated myself. *It's the disease. She can't help it.* The ugly part was my reaction to it.

In the crunch of moving, I had neglected quiet time with the Lord. What was the matter with me that I couldn't wake up at six anymore? I yearned for the stillness and sense of being on holy ground while sipping coffee and studying John's gospel. Prayer had opened me to strength beyond myself.

Autumn brought respite when Karen returned to School of the Blind. She was in the primary level for slow students where hands-on crafts took the place of academics. My kitchen drawer overflowed with woven potholders. Her room was in the older girls' section of Park Lewis Dorm, next door to the housemother's. Her roommate Dottie, one of her best friends, was helpful and patient, making allowances for the changes in Karen.

In October, the nurse called from the school infirmary. My throat tightened as she informed me of my daughter's accident. "Karen fell out of bed during a severe seizure," she reported. "When she regained consciousness, she was crying in pain."

Alarmed, I asked, "Was anything broken?"

"Yes, an X-ray revealed a broken collarbone. There's nothing much we can do for it except keep Karen quiet. She'd be better off at home."

How could I handle the demands of this needy child? I breathed a prayer, "O Lord, it's You and me together." Compassion and strength returned with my reinstated time with God. I read Psalms to Karen, brought her hot cocoa and cookies, and played her favorite tapes of gospel songs.

Rick, at five, a naturally loving little brother, crawled up in her bed with a notebook and pencil. He drew page after page of a stick-figure Batman in action, telling the story of his hero's exploits. Once Batman had to pull Robin out of Giant Grummer's toilet; another time the dynamic duo got stuck in Karen's bedroom window, trying to fly in for a visit. Her merry laughter warmed my heart. I missed her when she returned to school three weeks later.

A letter arrived the week after Karen's twelfth birthday in December. "We regret to inform you that we can no longer accept your daughter Karen as a student in New York State School for the Blind. Because her mental capacity and physical condition have deteriorated due to her neurological disorder, we are unable to meet her needs. The school cannot be responsible for her falling.

"A Developmental Center, such as the facility at Newark, would be better equipped to care for your daughter. Please come and pick up her belongings immediately."

After the broken collarbone, I had known that her days were numbered at the School for the Blind, but I was heartsick that this rotten disease was stripping this vulnerable child of loving teachers and friends. The last few days at home as she recuperated, Karen had been restless and eager to get back to school. How would I survive having this frail, declining girl at home all the time? Tears of self-pity clouded my vision as I reread the letter.

Steve called a family conference to enlist help from the troops. After explaining the situation, he asked, "What can we do as a family to help make your sister's life more fun?"

Rick volunteered, "She loves my Batman stories!"

"How 'bout playing toss with our big ball?" Jon suggested. He was six and in first grade.

Miriam added, "Karen loves to teach Cathy and me manners like saying 'please' and 'thank you.' We'll play the Beatles for her!"

"Me dance," Cathy offered, now two and a half. She'd twirl and gyrate to "Yellow Submarine."

For myself, I vowed to keep my early morning time of Bible study and prayer going. Only by God's grace could I give Karen what she needed. Housebound, I would have to drop out of church activities and my book club.

It was a difficult time for all of us. Karen, a naturally people-loving person, missed her friends in spite of our efforts to make her happy. "Why can't I go to school?" Over and over she asked this plaintive question. "The other kids go to school." How could I answer her? She needed the routine of a daily program.

Sue, a good friend and doctor's wife from church, occasionally came to take Karen to her home so that I could have a day of respite.

Karen enjoyed time with this caring woman with a light touch and sense of humor, and I enjoyed soaking in the tub and flopping on the sofa with a good book while Cathy tried her T-shirts on Baby Mary. How I relished the freedom!

As the winter months wore on, Karen's seizures occurred more frequently. I was on edge, afraid that she would fall. I often sat her in a chair close by as I cooked or cleaned. One morning, as I was making the bed in our room, I looked over at Karen who was trying to stand up. "I think I'm going down," she mumbled. I managed to place her on the bed before her body contorted in spasm after spasm. Her face was a mottled blue. I glanced at the clock. Ten minutes had passed before she began gulping for air. With trembling fingers, I took her pulse. She was chalk white, still as a dead person.

I *must talk to the doctor. Karen could have died*, my thoughts were fearful. Dr. Norris, the neurologist who had replaced Dr. Smith, answered the phone. "I just don't know how much longer I'll be able to handle Karen," I told him, after describing the seizure. "What about placing her in Newark?"

"Mrs. Castor," came his reply, "send her there only after she's lost all ability to understand. And then forget you ever had her." I recoiled in horror. "You can expect a personality change," he continued. "She will become violent and will have to be restrained. We will add tranquilizers to the medication she's already taking."

I hung up the phone in shock. I sat on the bed, weeping beside my silent daughter. In sleep, she was lovely. Color slowly returned to her face in a rosy tint. I touched the freckles that dusted her nose. "What kind of a devilish disease could this be that would make my dear one destructive? And who does Dr. Norris think he is, asking me to forget her?" I asked myself helplessly. "I can't stand it anymore!"

At that point, there came as clearly as if someone were speaking directly to me the words that Christ spoke to Paul: "My grace is sufficient for you; my strength is made perfect in weakness." (2 Corinthians 12.9)

"Yes, Lord, thank you." I again felt God's presence. "Only in Your strength can I walk this hard road with Karen." Soon, I would begin to understand the meaning of this verse.

It wasn't long afterward that Steve and I visited Newark Developmental Center which was thirty miles from Webster. It was an impressive campus, barren now as snow began to fall. The cottages were clean and homey. There was an indoor pool and a bowling alley, recreation that my daughter would never use.

"Where would Karen be living?" I asked. "In one of the cottages?"

Our guide, an older nurses' assistant, hesitated before answering. "The cottages are for fairly mobile, more independent residents. I am aware of your daughter's prognosis."

"Then where would she stay?" Steve repeated the question.

"Come with me to the women's infirmary," she directed. "This is where we place residents with medical problems." We entered the hall of a large brick building. The air faintly smelled of urine and Lysol. We wound our way through a long room, full of metal beds, as empty as a deserted barrack. My heart sank.

Next she opened a door. "This is the day room," our guide explained. "Our residents are usually attending a weekday program. Since it's Saturday, all of them are here on free time."

Two TVs blared, one at each end of the room. There were severely deformed residents, hunched in wheelchairs, and others with mouths open and arms flailing. Still others with large heads hardly moving at all. There were cries and grunts, subhuman sounds. This was my first introduction to seriously impaired people who were tucked away from the mainstream of everyday existence. A few aides walked among the women, offering snacks, feeding some, and placing straws in mouths for a drink.

One vignette that gave a touch of normalcy was a young woman at a table reading a Braille book to an older resident. Her body was bent forward in concentration as if to better hear the words. "Why, the blind girl seems almost like a teenager!" I exclaimed.

"Her name is Joyce, and she's just recently been placed in Newark," our guide informed us. "After a bout with cancer, she lost her sight."

Returning to Webster, Steve and I were silent for awhile as we tried to sort out the meaning of our visit. Our senses had been assaulted by a new pocket of reality. "I can't imagine sending Karen to such a place!" I was outraged.

"It's a far cry from School for the Blind," Steve's understatement was ironic. "But what are the alternatives at this point?"

"Honestly, Steve, I think I'm near the breaking point," my voice quavered. "I just can't cope with four active kids and Karen."

One awful evening two weeks later, I was edgy and exhausted. Karen had finished her bath. She babbled incoherently as she splashed water like a toddler. "Time to get out," I demanded.

"No, I wanna stay in." The next splash soaked me.

"Young lady, you stand up, and let me dry you." I tried to grab her slippery arms.

"No!" Another splash.

I slapped Karen on the back. She started to cry. On her white skin I saw the imprint of my hand. I knew I had crossed the line. I was in a dangerous state of burnout.

I wrapped the frail child in a towel and held her close, both of us miserable. "Forgive me, Karen, for hitting you."

"It's okay, Mom," she consoled me between sobs.

"I'll never do that again," I promised.

The next day, Steve filled out the application form for Newark. Within ten days, a letter of acceptance arrived, that very night, I was on my knees by our bed, talking to God. "O, Lord, when You said Your grace is sufficient, how come I've been so weak and such a failure?"

Silence.

"Now we're taking Karen to Newark next week. God, You know how awful that day room is. Please, please take care of my little girl. Give her a friend." The silence held a glimmer of hope. I knew my prayer was heard.

When we talked with Karen about the change, her face lit up with excitement. "I'll be going to school, too," she told her brothers and sisters. The same big suitcase packed for School for the Blind was dragged out of the closet and sat open on her bed.

The list of things she could bring was curtailed by lack of storage space. Each bed had a dresser. Her gospel and Beatles tapes with cassette player were packed along with blind Teddy and her potholder weaving loom. *Odd she chose that. She hasn't used it in ages*, I thought. I packed her Braille books of Psalms.

Karen could still read, slowly sounding out the words as her finger touched the raised code. Every night before bedtime, she would read aloud a few verses. Psalm 23.1, "The Lord is my shepherd; I shall not want," was her favorite. She shared it with me the day before our trip to Newark.

Then I knelt beside my daughter's bed as we said the familiar prayer from my childhood:

> *"Jesus, tender shepherd hear me,*
> *Bless thy little lamb tonight.*
> *Through the darkness be there with me,*
> *Keep me safe 'til morning light."*

I pictured Jesus carrying this little lamb who in innocent anticipation thanked him that she could go to school again. "Are you kind of scared about going away?" I asked as I tucked her in.

"Nope, Jesus is my friend. He's with me," was her confident reply. Weak in body but strong in spirit, Karen was much more ready than I was for what God had in store for her at Newark.

EIGHT
SOUL SISTERS

On a bleak day in March 1966, the station wagon was parked in front of the Women's Infirmary at Newark Developmental Center. Sleet pelted the car. A few dry leaves scudded over the sidewalk. Steve unloaded Karen's suitcase and boxes. In her white beret and new red wool coat, our daughter epitomized youthful beauty. "This is my school? We're here?" An eager smile revealed her excitement.

Misgivings held us, her parents, back from entering the building. "What do you say we have a prayer together?" I suggested. With our arms around Karen, we asked for God's protection and blessing on our child.

"Thank you for my new school," Karen prayed.

I added a P.S. "Lord, please give her a friend."

The door opened. "Come in, Mr. and Mrs. Castor," a nurse in a white smock warmly invited us. "Hi, Karen. I'm Mrs. Bentley. Welcome to Newark."

"My new school," Karen answered proudly.

"So that your daughter will have time to acclimate to her new situation here, we are asking that you not make contact with her for three weeks. A clean break from home is best initially," Mrs. Bentley informed us. "After we get you settled, Karen, I'm going to give you a physical." I handed her a bag of medications.

With a hug, Steve promised, "We'll come for a visit the first Sunday in April!" We walked down the hall, turning once to catch a glimpse of a slight young girl in her new red coat, walking toward the dormitory with the nurse. Once again, I felt the guilt and uncertainty of placing our child in another's care. "She looked so defenseless," I cried on the way home, "so full of hope."

"Are you automatically expecting her hopes in a new school to be dashed?" Steve's question sliced through my grief. I silently pondered.

"Remember what we saw in the day room?" I reminded him, "The TV blaring, the strange sounds, the people?"

Steve interrupted, "Connie, she won't be able to see the things that shocked us."

"Perhaps, her damaged brain helps her accept people just as they are—and her simple trust in the Lord Jesus," I added. I recounted for Steve our conversation the night before, Karen's firm statement, "Jesus is my friend. He'll be there."

"I think about Jesus taking the children in His arms and blessing them," Steve replied. "I know He will be holding Karen in that day room."

"Yes," I agreed. "She's got enough faith for both of us."

During the intervening three weeks in the early morning while the rest of the clan slept, I read the Psalms. "Turn to me and be merciful unto me, because I am lonely and weak," I prayed for myself. I inserted Karen's name in Psalm 23, her favorite. "Because the Lord is Karen's shepherd, she has everything she needs… He gives her new strength and guides her on right paths as He has promised." In my mind's eye, I pictured Karen with a new friend beside her. On my knees, I lifted her into the healing, gentle, warming love of God who knew exactly what she needed.

After a week, I mustered the courage to call Mrs. Bentley. "How's Karen adjusting? Is she homesick?"

"Mrs. Castor, Karen has acclimated amazingly well. She's made friends with Joyce, a new resident." I remembered the blind girl from our first visit. "Those two are working on a surprise for you," Mrs. Bentley reported.

I hung up and shouted a mighty, "THANK YOU, LORD!" I then called Steve at school with the good news.

"Yes, Karen's faith is rewarded," he breathed a sigh of relief.

"A friend! A friend for Karen!" My heart sang, sensing God's hand in meeting her need.

I was free to turn my attention to the rest of the family. With zest, I planned a party for Cathy's third and Jon's seventh birthday, all in one big celebration. The doings were to take place in the newly paneled and tiled basement family room, Steve's six-month project.

Jon and Rick biked around the neighborhood, delivering Batman invitations to five boys. Miriam and Cathy took Barbie "Come to my party" cards to five little girls. I inveigled Steve to blow up balloons which he did with such vigor that three exploded during the night causing everyone to jump out of bed. I shook with terror while the boys laughed. "Maybe Batman lit a firecracker," Rick told his brother.

"And Robin set off the other two," Jon added.

On the birthday morning, we hung the remaining yellow and white balloons from the family room ceiling with festoons of matching streamers. Cathy's blue eyes sparkled as Miriam decorated the tables with an Easter flair, rabbits and chicks. "And my job's the seats," Jon announced, toting church chairs and unfolding them in place.

At one end of the big room, Steve was "game meister" for the boys, beginning with a wild bout of ticking "hot potato." On the other side, I had the little girls blindfolded and sticking cotton ball tails on a bunny.

The cake was a coconut-covered rabbit. "Mom, you forgot his tail!" Cathy pointed out, strategically planting a cotton ball. Etched in my memory are two faces: one is impish with turned-up nose, two blue eyes straining to see seven burning candles on the bunny's back; the other is angelic with blond curls, dancing azure eyes, and mouth puckered to be the first to blow out her three candles on the rabbit's head.

In one frantic moment, the three-year-olds howled in anguish when they couldn't open Cathy's birthday presents. A grab bag gift momentarily appeased them.

Jon's gifts reminded me of an arsenal. He had circumnavigated the "no guns" rule in our house and had tipped off his friends. Water pistols, dart and cap guns, and a long rifle were among the loot. Steve and I groaned. After everyone had gone home, Jon beamed when his dad wheeled in a full-sized bike. Cathy hopped on her new red trike and pedaled it around the room.

As I pulled from the wall the last far-flung bunny tail, I realized how free I had felt to enter into the festivities for my birthday kids. The underlying anxiety about Karen falling or feeling lonely and unhappy was absent. Instead, I was aware of how delightfully unique the rest of my brood were.

Soon after, on a rare warm spring morning, I sat on the back patio with a family photo album open in my lap. There was Jon, a baby bouncing the springs out of his jumper. A close-up caught his dimples and sheer joy of being alive.

Baby Cathy, blond curls forming a halo around her cherubic face, was plunging a fist in her first birthday cake. Welling up in me was gratitude for the mystery of conception. These children, formed within me in utter seclusion, were unique creations and planted in their tender spirits was the seed of God's love. I understood at that moment that neither my anger nor fears nor the ravages of lipidosis—nothing could separate us from the love of God.

The robin's chirp, the raucous caw of crows, and the cardinal's whistle spoke to me. Yes, this is my Father's world. In that golden epiphany, I realized my purpose for living was to nurture that seed of faith in myself and in each of my children. Since we were made in the image of God, we were meant to delight in Him and in His creation.

After our first visit with Karen at Newark, Steve and I both understood, with a sense of awe, that a basic necessity had been met for our child—that of belonging. As Karen walked toward us, her face alight with pleasure, I noted her shining hair and new outfit of blue pants and red striped shirt. "Joyce gave them to me," she explained. "She's my new friend. I really like her. We make things together. Next week, you'll see what we're weaving for you, Mom!"

"Hey, we can't get a word in edgewise!" her dad laughed. "I want to meet your new friend." One of the aides escorted Joyce to Karen's side.

"Here she is!" Karen burst with pride. "My friend Joyce!" Part of the young girl's face had been disfigured by surgical removal of bone from her jaw. She wore a hearing aide and was obviously blind. Her voice surprised me—warm and melodious. A smile transformed her countenance as she held out a hand to us.

"I sure do have fun with your daughter!" she exclaimed. "Before Karen came, I was lonely. I was praying for someone to be my friend here. I'm new, too."

Isn't that just like the Lord? I thought. Beneath the externals flowed the pure sweet stream of Jesus' love, its current pulling two young girls together. I sensed something beautiful growing in the day room.

The following Saturday, Steve traveled to Newark to pick up Karen. As the bell rang incessantly, I ran to throw open the front door. There Karen stood, bursting with eagerness as she held a bulging plastic bag. She shoved it toward me. "Remember I told you Joyce and I were making you a present, Mom? Here it is!"

"Wait a minute! This calls for a family powwow!" Steve announced. "Hey, kids, come here! Karen's brought home a surprise!" Up from the basement came Jon and Rick who had been building a fort of pillows. Miriam and Cathy came out of the kitchen, licking their fingers from frosting cupcakes.

"Everybody has to guess what's in here," Karen challenged us, rattling the bag.

"An alligator," Rick ventured.

"Let me feel," Jon poked and probed. "I think it's a blanket."

"Close," his sister laughed.

Miriam's turn. "Maybe, it's a motorcycle jacket!"

"Or a puppy dog," Cathy chimed in.

"Mom, how about you?" Karen was teasing us, enjoying the attention.

"I think it's something for the bathroom floor," I guessed.

"Real close."

"Or a tent!" her dad piggybacked.

"Oh, Dad!" Karen reached in and pulled out a big rug.

"Wow!" we screamed. It was pieced together from dozens of hand-woven potholders. With all kinds of colors and sewn together with yellow yarn, it was an amazing creation. In wonderful abandon, some rows were longer than others. Hours of loving work had gone into its making, a joint offering of two generous friends. We patted it; Cathy sniffed it; the boys rolled on it; and I held it with tears brimming over. Steve laid it down and walked on it.

"Let's try it in the bathroom!" Miriam suggested. And that's where it found a home, in the powder room.

Sunday afternoon the doorbell rang. I knew who was there. "Karen, come here! Some special friends have come for a visit." I helped her open the door. There on the front steps stood Mrs. Slattery and all eight members of the junior high Sunday school class.

"Surprise, Karen!" they yelled in unison.

"Who?" Before she could say another word, Mary Jane Slattery gave her a big hug.

"Since you can't come to Sunday school, we decided to come to you! You'd better get your Braille book of Psalms." Mary Jane, a short woman with curly gray hair, looked into Karen's eyes, her own filling with tears of tenderness.

"Mrs. Slattery, my teacher!" Karen cried. A smile of recognition broke through her bewilderment. The children individually expressed their caring with a hug or a shy touch of hands. Each brought a small handcrafted gift and homemade card.

Once the class settled in the den, Mrs. Slattery asked Karen to read the twenty-third Psalm from her Braille book.

O, Lord, *help her remember*, I prayed. Reading had become difficult for her.

"The Lord is my shepherd, I shall not want."

It's embedded in her spirit, I realized.

Her fingers flew over the words. "And I shall dwell in the house of the Lord forever," she finished.

As the teacher drew out each child with questions, the ancient psalm became alive. "Karen, what gift has the Lord given you, something you really need?"

Without hesitation, Karen replied, "My friend Joyce." Miriam brought in the inimitable potholder rug and helped Karen hold it up.

"For Mom from Joyce and me," she proudly declared.

Despite signs including slurred speech and unsteady gait of the disease's progression, Karen's attitude remained joyful. The class had made Karen feel a part of them—accepted. She lived in the realm of the Spirit that brought health and simple acceptance of life to her inner self. The need for belonging went deeper than her friendship with Joyce and love from her family. Karen knew she was a child of God and belonged to Jesus.

• • • • • • • • • • • • • • •

My old Singer portable sewing machine chugged as I sewed twin rose jumpers with matching flowered blouses for Joyce and Karen. On our next visit to Newark, I was rewarded for my efforts with Joyce's exclamation after the girls had unwrapped their outfits, "Karen, we'll be twins!"

"Yeah, twins," she chortled.

Out on the front stoop several weeks later, Steve had an arm around each girl, both modeling their new jumpers. "Soul Sisters!" I laughed. On this relaxed weekend visit, I enjoyed getting to know Joyce and seeing the two interacting with each other.

I asked Joyce about her family. "I was living with foster parents, older people," she recounted. "Then I had to have surgery for cancer in my jaw. They couldn't care for me anymore." She paused, and her face darkened with pain. "I was placed in the hospital at Newark until I was well enough to live in the Infirmary."

The girl had no mental impairment. She showed me a letter she had typed to a sister in Kansas. "Joyce, you type well, especially with your vision loss."

"I learned in school before the operation. Cancer had gone into my optic nerve, too, and into my ear canal. They got it all but left me blind and partially deaf," she explained.

"With so many losses, aren't you bitter?" I was surprised at her inner strength.

"For a while I didn't have anyone but God." Her voice was low. "After my mom's death, my grandmother raised me. Every night, she'd read the Bible to me and said a prayer, kneeling beside my bed. On Sundays, we always went to Sunday school and church—until her death."

"Then what happened?"

"Since age eleven, I lived in foster homes. I kept going to church, sometimes catching a ride with a neighbor. But after the doctor told me I had cancer, I was scared.

"'You're all I've got, Jesus,' I prayed. I felt such peace. The Lord's been with me every step of the way."

We were silent. I was wordless in the face of such courage and faith. At last, I spoke. "Thank you, Joyce, for telling me your story. I'm glad you and Karen are friends."

"Karen and I, we're kind of like a little church in the day room."

"What do you mean?"

"Alice, she can talk. She was real nervous one day when the doctor said her heart was bad," Joyce explained. "Karen told her, 'I'll pray for you,' and she did, right then and there. I joined her, and we've prayed for other people, too."

A witness, a center of peace in the cacophony of the day room! I was deeply moved to discover how these two humble girls were blooming where they were planted. The barriers that kept me from sharing my faith with others just weren't there in Karen and Joyce. Living each day with their friend Jesus made reaching out to needy ones as natural as breathing. I was learning from them and ready to grow as a Christian.

NINE
UNEXPECTED ANGELS

L ike the refreshing wind of the Spirit, Chuck Rheinholt blew in one day to begin a Young Life club in Webster, New York. Since Steve was his connection to the high school, he often dropped in for a visit. Funny, young, and enthusiastic with a childlike capacity to enjoy the moment, he was full of creative ideas.

"A Yokefellow group," he announced one afternoon as I tackled a back-load of ironing, "that's what I need to keep me growing in my Christian faith. I think your home would be a great place to meet."

"A Yokefellow group, what does it do?" He had touched a needy spot in me, too.

"Mainly, we're yoked together in Christ to help carry each other's burdens," Chuck explained. "Read this, Connie. It tells about its Quaker beginnings when a guy named Elton Trueblood caught the vision and moved on it. Yokefellow groups are all over the country now."

Within the month, nine of us were meeting on a weekly basis in our living room. The combination of Christian psychology, Scripture, honest sharing, and prayer was a catalyst for growth in my walk with the Lord. I was learning how to listen and care as group members revealed concerns, and our prayers were being answered. We kept in touch by phone between meetings. Indeed, it was the backing of these friends that helped me through one of our most challenging times with Karen.

Yearly, Steve traveled to New York City with Karen and Jon to meet with staff at the Einstein Medical Research Center. Dr. Rapin, a children's neurologist familiar with juvenile lipidosis, thoroughly checked over Karen and Jon, including administering an encephalogram, which is a process for recording brain wave patterns. To continue much-needed research on this rare disorder, Dr. Rapin kept us informed on the need for living brain tissue from an affected child. In the spring of 1966, a phone call from a doctor at the Research Institute brought the issue to a head.

"Please consider a brain biopsy," she requested. "It's not a serious operation. A small piece of tissue would be extracted from Karen's brain. The reward might be a breakthrough in our knowledge of the disorder."

We argued the pros and cons. "The doctor said it was a simple proce-dure," Steve stated. "If we could further research…"

"But what about Karen?" I countered. "She's happy now, content at Newark."

"Yes, I know," Steve agreed. "Let's ask the New York doctor more about what's involved for her."

"Really, it's a minor operation," the neural surgeon reassured us. "Recovery time would be two or three weeks."

The decision was difficult. We brought it before the Yokefellow group and asked for prayer. A deciding factor was knowledge resulting from the biopsy that might even help Jon. A date was set for surgery at Albert Ein-stein Hospital in the Bronx during the third week of August 1966. Steve would drop off Karen and me and then return to cover the home front in Webster.

As the time approached, doubts bombarded me. My emotions ran a roller coaster of fear, guilt, and hope. Chuck Rheinholt and a few Yoke-fellows encircled Steve and me with prayer just before the journey to New York.

Karen slept most of the way there, unaware of what lay before her. At age thirteen, her understanding was limited, yet at the hospital, she was talkative and alert as a battery of doctors examined her. With a smile, she cooperated with all the tests and chattered about good times with Joyce at Newark. "I am amazed," the neurologist in charge told us. "This child has compensated for the disease in a remarkable way."

Tuesday morning before surgery, reality dealt us a blow. Karen had slept soundly the night before with me beside her on a cot. At six A.M. a voice awoke us. "It's time to shave your daughter's head," a nurse crisply explained. "Her biopsy is scheduled at seven." The shock of seeing Karen shorn of her thick brown hair stabbed my heart. She was disoriented and afraid.

"Mom, where's my hair gone?" she whimpered. Next, the nurses gave her a shot to quiet her and then transferred Karen to a gurney. As they wheeled her off to the operating room, I heard Karen cry out, "I want my friend. I want to see Joyce."

Weeping beside her bed, I felt deep regret for putting her through this unnecessary ordeal. She'd asked for Joyce, her faithful companion. Here in this huge metropolitan hospital, I felt totally alone. I heard a tap on the door, "May I come in?" and a maintenance man arrived to mop the room. I looked up into the kind brown eyes of a very tall black man. His hair was grizzled, and his shoulders stooped. "You're feeling bad," he noted. "What's the matter, Ma'am?"

"Oh, they've just taken my daughter to surgery. They shaved her head, her beautiful hair, and she was crying for her friend Joyce," I mumbled.

"You're scared, aren't you?"

"Yes."

"And feeling like it's your fault."

"Yes, Karen didn't have to have a brain biopsy."

"Well, let's give Karen to Jesus right now!" Still holding his mop, he stood beside me in my chair and offered a simple prayer, "Dear Lord Jesus, please guide the surgeon and hold Karen in the palm of your hand. Let this mother know you are right here now with her and with her girl. Thank you, Jesus. Amen." The compassionate petition of a godly man was a sign. I continued in prayer.

Peace enveloped my fretful self. I turned in my Bible to Romans 8.28. "All things work together for good to them that love the Lord."

It wasn't until noon that I saw Karen in the Intensive Care Unit of the children's ward. She lay on her stomach with her head swathed in a white gauze turban. Her face was swollen beyond recognition. "How did surgery go?" I asked the attending nurse.

She avoided the question. "The doctor will be here shortly," she replied curtly. Karen began to thrash in the familiar spasms of a seizure. The nurse ran to her side, joined by a doctor, still in scrubs. "Start a valium IV stat!" he ordered.

"She's been doing this every fifteen minutes," the nurse reported.

Karen gasped for air. A spurt of vomit pooled on the bed. "Make sure the patient doesn't ingest that!" the doctor warned.

"Doctor, please," I interrupted, "tell me how my daughter did through surgery."

"The surgery went well. We got the brain tissue." Her voice was cold, matter-of-fact. "It's the seizures I'm concerned about. It's important to stop them."

"What if they continue?" I asked, frightened.

"More brain damage."

"Could she die?" The doctor didn't answer me. The valium induced a deep sleep and rasping snore. I looked at Karen's bloated face and bandaged head, blaming myself for her condition.

In a curtained cubicle nearby, a black family gathered around a crib. A newborn baby struggled to breathe and lay in a respirator. I overheard the grandmother's prayer for her tiny grandson, "Jesus, he's in Your hands now. Thank you for holding him safe." Others joined in, offering thanksgiving for the Lord's care.

A sharp pang of aloneness brought yearning for my friends in the Yokefellow group. Just a touch from another understanding person would help. The grandmother parted the curtain and looked over at me, a young mother weeping beside her daughter.

Soon, I felt the comfort of her arms around me. "Honey, this is your girl?" She lightly touched Karen's still hand. "Don't be afraid. Jesus is right here with her and with you, too."

I voiced my fears and guilt in a jumble of words, and she listened with compassion in her wise loving eyes. This woman of faith lifted Karen and me into God's healing light. *The Lord sends His angels in amazing ways*, I thought, *just when I need His strength the most*.

Karen began to speak again after five days of silence; the seizures were under control; and she was enjoying eating. The doctor suggested I return home while she stayed a second week in the hospital. I was reassured when Karen asked, "When can I see Joyce?"

The morning before my departure, the nurse arrived carrying a pink box with a white ribbon. "Open it, Karen!" she demanded. I helped lift the cover to unwrap from tissue paper a short brown pageboy wig. Karen held it, mystified.

"Your new hair!" I exclaimed.

"This one's made from human hair, none of the acrylic stuff!" the nurse boasted. "Try it on." She slipped the wig over the light gauze bandage. "Wow, you're a glamour girl!"

For the first time since surgery, a smile brightened Karen's face as carefully she felt the strands of hair.

"School soon?" she questioned.

"Soon as you're better," I assured her.

To prepare for Karen's homecoming, Steve and I transformed the den into a bedroom. A wheelchair, the talking book machine, her favorite stuffed animals, Baby Mary, and her Braille book of Psalms made the room Karen's. I set up a cot for sleeping close by to help her to the bathroom at night. Rick's Batman cartoons and Miriam's soft velvet lavender pillow were signs of welcome from the children.

When Steve drove in Saturday afternoon, the clan was there to greet them. To see their sister in a wheelchair troubled her brothers and sisters. They crowded around Karen, questions flying. "Glad to be home?" "Wanna play ball?" "Let me see your scar." She sat hunched over, mumbling incoherently, and unable to connect with her family.

Later, eleven-year-old Miriam grabbed my arm and pulled me into a chair as her big sister napped. "Mom, what's happened to Karen? She can't do anything after that operation! Is she going to die?" Her eyes were full of tears, her pixie face sad.

"Honey, she'll be improving, but I...I..." A vise of grief tightened my throat. "I just don't know."

There were some changes for the better over the next few weeks, but incontinence, slurred speech, and immobility marked Karen's decline. However, one part of her remained untouched—her loving spirit.

The reunion with her best friend at Newark was unforgettable. Joyce walked to the wheelchair, touched her friend's new hairdo and laughed. "Hey, Karen, you're a beauty queen." A chortle and then a warm hug spoke of the bond of love between them.

TEN
THE VALLEY OF THE SHADOW

It started as a gentle snow falling in hefty flakes that soon covered our backyard in a blanket of white. On the way home from church this first Sunday in January 1967, spirits soared. Packed in our station wagon, the children welcomed the gale-force wind that whipped sheets of snow against the windshield. "Betcha there's no school tomorrow!" Jon wagered.

"Yeah, we can try our new sleds on the golf course hill," Rick exulted.

Steve was concentrating on driving. "It's tough visibility. These white-outs are dangerous." An anxious note in his voice quieted the children. On Route 104 gusts of swirling snow slowed us down to five miles an hour. The cargo of lively humanity was at risk in the midst of a full-blown blizzard, and I was carrying a tiny new life, only seven weeks along.

"Let's pray, everybody," I suggested.

One after the other, the children spoke to God. "Just help us get home safely, so I can have a grilled cheese sandwich."

"Help Dad not to bump into another car."

"Protect us all, O Lord," I ended.

"And thank you for the snow," Cathy's voice added a P.S. At last, we turned into Woodard Road and plowed a car's length into our driveway. Stuck.

"Carry me, Dad," Cathy begged.

"Grab a hand," Steve organized the troops. Negotiating a path around the drifts, we tumbled into the front hall, leaving a melting pile of snow on the floor. I plugged in the lights of the Christmas tree which was still up, lit the candles on the mantle, and soon Steve had a merry blaze crackling in the fireplace. I threw a few old quilts on the living room floor, and the children sprawled out while they munched on grilled cheese sandwiches and soaked in the warmth of the fire.

"Look at that drift!" Miriam pointed to the window, almost entirely blocked with snow. "Wow! This is a big one!"

Steve and I sat companionably on the sofa. "Connie, how are you feeling after the struggle of getting the family off to church plus the surprise of this blizzard?" He put his arm around me.

"Still queasy in the morning and awfully tired," I admitted. "But I feel good about our decision."

"Me, too," he agreed. "Of all the kids, this one's the biggest shock, but…"

"A gift from God." I finished his sentence.

After hearing about another child, Dr. Norris, Karen's neurologist, had offered to arrange an abortion. "With the high risk of lipidosis, you'll want to weigh the consequences of a full-term pregnancy," he counseled. "Talk it over with your husband."

At age thirty-seven, I quickly approached middle age, not prime childbearing years. More daunting was the threat of this pernicious disease in another offspring. Steve and I had debated the pros and cons. Already I loved that embryonic being growing within me. "I believe this baby is a gift from God, sent to comfort us and give us hope," I concluded.

"Karen's going downhill," Steve added. "Maybe in His way, God is replacing her with this little one." We embraced, expressing our commitment to the small growing life within me.

Once again, as I glanced around the circle of faces on that snowy afternoon in January, I sensed the vital individual goodness in each child. The connection of sisters, as Miriam rocked Cathy; the affection of brothers, as Rick and Jon played with Matchbox cars—who could calculate the treasure of family love?

• • • • • • • • • • • • • • • •

Winter soon passed. Spring was blooming in tulips and daffodils along Woodard Road. On a sunny April weekend, Karen came home for a visit. Since her surgery, there had been times when she did not recognize her brothers and sisters, but pleasant surprises punctuated the shadows, and by Christmas, three potholders in my stocking reassured me that the Newark weavers were busy again.

Sunshine and a refreshing breeze filled the dining area off the kitchen. Karen now sat on the sofa. Rick laughed as he hurled a pillow. "You're good at catching, Karen! Throw it back!" It wasn't much of a pitch, but he caught it in midair.

Later, I carried in a basket of clean laundry, fresh from the dryer. Karen folded towels and washcloths, chattering while she worked. Steve was taking a break from the first mow of the season. "Karen, let's go out, and I'll show you my new ride 'em lawn mower," he offered.

"Wanna ride with you, Dad," she requested. It wasn't often that we could decipher her words, but this was clear. Her father put an arm around his daughter and guided her to the tractor and up into the driver's seat.

Karen thrived on being busy. I marveled at her energy that weekend. I held her up so that she could scrub the kitchen counter. Later, dishtowel in hand, she sat in a chair and dried pots and pans. Her hair had grown into a becoming pixie cap, and she wore the rose jumper and flowered blouse I had made her. Something prompted me to grab the camera and capture her smile of delight in being able to help.

Tired, she dozed as Steve drove her back to Newark Sunday evening. "I think Karen's getting better, Mom," Miriam commented later. "There are still lots of things she loves to do."

"And this weekend she had a chance to do them all," I agreed. Before bedtime, we shared a prayer of thanks for Karen's loving self and her enjoyment in helping.

The following week as I was out in the garden raking dead leaves away from the perennials, I heard the phone ringing. I ran to answer it. "Mrs. Castor, this is Dr. Randall from Newark." Icy fear constricted my breathing.

"Is something the matter with Karen?" I asked.

"I'm not sure if it's a psychological problem or caused by her disorder, but there's been a change," he continued. "Karen is now completely bedridden."

"You mean, you mean…" I was grasping for words. "She can't sit up or stand? Can she speak?"

The doctor cleared his throat. "She said only one sentence, 'I think I'm going to die.'" His voice was gruff with emotion. I began to cry. "Please come and see her as soon as possible. I'm interested in how she reacts to you," Dr. Randall requested. "You'll find her in our hospital, right next door to the Women's Infirmary."

With my head in my hands, I sat down on the sofa. I felt as if an unbearable weight were pulling me down into blackness. I *think I'm going to die*. The words echoed in my mind. "Oh, God, she knows," I wept as I prayed. "How lonely and scared she must be, knowing that she is dying! Please hold her close to Your heart, Lord Jesus." Now, it was happening, the fact of my daughter's death. I had to face it, but I was unable to bear it.

Steve was away at a teacher's conference. I needed to talk to someone. Phyllis from Yokefellows would understand. Often when I had shared my feelings about Karen's decline, her empathy had reached me through a touch or eyes full of tears. She listened as I poured out my grief. Her voice was husky as she offered, "I'll be glad to drive you to Newark tomorrow, Connie. And just know I'll be praying for you and Karen."

As I waited in the reception room of the hospital, the familiar smell of Lysol and urine evoked in me the memory of our first visit to the Women's Infirmary three years before. A nurse arrived to escort me to Karen's bed in the hospital ward. "Do you want me to come with you?" Phyllis had asked.

"Thank you, but I think I'll see her alone," I decided.

Karen's eyes were wide open, her face peaceful. Her thin body seemed diminished under a white sheet. The stillness, not a sound or a movement, was eerie. I sat beside her and held her hand. Five and a half months pregnant, I felt the flutter of life within me. I longed for a sign of response from my frail daughter. "Karen, it's Mom," I spoke to her. Not a flicker of reaction. I told her about happenings at home. "Last night, Rick and Jon tied some blue towels around their necks and jumped off the top bunk," I recounted. "Boy, was I scared when I heard that loud crash!"

"'We're Batman and Robin,' they explained." Her blank stare was replaced by an expression of delight as a smile spread over her face. Then, I heard the familiar chuckle that told me her sense of humor was still intact. There was no ability to grip my hand; her arm was limp as I moved it. The disease, with its lesions of clogged dead cells, had shut down a crucial part of her brain, but I knew her spirit was untouched.

Phyllis joined me, each of us holding a hand as we prayed for my daughter. I sensed another Presence by her bed, a Presence of infinite love reflected in Karen's peaceful face.

Dr. Randall kept us informed of changes and concerns. Feeding her was difficult. At times, she could eat pureed food and drink fluids through a straw, but she often refused nourishment. The loss of weight made her body emaciated like the starved children I saw on TV. One time, I gathered the courage to look beneath the hospital gown. Her body was a skeleton covered with skin. Good care had avoided bedsores.

Another time, we were wheeling Karen in a Gerry chair and bumped her foot against the bed. She wailed like a mewing kitten as her face contorted in pain revealing her vulnerability. I moved her with great care after that incident.

Karen's transfer to the hospital was difficult for Joyce. During one of my visits to Newark in the summer of '67, Joyce and I sat under a maple tree, talking. "Mrs. Castor, it's awful hard for me to see Karen so weak." There were tears as she spoke. "We used to have such fun together. Sometimes, I just sit beside her bed and cry."

"I do, too, Joyce. Know what cheers me up? That amazing rug you two made!" I tried to give her spirit a lift.

"Karen and I were like a factory," Joyce recalled. "In and out, in and out, we wove those strips and hooked them to our looms. As fast as we could, we produced potholders."

"Didn't you get tired?" I asked.

"We had a goal—to get it done as a present for you," Joyce reminisced. "Sewing 'em all together, I was really tired."

"The potholder rug is a reminder to me of two friends and their gift of love. Hey, you like to type. Let's write each other letters." For a year, Joyce and I kept in touch until our family moved away.

In the meantime, the burgeoning fetus created a shelf atop my enormous belly on which I could balance a cup and saucer. Of course, a good inside kick would send them flying! I had been studying books on natural childbirth and practicing deep breathing because I was determined to work with the contractions. No drugs this time.

In the wee hours of the morning, August 8th, I was practicing the script encoded in my subconscious. As each contraction peaked, I pictured uterine muscles, fueled by the Creator's power, pushing the baby along to the birth canal. I rested peacefully in between.

I thanked God for this new life and for the amazing birth process. Once I overheard Dr. Merrill speaking to the nurse out in the hall. "These old mothers are slow. It will be a while." After three hours, I was only five centimeters dilated. The nurse agreed, "Especially for a baby this size. It's a big one!"

My morale plummeted. Was this going to be a long twelve-hour labor like the others? But again the uterine clamp of a strong contraction focused my attention on giving birth. At five A.M. the nurse wheeled me into the delivery room. "How about something to take the edge off?" she offered, a gas mask in hand.

"Nope. I'm fine," I grunted. Dr. Merrill arrived in time to encourage me to "Push! One more time, PUSH!" Only a mother knows the joy of that final whoosh and then the music of a newborn's cry. David Mark Castor weighed nine pounds twelve ounces. The euphoria of motherhood enveloped me once more as I held a very alert baby boy who peered up at me from deep blue eyes. Yes, God's gift of love and comfort had arrived just in time.

In October, Karen met her new brother. Steve, Suzy Gazlay, our guitar-playing friend, and I plus baby David stopped off at Newark for a visit. We were returning home from a "Faith at Work" weekend. The nurse agreed to transport Karen down to the reception room.

Toting a diaper bag on one arm and a howling Davey in the other, I arrived just as Karen's bed rolled out of the elevator. "Lord, calm him down," I prayed. "Karen doesn't need the bellowing." Steve held his son, tummy down. Sure enough, he began to coo and gurgle as I helped Karen feel his fuzzy head, little ears, button nose, and his diminutive hands and feet. "Karen, this is David, your baby bother," I introduced them.

A soft sound parted her lips. "David," she whispered. A smile wreathed her face.

"Thank you, thank you, Lord," I prayed silently. Suzy Gazlay began to strum her guitar. "Jesus loves me this I know," we sang. The elevator door opened. Other nurses, patients, and aides arrived to join in the hymn sing. Karen was aware and listening, obviously enjoying our spontaneous worship. With the baby asleep in my arms, I gathered with others around her bed to offer prayers of praise and petition. The oldest had met the youngest!

In December, just before her birthday, we were surprised to hear Karen distinctly counting, "One, two, three, four, five, six, seven, eight, nine, ten, eleven, twelve, thirteen, fourteen, fifteen…I am going to be fifteen," she announced. I was flabbergasted.

"Did you hear that, Steve?"

"Unbelievable!" was his reaction.

The nurse smiled when I exclaimed over the way Karen had broken the silence. "There's a foster grandmother who has unofficially adopted your daughter," she explained. "Several times a week she comes to visit."

"Has she been teaching Karen to count?" I asked incredulously.

"For at least a month Mrs. Perkins has been working with her on numbers and talking about her birthday."

"Another angel!" I thought, "Someone who loves Karen and can still see the potential for learning. Thank you, Lord."

On her birthday, Karen was agitated. Thus far, lipidosis had not caused aggressive behavior, but it now became difficult to watch her reflexive biting and thrashing. Still, Karen enjoyed the soft ice cream, sips of juice, and our family's off-key rendition of "Happy Birthday." We just missed a disaster with the lighted cake when her hand flew out. As she became calmer, I slipped on her the new pink satin quilted bed jacket. I brushed her hair and stroked her cheek until she fell asleep. I knew instinctively that this was Karen's last birthday on earth. How much longer could her frail body keep going?

I had come to dread telephone calls during Karen's ten months in the hospital. Again, I heard Dr. Randall's voice on the other end of the line, "Karen has pneumonia," he relayed the information with sensitivity. "She's too weak to fight the disease."

"Are you saying she's going to die?" I asked with my heart in my throat.

"Yes," he replied. "I hate to see her go, there's something about her—a goodness—that I like."

Davey, at six months old, rolled around in his playpen. His long-lashed blue eyes, dandelion crop of hair and wide toothless grin made him an antidote to grief. I held his warm, chubby body against me, and rocked him back and forth. "Oh Lord, thank you for Your presence in life and death. You are with Karen now even in her weakness," I prayed. "Thank you for the gift of Davey. Strengthen me one day at a time."

Steve and I could hardly communicate our feelings, each so burdened with grief that we had little to give to each other. Yokefellows continually rallied around our anxious family. Phyllis sat with me by Karen's bedside while she slept. The thin body under the sheets at times struggled to breathe because her lungs were congested. Ashamed to admit it, I was afraid to be alone with her. What if she should die while I was with her? How could I stand it?

Her brothers and sisters were also full of questions. We told them that Karen would soon be with the Lord. Where would she go when she died? What was Heaven like? Was she sad about leaving? Was she in pain?

"Come on, kids," I invited them. "Let's sit around the kitchen table and see what God's Word has to say about the questions you asked."

Miriam read aloud from John 14.2. "In my Father's house are many rooms…I go to prepare a place for you."

"A special place for Karen?" Rick asked.

"That's right," I answered. "Rick, you're a good reader. Look all the way to the end of the New Testament at Revelation 21.4. What does it say about Heaven?"

"And God shall wipe away all tears from their eyes; and there shall be no more death, or sorrow, or crying, or any more pain," Rick read. "Karen's going to be very happy in Heaven."

Jon joined in, "She'll have a new body, too. My Sunday school teacher told me."

"That's true. Listen to this." I read 1 Corinthians 15.48 from my Phillips translation. "The body is sown in weakness; it is raised in power … As there is a natural body, so will there be a spiritual body. That means Karen will be strong and alive." Our little Bible study not only reassured the children but also gave me promises to strengthen my spirit.

Steve and I knew it was important for the children to say goodbye to their sister, so on a Sunday in March, a sunny pre-spring day, we left for Newark immediately after church and stopped for burgers and fries en route.

There was the customary wait in the reception room as the nurse prepared Karen for our visit. She had received excellent care in her private room. Later, in a poem addressed to Karen, I was able to express my feelings during this last visit:

I hesitated outside the hospital door,
Clutching at me, a knot of fear.
Today would you know that we were here?
You had been sleeping the two weeks before.

You were awake, lying on your side,
Quietly knowing we were there.
Your eyes not seeing, yet somehow aware,
Of something eternal, beyond us, outside.

Your face was beautiful, tranquil, bright;
Fragile body covered with an aseptic spread
Had wrenched me, so thin after months in bed.
Today I saw only your face, transparent with light.

A flicker of response as your dad held your hand,
You were too weak to play "Magic Ring."
Happenings at home, we told you everything.
Somehow I felt you could understand.

Once we watched you struggle for breath.
Helpless, I knew with a twinge of dread.
One heartbeat maintained the tenuous thread
That held you from the shadow of death.

Before we left, we wanted to share
'Jesus Tender Shepherd,' last words by your bed,
Expressing the love more felt than said.
Your spirit was joining us in this prayer.

The sense of being on holy ground, with our pure sweet Karen about to enter eternity, hushed all of us. Tears wet Miriam's cheek laid on Karen's as she said goodbye. Rick and Jon came together as Rick cried, "Don't forget Batman!" Jon masked his feelings, mercifully protected from associating himself with Karen's illness, whereas Cathy didn't understand. "Why doesn't she talk?" she wondered.

After the visit that Sunday afternoon, I felt a need to shut myself away. I locked the door of the bedroom and knelt beside the bed. It was an urgent prayer of a mother, asking the release of her daughter. "O God," I pled, "Tonight set her free from her weak body, from the struggle to breathe." From the intensity of prayer came an inner release. It was as if He said, "Leave her in My hands now. You will have your answer soon."

Friends from church dropped in for a visit that evening. At 9:10 P.M., the call came from Newark that Karen had gone peacefully. We wept together while our friends comforted us. We joined hands, thanking God that she was now with her friend Jesus, the one she loved so much. Her prayer, "Jesus heal me some day whole," had been answered.

"I just can't believe my sister is dead!" Miriam cried. She elected to stay home from school and help me with preparations.

I sensed that with Rick and Jon the Bible study had made a difference in their acceptance of Karen's death. "We want to stay home, too." They sorted through photos with me to put together an album of her life.

Plans had been made through the Research Institute and Strong Memorial Hospital that there would be an immediate autopsy to provide tissue for further research in juvenile lipidosis. On Wednesday, I received a box from Strong. A note verified that inside were Karen's ashes. As I held it, strange emotions welled up. "Is this all that is left of you, Karen?" I cried. "O Karen, my daughter, my daughter!" With great gulping sobs, I wept for the loss of one truly good person who gave all she had—simple love and faith in God. Over and over, I read Paul's words of comfort, "Eye has not seen, nor ear heard, nor entered the heart of man the things God has prepared for them that love Him." (1 Corinthians 2.9)

● ● ● ● ● ● ● ● ● ● ● ● ● ●

A triumphant celebration took place at Brighton Community Church on March 10th, 1968. The sanctuary overflowed as we remembered together one small life lived for Jesus. On the altar was a simple bouquet of lavender and white mums. "Open our eyes, open our eyes," a high sweet tenor began the anthem. Thirty voices from the chancel choir joined him: "That we may see You, O loving and compassionate Jesus, walking beside us in our sorrow. For through the portals of death we enter into the presence of the living God."

The words rang true. Joe Bayly had admonished us, "Be prepared to walk with Karen through the valley of the shadow of death." All the way through her short life, Jesus had been with her as her Shepherd, and He now walked with us in our loss.

As Pastor Crawford read Steve's and my memories of our daughter and shared his own experiences with her, I was amazed at the impact of her life. Her father's words said it well: "In Karen, who gave herself early to Christ in a simple, unquestioning faith, we have seen how God has infused her life with a purpose many times beyond its apparent potential... If the beautiful account of Christ's taking an unknown boy's lunch of two loaves and five fish to feed the hungry could have a spiritual counterpart, it is illustrated in how He has taken Karen's life, blessed it and broken it, and nourished our own inner life through it."

• • • • • • • • • • • • • • •

A year later, almost to the day of Karen's death, the Castor family had decided to worship at the United Methodist Church in Batavia. After a recent move, we had been searching for a church home. This was our first Sunday morning at this particular house of worship.

A simple arrangement of lavender and white mums adorned the altar. It was time for the anthem. A high sweet tenor sang, "Open our eyes, open our eyes..." The choir joined in: "O loving and compassionate Jesus, that we may see You walking beside us in our sorrow."

"Got a Kleenex, Mom?" Miriam was remembering. Steve and I wept. God's sign to us was clear: His love was encompassing Karen in Heaven and us on earth. I knew that "Nothing can separate us from the love of God which is in Christ Jesus our Lord." (Romans 8.39) Jesus was still walking beside us in our sorrow, and for the first time, Steve was free to grieve.

But in all these things we overwhelmingly conquer through Him who loved us. For I am convinced that neither death, nor life, nor angels, nor principalities, nor things present, nor things to come, nor powers, nor height, nor depth, nor any other created thing, shall be able to separate us from the love of God, which is in Christ Jesus our Lord."

PART II

JON

ELEVEN
RENOVATION

There wasn't much to distinguish Elba from hundreds of other quiet little towns in New York State except perhaps that place on Main Street. We drove by slowly, taking in the details of the decaying old townhouse, a surprising blemish in an otherwise tidy neighborhood. Weathered clapboards were peeling off the second story—not a trace of paint anywhere. The porches sagged, and ornate pillars threatened to cave in from the weight of the roof. In front, a wild grapevine climbed luxuriantly over the posts and up into the attic through broken windows. The barn spewed an assortment of junk into the driveway. A mammoth place, it had probably been the pride of the town in its day, but now a FOR SALE sign hung dejectedly on its front door.

Steve turned the station wagon around and drove by again. "You know, Connie, that house could really be something if it were fixed up," he mused aloud. I was getting nervous. "Just look at the lines! And I bet it has a magnificent staircase!" We were now parked across the street. I could see Steve was about to go over for a closer look, a visionary gleam in his eye. My nervousness was becoming acute anxiety.

"If you think I'd even inspect that…that…DUMP," I sputtered, "you're out of your mind! And how can you tell about its lines under all that Victorian folderol and jungle growth?" Over the front porch hung a Juliet-type balcony, replete with intricately detailed railing. Huge maples shut out the summer sun, casting a funereal gloom. "I wouldn't be a bit surprised if that house were haunted," I added, keeping a firm grip on Steve who had opened the car door.

Reluctantly, he started the motor, giving a last long look across the street. I thought of the colonial on Woodard Road in Webster which had been ours the last four years. When Steve had accepted a new position as curriculum coordinator of Batavia schools, we sold it. Closing was set for

85

the end of August. All spring, we traveled the fifty miles back and forth between towns, tracking down every possibility of a home. The selection was sparse. Apparently, people settled in the Batavia area for the rest of their lives.

• • • • • • • • • • • • • • •

After Karen's death, I had times of missing her intensely. Our family circle had been broken by a silent predator, Batten Disease, the newly designated name for juvenile lipidosis. On restless nights, I would sometimes be haunted by flashbacks of my daughter in a hospital bed, thin and still, ravaged by the disorder. Anger at the unfair ugliness of it flickered inside me. I knew in my heart that she was with Jesus and complete and joyous, but nevertheless, residual hurt had wounded me.

In contrast, Jon at age ten, was tough and strong, the picture of health. Blind, yes, but he was convinced his life could be full and satisfying despite the handicap. Since first grade, Jon had enjoyed being a student at School for the Blind in Batavia. His keen mind was untouched by the disease. History of the United States fascinated him, especially accounts of the Revolutionary and Civil Wars. Wrestling was his sport, and he was coached by Mr. Gugel, his hero.

I refused to harbor thoughts of his decline. Jon was different from Karen. God was guarding his sinewy young body and questing intelligence.

One night a week after driving by the Elba house, Steve and I were wide awake in the big antique double bed, so we talked over our latest futile house-hunting trek. He cautiously broached the subject of the house in Elba. "Wouldn't it be fun to turn that old place into a real home again? It would be a natural for our antiques." I stiffened beside him. "In fact," he continued undaunted, "I found out we could get it for $9,000. The realtor's going to take us through this weekend."

"How on earth would you find time to work on that wreck?" I snorted, ready to clobber him with a hundred objections. "With your schedule, you hardly have time to mow the lawn now!"

"The profit we've made on this house would be enough for hiring a contractor to do everything," he retorted.

"How about Jon?" I questioned. "We have to consider his needs. Can you imagine trying to navigate without sight in the midst of remodeling?"

"You know Jon, Connie," Steve countered. "He loves a challenge. Let's not worry about that until we've seen the inside."

And so, I found myself on the dilapidated side porch, gingerly turning the doorknob after the realtor unlocked the door. "Solid brass, underneath the tarnish," Steve breathed in my ear. I braced myself for a snow job. He was acquiring the proprietary air of a king surveying his castle. We entered what must have been the dining room. Twenty-eight feet long and with a tall bay window on the far end, it was surprisingly gracious. Two sitting rooms on either side of the large hall appeared in fairly decent shape. One boasted a corner fireplace with a handsomely carved mantle. And Steve had been right about the staircase. It curved regally up into the second floor.

"Notice the excellent condition of the woodwork—cherry, I think," the realtor pointed out dutifully. I was noticing quite a few details—the heavy paneled sliding doors, the spacious, high-windowed rooms that somehow seemed homey in spite of cauliflower wallpaper. Steve was keeping an alert eye on my reactions.

"Can I see the kitchen? And how about the bathroom?" I asked, not bothering to hide my interest.

"You'd probably have to have some plumbing done before you could move in," the realtor warned us in one of her many understatements. In the kitchen, an iron sink on spindly legs was equipped with one faucet that dripped rusty water. No cupboards at all, but there was a long many-shelved pantry. Next to it, a shed-like room packed with metal parts, magazines and two bulging closets that emitted a musty odor. Ugh! I shuddered at the mess.

Steve, ignoring the debris, was mentally measuring the shed. "Hey, this could be our family room! I'd knock out the pantry wall, put an old beam up there for reinforcement and a brick wall with a fireplace where the two closets are now.' The dip in the floor was obvious even under the junk, yet I could almost envision a crackling fire and a shiny linoleum brick floor.

The scurry of a rodent brought us back to reality. "I'm getting out of here! You can have your ratty shed!" The bathroom with its smelly unflushable toilet was an added dampener to the adventuresome spirit that had almost gotten the better of me.

"Shall we go upstairs?" The realtor was anxious to leave. The hall, with six intriguing doors opening off it, was long enough for a bowling alley. The bedrooms were large, each with its own walk-in closet. Even the plaster lying in heaps on the floor and the bare lathing on some of the ceilings couldn't hide the basically livable layout. A claw-footed unhitched tub was the only sign of a bathroom.

"Well, it would take plenty of work," I admitted grudgingly. A bear hug from Steve told me how glad he was that I'd caught the fever. The realtor looked at us uncertainly, quite sure we'd lost our minds.

"We won't decide anything until we've had a contractor look the place over," he reassured her.

Within a few days, we'd found ourselves a builder, a burly ex-Marine who took on the old house with obvious misgivings. He beckoned me aside after his initial inspection. "Listen, lady, I gotta nice split-level near here, two and a half bathrooms, just perfect for your family." He cast a disapproving eye on the fallen ceiling by our feet.

"Nope. We want the atmosphere and spaciousness of an older home, like no other house anywhere!"

"Do you have any idea how much this'll cost ya, lady?"

"Couldn't you give us some kind of an estimate?" I asked naively.

"Who knows," he shrugged, "just getting rid of the stuff in these thirteen rooms…" He shook his head. Later, when we signed the papers that officially made the home ours, I wondered what we had gotten ourselves into.

Part of me, however, looked forward to the move. A new location and the challenge of rebuilding an old house roused my nesting instincts. The sagging mansion was like my torn self. The renovation process could be healing, and working with Steve might bring two grieving parents together.

In the meantime, we had moved out of the Webster colonial into a three-room cottage on Horseshoe Lake in Batavia. It was a tight arrangement with our camper set up nearby for the boys' sleeping quarters. Steve and I worked over plans, picturing the sunny kitchen with its cherry cabinets, a green and gold bathroom off our room, and,—oh joy!—a playroom with shelves for the kids' toys.

It's a good thing our imaginations were in healthy condition because there was certainly no indication of our plans becoming reality. In fact, the old mansion began to look more woebegone than ever. Workmen tore the weathered clapboard away, revealing its skeletal innards. It was sad to see the grapevines come down. Minus the bric-a-brac and foliage, the house took on the air of an emaciated old pachyderm, shivering in the autumn breezes.

Inside, work was in progress, difficult to discern through the plaster dust, tangled wires, and bales of insulation. As soon as the children were off to school, I'd pack up one-year-old Davey, make the six-mile jaunt to Elba, and wade through the debris to work upstairs. When the plasterers had installed new ceilings, I came through with my buckets of hot water (bummed from neighbors) and monstrous sponges to soak off the old wallpaper. The hissing of a rented steamer with its unpredictable eruptions of scalding water was too much for me to handle. I counted as many as nine layers of paper in the scraping process. Now, the bare cracked walls were ready for repair. Thank God for a mild sunny fall when Davey could curl up for a nap in his porta-crib outside under the trees or play contentedly in his playpen.

The wiring completed upstairs and the walls ready for papering, Steve and I discovered our Yokefellow friends from Webster were willing to put love into action. On weekends, a small battalion would converge on "Castors' disaster" (as several dubbed our private urban renewal project) with their paintbrushes and rollers in hand. Scraping, sanding, and painting the old woodwork as the coffeepot steamed in one corner, we gradually saw dingy places transformed into bright cozy bedrooms.

Steve caught the paperhanging fever. A quick supper at the cottage, and the mob would be packed into the station wagon for another onslaught on the "mansion." Our bedroom, inviting in soft aqua carpeting, was the first to be completed. Spreadout sleeping bags and a lamp rigged up for homework, the children made it their headquarters. Into the early morning hours, I measured and pasted. Steve hung the strips of paper until weariness overtook us. "What do you think? Is it worth it?" we'd ask each other, surveying our handiwork bleary-eyed.

The children explored the nooks and crannies typical of an old house. Jon saw possibilities in the laundry chute with its trap door in his brother's room. "Hey, Rick," he called down the passageway. "Ready for a secret message?" Down clunked a box holding a map with an X marking the site of their planned fort. Already the boys were hoarding a pile of leftover lumber for building a hideout.

One Saturday afternoon while hanging wallpaper in the kitchen, I heard a muffled scream coming from the corner cupboard in the family room. I opened the door to find two legs dangling from the laundry chute. "Help, I'm stuck!" Cathy yelled.

Upstairs, Jon's voice echoed down the escape hatch. "Need a push?"

"Hey, I'll handle this," I took charge. Carefully, I extracted a bedraggled little seven-year-old from the cupboard.

"Wow! That was fun!" Cathy exclaimed.

"Secret tunnel," her brother's voice bellowed from above.

"No more trial runs," I announced. "Use the back stairs."

Rumors were spreading among the relatives about the monstrosity we had acquired. In October, Steve's brother and his family arrived to survey the place which was now in the process of being sided with six-inch clapboards. Shiny polyurethaned floors gleamed upstairs, bringing out the mellow coloring of the old pine flooring. Impressed with what they could see of the still-sticky upper story, Dick and Diana joined us for a tour of the ground floor. Chaos prevailed—one wall knocked out where the family room connected to the workshop, bricks in a wheelbarrow by a half-finished fireplace, and gaping holes in the floors where the old registers used to be. Our furniture clogged the two side rooms that would someday be the playroom and library. At least the powder room, with its gleaming tile and flushable toilet, was an accent of order. "Do you think you'll be moving in before the snow flies?" Dick asked.

"You can't be serious about having us for Thanksgiving!" Diana added. Seen through others' eyes, it was a disheartening mess. And just when we were hoping for a final push from the contractor, the work crew mysteriously disappeared.

The fall winds whistled around the little cabin on Horseshoe Lake where Steve and I sat at the kitchen table, taking inventory of the situation. "Promises, promises," Steve muttered morosely. "He says he'll be there tomorrow with his men, but all he's interested in is finishing the new houses in the development."

"Yeah, the guys are bugged by our old place," I added my touch of gloom. "You should have heard the mason swear at the uneven bathroom floors!"

"We sure can't move in before the wiring's complete downstairs," he continued. "With the weather getting colder, we've got to have heat. Maybe the whole thing's a terrible mistake!" Depressed, I almost agreed with him.

The next morning, the wind carried with it whirling snowflakes, clinging to my sneakers and stinging my face as I trudged over to the camper to awaken the boys. Rick and Jon, snug under electric blankets, awoke with whoops of joy over the first snowfall. Steve was uneasy. "If this keeps up, be prepared to move out of here today," he warned.

"But the stove's not even hooked up, and what about the heat?" I sputtered.

"The car will never make it up the hill on a slippery road," he replied. "You know they don't plow back here."

All morning, the fresh snow drifted, coming down thickly. At eleven o'clock, Steve burst through the kitchen door, carrying a load of boxes. "Pack up everything you can lay your hands on—fast!" he ordered. "They're predicting a blizzard!" An hour later, the station wagon was crammed to the gills with our belongings. We journeyed down the hill to Elba. Snow drifted into the barn, settling on bikes and boxes stored in the back.

"I have no idea where to look for the kids' boots," I complained. "Sometimes, I hate this whole mixed-up mess!" Steve stalked into the house. I sat in the car, crying angry tears of frustration.

Our unexpected arrival convinced the contractor that we were serious about living in the house. Suddenly, there was a flurry of activity as the electricians put in long hours on the wiring. The carpenters hung kitchen cabinets, and the mason finished the fireplace. In the meantime, we operated on one-third voltage, blowing a fuse whenever the stove and toaster were on simultaneously.

During this time, I received a visit from my chic Rochester friend, Eileen, who brought along Gwen, her elegantly coiffured blond sister-in-law, I greeted the two in my paint-smeared dungarees and sweatshirt, offering them coffee at the picnic table in the family room. The plaster, a virile type on stilts, was obviously appreciating the rare touch of glamour. He'd come clomping over, as close as he dared, and would slap joint compound on the taped wallboard directly above us. The girls viewed the chaos wide-eyed. "Connie, how can you stand to live like this? I'd be out of my mind!" At that moment, a wad of plaster plopped into Eileen's coffee. We ended up laughing hysterically.

There came an evening when I stood back quietly, taking a long look at the dinner table just before Steve came home from the office. Soft firelight lit up the family room, which now boasted early American wallpaper and warm red drapes. Even the old settee and chairs looked handsome in fresh slipcovers. Candles glowed on the antique cherry drop-leaf. The white brick-patterned floor, finished the night before, reflected dancing flames. In the kitchen area, cherry cupboards were hung efficiently, polished in the light of hob-nailed lamps. Steve hung up his overcoat and joined me, the proprietary gleam kindled again in his eyes. "Nice, isn't it?"

"Just as we'd imagined it would be!" I replied.

"Think it's worth the struggle?" he asked.

I had to stop and think a little on that one. "Yep, it's home now!" The oasis of order in the kitchen and family room was a retreat as we tackled the rest of the downstairs.

A phone call from Steve's secretary one early December morning roused the painting and papering team into frantic action. "Connie, I thought I'd better let you know about a rumor that's been floating around the office," she reported sotto voce. "The administrative staff is planning a surprise housewarming for you a week from now."

"How many do you think will be coming?" I asked nervously.

"Probably thirty or forty."

I hung up the phone and looked around the place, wondering where we'd put that many people. The living room had been papered and painted but now held leftover bales of insulation. Apparently, the contractor had bought enough of the stuff on sale to insulate three houses. Okay. Get him to move 'em out of here, I mentally noted. That left the dining room still untouched, dismal dark woodwork beetled with old varnish and lurid roses peeling off the walls. Could we clear out the two rooms before the housewarming?

Every night, we scraped and painted, pushing ourselves with new energy. Off-white woodwork brightened the long dining room considerably. A pale blue above the wainscoting and wedgewood below picked up the colors in the fishing village mural that Steve hung on the far wall. At four-thirty A.M. of the big day, he smoothed on the final strip. "The most expensive paper in the house, and it's not even plumb," he groused wearily, patching a spot near the molding.

A few hours sleep and we were up moving furniture into the dining and living rooms. No decent rugs or drapes yet, but still the red velvet Victorian loveseat looked handsome against the gold and white paper. Grandfather clock ticked away in the corner, sonorously gonging the hours. The children helped me unpack antique glass pieces I'd almost forgotten we owned, and we carefully placed them in the pine corner cupboard. A quick swish of a dustcloth over the cherry drop-leaf with its familiar scratches, and we were braced for the "surprise" housewarming.

As Steve's staff people and cohorts from central office arrived with gifts and words of welcome, our home must have struck them as an overwhelming undertaking. The splintery pine floors downstairs were unfinished, the tall windows gaunt without drapes, yet firelight and candleglow softened the bareness of the rooms. That evening a house full of people laughing and eating gave us a preview of the kind of warmth we'd be experiencing.

• • • • • • • • • • • • • • •

The following November, the family gathered twenty-five strong to celebrate Thanksgiving. Just as I lifted the golden brown twenty-five-pound turkey out of the oven, a high-pitched "Help!" emanated from the family room cupboard.

"Not again!" I muttered, plopping the bird on a counter. I opened the door in time to catch Natalie, a tiny three-year-old niece, as she shot out of the chute.

Her cousin Jon chortled down the hatch, "Nat's just the right size."

"I wanna do it again," she agreed. From one end to the other of the red-carpeted dining room, the clan sat around a strung-out conglomeration of tables. The house was almost completed now from carpets to brocade drapes to federal blue clapboards outside. Young and old voices joined in the doxology, that ancient hymn of Thanksgiving:

"Praise God from whom all blessings flow,

Praise Him all creatures here below,

Praise Him above ye heavenly hosts,

Praise Father, Son, and Holy Ghost."

Our Heavenly Father's love encircled the family. The old house had come into its own.

TWELVE
DO YOU SEE WHAT I SEE?

An evening alone! I savored the thought of stillness and the time to dip into Catherine Marshall's book, *Beyond Ourselves*. Darkness came early in November 1969. In the yard, maple trees lifted bare branches in rhythm to the gusting wind, and autumn leaves rustled on the porch.

It had been a year since the family had moved into the old blue mansion on South Main Street in Elba, and the clan was settling in. Rick and his dad were away with friends, Roy and son, cheering Batavia's championship football team; Miriam was listening to records with a girl down the road; Cathy and Davey were tucked in, and Jon had just left for an overnight with a family from church.

Red candles glowed on the mantle. I was mesmerized by the flames of birch logs crackling in the fireplace. A spicy sip of Constant Comment tea warmed me, but I still needed something to rekindle my spirit.

The crunch of late night papering and painting had depleted my inner self. At last, the house project was completed. Drapes had just been hung in the library and books lined the shelves. I felt the need for personal renovation. Catherine Marshall made it plain when she said, "God is for us, first, last and always. By every word and action, by all the force of His personality, Christ sought to tell us that the Father is always nearer, mightier, freer to help us than we can imagine."[6] Yes, I had experienced this.

I recalled the sign God had sent to us the first time we had worshiped at the Methodist church in Batavia. Lavender mums on the altar and the words of assurance in the anthem on the anniversary of Karen's death had healed the bitterness of loss. The Father was holding my dear one in light eternal.

Surely, God was taking care of Jon as well. I thought about his amazing fort-building project. His cousin Andy had visited during the summer, and the two of them had dismantled Jon's first effort, a flimsy model that was "not big enough to keep the girls in jail." The search for a discarded window, the discovery of a hunk of leftover carpet, the pounding of nails, and the excitement as the gangplank was secured—I could hardly wait to see it.

"Not yet, Mom, not until we're finished," Jon warned me.

"Are you planning a celebration when it's all done?" I asked. "I'll make chocolate chip cookies and Kool-Aid."

"The first thing we're gonna do is capture the girls," Andy declared.

"And try out the jail," Jon added. "Ransom is twenty-five cents to spring 'em."

"How about fifteen cents on opening day?" I bargained, "And some refreshments?"

Jon allowed me to tour his fort the day after Andy went home. It was a rambling structure, built around an old lilac bush as big as a tree. A sign, "Girls Watch Out" was nailed to a creaky door. Jon straddled a high limb, intently hammering the last board on the roof. "Hey, Mom," he called down, "What do you think of it?"

"Some pad," I replied, surveying the cage-like contraption that held the platform up on the lowest branches of the gnarled tree. "What's this place for, with the bench in it?"

"Oh, that's the jail," he explained, backing down the rickety ladder. "We'll keep prisoners here after we catch 'em." A very long wide board leaned at an angle from a branch higher up. On it was tacked the scrap from our blue living room rug. "That's a look-out tower," Jon proudly informed me. "Good place for relaxing, too." He spread his eleven-year-old body out on the piece of lumber, managing to look comfortable even at a forty-five-degree angle.

"And what's this thing out in front?" I asked, peering up at what looked like a diving board.

"That's the gang plank," Jon grinned. "If the girls don't come across with a ransom, we'll make 'em walk the plank." I had almost forgotten he was blind that late summer morning as he introduced me to his fort.

• • • • • • • • • • • • • • • •

I sat in silence as I read, "Only if I can depend upon the Creator as a God of love shall I have the courage and confidence to turn my life and affairs over to Him."[7] The ringing of the telephone interrupted my train of thought.

"Connie, it's Rindy," her voice was shaky.

"Any problems with Jon?" I asked.

"He just had a spell. He was sitting on the floor watching TV, and suddenly, he toppled over, his arms and legs shaking. He's sleeping now."

A seizure. Fear constricted my throat as I hesitated before replying. "Oh, Rindy, I'm sorry you had to go through this. It's his first seizure."

"I was scared," she admitted. "Jon is just waking up now. I'll bring him right home."

Jon was groggy as I helped him into the house and up the stairs to bed. During the weekend, a pall of sadness covered my spirit. *Not Jon*, I thought, *not my vital strong son!* Steve, too, felt the pain. Our hope that somehow he would escape the inroads of Batten Disease was destroyed.

"I can't even think about Jon suffering what Karen did," Steve's voice broke. "Can you, Connie?"

"I'm struggling with flashbacks of Karen's last days," I wept. "Look at him! He loves life!" We sat in silent grief, caught up in the current of Karen's decline and Jon's inexorable future.

On Monday, Dr. Norris at Strong Memorial Hospital phoned in a prescription for Phenobarbital and Dilantin. I hated to put this lively bright boy on drugs. With no memory of the seizure, he was puzzled by new medication. "It's something your body needs," was my weak explanation.

"Wrestling practice after school," he reminded me. "Dad will bring me home." I was afraid the exertion would bring on another seizure.

"Jon, are you feeling up to it?" I asked anxiously.

"I'm fine. I feel great," Jon asserted.

The busy schedule of that week with church and tending to the needs of five children had kept me from facing the implications of Jon's seizure. Now there was a lull as Davey snoozed during his afternoon nap. I sat in the living room rocking in the old needlepoint rocker, my New Testament open on my lap. Turning to Romans 8.15, I read, "For you did not receive a spirit that makes you a slave again to fear, but you received the Spirit of sonship. And by him we cry, 'A*bba*, Father.'" (NIV) Yes, I had reverted to raw fear, akin to horror, over Batten's encroachment on my son. He, as a child of God, lived life with gusto in spite of limitations. I, despite knowing the reality of Christ's presence throughout Karen's illness, was shaken by doubts.

Paul continued: "Not only so, but we ourselves, who have the first-fruits of the Spirit, groan inwardly as we wait eagerly for our adoption as sons, the redemption of our bodies." (Romans 8.23, NIV) I realized that blight and disease are built into the very framework of creation, originating with the fall. Living as a child of God in my own slice of suffering was the challenge.

But how? I sat rocking and thinking. I wanted to pray, but only tears and sighs came from deep within. Through the blur, I kept on reading Romans 8.26–27, "In the same way, the Spirit helps us in our weakness. We do not know what we ought to pray for, but the Spirit himself intercedes for us with groans that words cannot express. And he who searches our hearts knows the mind of the Spirit, because the Spirit intercedes for the saints in accordance with God's will." (NIV)

"Oh, Father," I cried out, "I don't know how to pray for Jon. I am crushed under the weight of Batten's damage to his brain." Back and forth, back and forth, I rocked. "Holy Spirit, You pray for Jon," I beseeched. Inwardly, I stepped aside, aware of deep calm. Words in another tongue were formed and expressed. The Spirit was praying through me for my dear son. The core of me was united with Christ in petition and praise that only God understood. Peaceful as the prayer language ceased, I rested in the knowledge that Jon was secure in God's hands. "Neither height nor depth, nor anything else in all creation, will be able to separate us from the love of God that is in Christ Jesus our Lord." (Romans 8.39, NIV) The burden of fear and despair was lifted from me that afternoon. I walked again in the light of Jesus.

• • • • • • • • • • • • • • •

In the summer of 1970, my brother flew in from Florida for a weekend visit. A diabetic since age nineteen, Phil experienced serious complications from the disease. He was losing his sight, and there were signs of kidney damage.

Jon and Phil had a bond of understanding between them, a free flow of communication. Flopped on the living room floor, my brother plied his nephew with questions. Jon poured out the story of life at School for the Blind and about Gerald, his big black friend, section five heavyweight wrestling champion. "Nope, Uncle Phil, I haven't won a match yet, but Gerald's coaching me."

The last day of Phil's visit, the two buddies sat on the settee in the family room in earnest conversation. Phil held Jon's hand and prayed for him. The rest of us left, knowing this was a holy moment between uncle and nephew.

"Hey, Connie, come on out here," Phil called. "Jon has something he wants to tell you."

I sat down beside my son on the settee. The combination of a big smile and tears in his eyes signaled to me that the Spirit was at work. "Mom, I have Jesus in my heart," he declared. "Uncle Phil helped me understand that Jesus died to save me. He loves me very much."

"Jon, I'm so happy!" Phil beamed. My eyes were misty. "How do you think this will make a difference for you?" I asked.

"I have the Lord for my friend," he explained simply. "I can talk to Him anytime and know he's right there."

Just like his sister, Karen, I recalled.

Later, talking with Phil, I was moved to hear how Jon had impacted my brother's outlook. "Connie, I'm going blind, and frankly, I'm scared." His brow was furrowed with worry. "The next optic hemorrhage will take the last of my sight. And it won't be long until I'm on dialysis."

I held his hand, aware of his frailty. "But being with Jon and seeing how full his life is in spite of Batten Disease gives me hope," Phil continued.

"Phil, thank you for sharing Jesus with Jon," I said. "You have introduced him to the source of all hope in the person of Christ."

"Yes, He's with us every step of the way," my brother agreed. "I haven't got much time left. And Jon?" his voice trailed off.

"One thing I'm learning from that kid," I interrupted, "is to grab each day and live it full throttle."

That same summer, Byron, a little town next door to Elba, buzzed with excitement. A new minister with a strong belief in signs and wonders opened the church doors for a weekly healing service. Sick and needy people flocked to the altar. The word was out, and miracles were happening.

One Wednesday afternoon in August, the doorbell rang. I was surprised to see a distinguished older man with a trim white beard, piercing blue eyes and a clerical collar. "How do you do, Mrs. Castor." He extended his hand. "I'm Pastor Bob McPherson from Byron. I heard about your son, Jonathan, who is afflicted with a rare disease. May I come in?"

Part of me resisted. Was he going to reopen the question of healing? Hadn't I put that one to rest in Pittsburgh at the Kuhlman mission? Common courtesy demanded that I invite the reverend in to state the reason for his call.

I thought of several friends whose lives had been changed through his ministry. As Pastor McPherson once again described the vesper service in his faint Scottish brogue, the yearning for Jon's healing took hold of me.

Steve and I talked it over. My friend urged us to visit, and Jon was eager to come with us.

So it was that Steve and I, one on either side of our son, knelt at the altar on a Sunday evening two weeks later. People gathered around, first laying hands on Steve and then on me. Some prayed loudly in tongues. One claimed to have a revelation of seeing sin in either Steve or me that blocked healing. Others were compassionate and gentle in their prayers. Then, the pastor knelt before Jon and held his head. All hands joined as he claimed the power of Christ to heal our son. Elders of the church encircled the pastor and the boy as they anointed Jon with oil. Prayers rose to a crescendo and ended with a song of praise. I was uncomfortable. How was Jon feeling as the focus of all this?

After the service, we traveled home in silence. Steve went inside while I took my son's arm. Together, we walked through the hedgerow to the field in back of our house. Inner questions were demanding an answer. A gentle breeze cooled us after the crush of people. "Feels good, doesn't it, Mom?" Jon commented.

I looked up into the night sky where the evening star twinkled bright and pure. I remembered my mother, holding Karen's hand in the field behind our Webster bungalow.

"Do you see the evening star, honey?" she had asked.

"Only the darkness," Karen replied.

Now, I asked Jon the same question. "What do you see when you look up into the sky?"

"Just the black night," he answered.

I began to cry. "What's the matter, Mom?" He put an arm around my shoulder.

"Oh, Jon, I wanted your eyes to be healed tonight."

"Hey, Mom, I'm okay." His voice was firm. "I have my friends at school, my tree fort, everybody in the family—and I have Jesus in my heart. I'm fine just the way I am."

I stopped crying and took a deep breath. Jon was whole. I was the one who needed healing. I hugged my son. "Thank you, Jon. You taught me something very important tonight."

"What's that?"

"To be thankful for my blessings—especially for you!" It was a lesson I would need to review, and this sturdy child of faith would be my teacher.

THIRTEEN
CONQUERING THE SLOPES

In the bleak mid-winter, frosty wind made moan,
Earth stood hard as iron, water like a stone.
Snow had fallen, snow on snow, snow on snow,
In the bleak mid-winter, long ago.[8]

Christina Rossetti's icy description of winter sent shivers down my spine. I drew my rocking chair closer to the fire burning on the hearth.

For the rest of the Castor clan, a big snowstorm meant school was closed. It was time to strap the skis on top of the wagon and head out to conquer the slopes. It all began when Jon was seven. A nearby winter resort offered lessons early Saturday mornings to teach blind children to ski.

Steve asked, "Jon, what do you say you and I travel over to Bristol Mountain next weekend?"

"Oh boy! Let's do it!" Jon knew all about it because School for the Blind co-sponsored the program. "Dad, do you know what my coach, Mr. Gugel told me?"

"What did he tell you?"

"They have everything I need right there—boots, poles, and skis!"

Miriam overheard plans for skiing. "Can I go, too?" she requested.

Steve made a phone call, "May I bring my daughter?" The two shopped for used equipment. Early Saturday, I packed lunches, and the neophyte alpine athletes were ready to hit the slopes.

One forlorn six-year-old grabbed his dad's jacket. "How about me?" Rick asked plaintively as tears trickled down his cheeks, "I wanna come with you."

"Rick, you don't have any skis."

"I have two dollars from Grammy Jackson."

"You put your money under the tree and see what Santa brings you."

Sure enough, two weeks later on Christmas morning a pair of bright red skis with boots and poles greeted a small boy's wondering eyes. Rick's face lit up with a huge smile. "I'm ready! Let's go!"

"You should see the ski instructor's nose!" Rick reported after his first lesson. "It's real shiny and made out of plastic."

"Maybe he hit a cliff when he was skiing," Miriam ventured.

"Or his motorcycle smashed into a car," Rick countered. "Anyway, he's real patient with the blind kids."

"I bet his accident helps him understand people with a handicap," his sister said.

The ski instructor at Bristol discovered in his small class that Jon was an eager learner. Rick and Miriam, as unofficial students, picked up the essentials along with their brother. The face of a clock was his compass. Carefully, the young man trained his students to listen for instructions— three o'clock turn right, nine o'clock left, with gradations in between.

On the bunny hill, Steve later worked with the children on the "snow-plow." Miriam learned to give Jon directions down the hill. He always wore an orange vest that signified "blind skier." It wasn't long until the clan was zigzagging down the intermediate slope.

Steve later vividly described for me their adventures. "Connie, I wish you could see the kids in action." Steve's eyes sparkled. "Jon's hearing is acute. He picks up every clue accurately, and he has no fear."

"How's Rick doing on his magic red skis?" I queried.

"He's a natural, full of unbridled energy. Already he likes the bumps," Steve continued. "And Miriam—ask her."

"All of us riding up the hill on the T-bar with snow on the trees and sun sparkling on the drifts—it's a whole new world!" Miriam exclaimed, recalling the beauty. At age seven, Cathy, too, would go through the rite of passage that brought her into the winter wonderland of skiing Castors.

Hidden in the piney hills of North Creek in the Adirondacks was a chalet. Spacious yet cozy, it was built by family friends for use during the season. During the February break, we rented it for a week. Now, we were en route, packed into the station wagon with skis strapped on top. The children were exuberant as snow began to fall.

"Wow! Look at those drifts!" Rick yelled.

"How high?" Jon wanted to know.

"Eight feet!"

Davey was squirming. "When are we going to get there?" he asked. "I want to try out my new green snow disk."

"I hope the road into the chalet is plowed," I voiced my concern. "This year has been a big one for blizzards up here in the Adirondacks."

"Remember the balcony on the roof?" Cathy asked her sister. "I bet we can jump into a drift from up there."

"Is it okay if we girls have that upstairs room?" Miriam requested.

"First of all let's pray we make it through the snow," Steve was peering out through a windshield that even the wipers couldn't clear. "North Creek! I see the sign!" He turned down a familiar road and past the main lodge with Christmas lights still glowing.

Yes, our long driveway was freshly plowed. "We're here, thank you, God! And it's so beautiful," I breathed a prayer of gratitude. As the children and Steve toted boxes and suitcases into the chalet, I stood alone in the circle of light now illuminating each flake falling from a dark sky. Silent sentinels of pines and hemlocks bowed beneath their blanket. No breeze stirred the contours of whiteness. I heard only the whisper of softly falling snow as peace caressed me. My heart welled up in thanksgiving to my God, the Creator of such artistry.

Reality penetrated my reverie. "Grab that last suitcase, please, Connie," Steve called down from the porch. It was my old red hard plastic model from college days that I dragged up the stairs. Inside, everybody was talking at once. "Let's plug in the Christmas lights on the mantle."

"Light these candles, Cathy."

"Here, Jon, you and Rick carry some wood to the fireplace."

"And I'll get the popcorn cooking!" I bellowed. A festive atmosphere erupted as hands reached out for cocoa and bowls of buttery popcorn.

"So, when are we going to hit the slopes?" Rick asked.

"Yeah, I can't wait to try the big one," Jon added.

"Gore Mountain opens at nine," Steve announced. "Everybody hit the sack so that we can roll out of here by eight-thirty."

The next morning, I packed peanut butter and jelly sandwiches, Pringles, oranges, bananas, Little Debbie cupcakes, and a carton of milk into our big cooler. Boots were warming by the fireplace. "Bundle up! It's a cold, cold morning," I clucked over my brood like a mother hen. "Don't forget Jon's meds—and the cooler!"

A tug on Steve's sleeve caught his attention. "When am I going to learn to ski?" Davey looked up at his dad with imploring blue eyes. Steve tousled his blond hair. "When you're seven, Davey."

The little boy counted on his fingers. "Two more years, huh!"

Outside, the motor coughed as the station wagon plowed under an archway of glistening fir trees. Inside, the aroma of fresh coffee and the crackle of logs in the fireplace drew me into an aura of well-being. There were no phones to answer, no lessons to prepare for my women's study group. I was delightfully free of "shoulds." I stretched out on the sofa under the picture window. The sky was azure. A cardinal's dash of red punctuated a hemlock's snowy branch.

Davey "brum-m-med" a matchbox car up and down on my stomach. It felt good, like a tickle. I marveled at this last child who had come at a time of mourning. During Karen's final days of Batten Disease, his wide smile and baby sweetness had cheered my spirit.

Under the rough thumb of Mrs. Franklin, Davey had survived a half year of kindergarten. How such an unbending person had ever been chosen to teach little ones was a frustrating mystery to us parents. A former officer in the WAVES, Women Accepted for Volunteer Emergency Service, which was a women's division in the US Navy, she ran a tight ship. "Heads up," she commanded her class.

"She grabbed my chin, Mom," Davey told me, his eyes sad. "And she says I'm a sloppy writer."

Other parents were unhappy as well, so we had all signed a petition for her removal. My bouncy sprite who had started school with excitement now dreaded facing Mrs. Franklin each day. This week off for sheer fun was good for him.

"Hey, Mom, can I try my snow disk?" Davey asked.

"Snow pants, jacket, and mittens are hanging up over there on the pegs. Need help?" I offered.

"I can do it myself," he asserted.

The green disk was a perfect vehicle for this kind of terrain. I helped Davey up a big pile of snow. "Wow!" he peered down from the top. "You go with me, Mom." We gave a shove and whirled together down the hill, turning in circles. Across the icy plowed drive we flew, landing in a drift. Over and over, we climbed and slid down the monstrous drift until my middle-aged legs screeched, "Halt!"

After lunch, while Davey napped, a dark shadow crept into my mind, one that I had shoved into a far corner of my subconscious. What if Davey had Batten Disease? Impossible! Out of the question! God had sent him as a special gift. That afternoon I wrote a letter to my Heavenly Father in a journal. "Dear Lord, thank you for this time away in this pristine place of pure beauty. The icicles sparkle over the picture window. Your suncatchers are dazzling.

"Thank you for the gift of my little son David. His soft hair and pink ears and long-lashed blue eyes are all your perfect handiwork. Lord, he's five now. The shadow of Batten Disease is a question mark on this beautiful child. As yet, there are no signs of eye problems, but my mother's heart wonders. I give him to you, Lord Jesus, to hold close to Your heart of love. For now, I will cherish each day with Davey in Your exquisite world of snow. In Jesus' name, Amen."

The next day, Steve picked us up for a visit to Gore Mountain. I would at last see the ski bums in action. We swung up the mogul run in the gondola. Huge mounds of packed snow rose up at intervals down the steep trail. Rick waited for us at the top, eager to show off for his mother and little brother. In faded jeans and well-worn old jacket, he flashed a smile and shoved off down the hill. Crouching low, ski poles close, he skied the bumps, sometimes around, sometimes over. Then with a whoop of joy, he sailed into the air and down again. Could that kid ski! From my safe perch, I was amazed at my son's skill and daring spirit.

"Man, is Rick ever cool!" Davey exclaimed.

Down, we descended in the gondola. From the bottom of the hill, we watched Jon in his orange vest ski on the intermediate slope with his dad. Calling out directions, Steve guided Jon along a perfect run. Cathy and Miriam gracefully traversed the hill, and, rosy-cheeked, stopped in front of us.

Steve felt deeply the awesome responsibility of directing his blind son down a crowded trail. Years later, he would recount the lessons he himself learned in working with Jon:

"I learned much about 'blind trust' one Saturday when I was skiing with Jon, a young teenager. I inadvertently said 'left' when I meant 'right' and steered him sightless off the ski trail into the woods. By the time I reached him, he had collapsed at the foot of a large tree, the marks of an ugly bruise forming on his forehead with a trickle of blood. The collision was painful, but not serious, and in no time, we had Jon back into skis, cap and gloves in place. Apart from the discolored bruise on his forehead, he seemed more ready to ski again than to call for the toboggan patrol. I apologized profusely for my stupid carelessness. 'Jon, can you forgive me?'

'Of course. You didn't do it on purpose.'

'But Jon,' I asked, afraid I might repeat the same error, 'can you trust me to get you down the rest of the mountain?'

'Sure, Dad. You got me this far, didn't you? I trust you.'

We skied onward, his trust somehow unshaken. But I was shaken and awakened to the meaning of 'blind trust' as the only path to progress, to growth, to a life of adventure rather than a life of timid safety. I realized how much of reality is unseen by me, in my blindness and limitations, how much I must—like Jon—live out my life in 'blind trust,' a gamble on the goodness of God, so often hidden from my own view by the clouds of circumstance. And who could not love such a lad, whose very life was a teaching parable? Who could not learn from him?"

That night around the dinner table, a tired, sunburned, and hungry crew of skiers gave thanks for the food and for an unforgettable day on Gore. Roast beef and apple pie were demolished with gusto. Later by the fireside, Miriam and Steve played chess. Jon settled into a recliner, reading a Braille book on the Civil War. Davey and Rick flopped out on the sofa, comparing notes on disk sliding and skiing the bumps. "We were both whirling through the air!" Davey concluded.

Cathy and I were cleaning up the kitchen. "What was your favorite thing about today, Cathy?" I asked her.

"First was lunch." She laughed, "After skiing hard, we were famished. Your PBJ sandwiches never tasted so good—and the Pringles!"

"And second?" I prodded her.

Her eyes had a dreamy far-away look. "It was at the end of the day," she recalled. "We were playing follow-the-leader down a long winding slope. The sun was setting and soft golden light touched the trees and trail." Her voice was quiet. I knew we had both experienced God's artistry and nearness during our time away.

Toward the end of our vacation, there was one day when I was surprised to hear steps on the porch late in the morning. Steve was holding Jon up, helping him to a kitchen chair. "Seizure on the T-bar," he said curtly. Incontinence had soaked Jon's ski clothes. We washed him, dressed him in pajamas and tucked him to bed. "Jon was ahead of me on the lift, so I could catch him," Steve explained. "The ski patrol was right there to strap him into a toboggan and pull him down the hill."

After a long nap, Jon awoke, a bit groggy.

"What am I doing here?" he asked. "Are the rest of the guys skiing?"

"You had a seizure, Jon. I'll read you your favorite story about David and Goliath." He was content to listen.

After supper, it was Rick's turn to help wash dishes. "Were you there when Jon had the seizure?" I asked, "Were you scared?"

"No, I was really embarrassed," Rick admitted. "They had to stop the T-bar and call the patrol. Everybody worriedly crowded around Jon. It just felt weird for our family to be the center of attention."

My eyes were being opened to those vulnerable teenage feelings of having a handicapped brother. The tentacles of Batten Disease were reaching beyond just Jon.

"The great thing was being free—Dad, Cathy, Mim, and me—to ski without that weight of responsibility," Rick continued.

Cathy chimed in. "We take turns guiding him down, but I'm always afraid I'll crash him into a tree."

"Or that he'll go into a seizure," Rick added. "Dad's the one on those slopes that carries the load for Jon."

"Thanks, you two, and I thank Steve for including him. Jon's life is rich and full because you give him time." Words were inadequate to express my appreciation. "It's not easy, and I love you for it."

"Thanks, Mom, for understanding," Rick hugged me.

FOURTEEN
NOT OUR SPECIAL ONE!

I missed the Yokefellow weekly meeting. The absence of friends who listened and cared left me feeling bereft after our move to Elba. The Yokies had arrived to put the finishing touches on the old blue mansion, but there was no time for sharing and prayer.

God had something else in mind to meet my need. It all began with an empty bucket. During renovation, I was desperate for hot water to loosen layers of wallpaper. Pail in hand, I had knocked on the side door of my neighbor's house. Slowly, it opened, and shy brown eyes peered out at me. The woman was in her fifties and looked disgruntled. She abruptly announced, "I've just gotten a divorce. Help yourself to water at the kitchen sink." She looked away, her face a mirror of pain.

Over many cups of coffee in the months that followed, Dora told me of her unhappy marriage and secluded life. Her suffering and bitterness were hard to hear. It was time to become more than a comforting listener. Directions came clearly when I asked God for help. *Next time Dora mentions her ex-husband, offer to pray for them both—out loud.* Out loud?

The next day, I trudged with heavy feet over to her back door. Once again, she began to express the anger inside. "Dora," I asked awkwardly, "Do you mind if I pray for you and your ex-husband?"

Surprised, she replied, "No, I guess not, Connie." Stumblingly, I blurted out a prayer, asking God to let His love be known to these two hurt people. I looked up to see tears in my friend's eyes.

After that, it seemed natural to explore a chapter in John's gospel together and end in prayer. Activated in my friend was a deep well of love for Christ that had stayed dormant for years. Her family and ex-husband began to see a difference. Her bewildered expression gave way to a ready smile.

After several months of sharing together, we considered inviting a few neighbors to our study. Virginia, a friend from Weight Watchers, and I had talked about our mutual struggle with diets and the woes and joys of mothering five kids. Finally, I mustered up enough courage to ask her to join us. "We want to find out whether God can be real in our lives right where we are," I challenged her.

"Sure, I'll try anything!" she responded.

Miriam, a Houghton College graduate, brought her solid Bible background and a need to put it into action. Midge joined us, wondering whether she could ever get rid of the dislike she felt for herself and the resentments she carried. Joanne came in loneliness, newly divorced with a bunch of children to mother. Gen, a Catholic, was eager to discover what it meant to trust God. Barb, a member of a Unitarian Church, questioned Christ as the way to God.

We were a motley crew that met around the kitchen table, timidly revealing a little of our real selves and learning to listen to each other. Catherine Marshall's *Beyond Ourselves* served as the catalyst that opened several women to entering into a commitment to Christ.

A study in First John introduced the depth of God's love for us in the gift of Jesus. Barb saw that love in action when, after a dinner for thirty-five, her fundamentalist friend Miriam mysteriously appeared to clean up the whole mess. Barb then began to explore privately a New Testament she hadn't read in years.

Now, on a May morning four years later, I looked around the table, aware that I was blessed with Christian friends who truly cared. Could they carry with me the heavy load on my heart? Just yesterday, the school nurse had called from Elba Central School. "We are concerned about your son David's vision." For the last two weeks, I, too, had been aware of the familiar pattern: Davey closely clutching picture books and straining to see them. Again, I had devised eye tests. My little son was definitely having problems.

It was now time to share prayer requests around the table. "It's Davey," I could hardly speak. Already, tears flowed. "He's having trouble seeing, just like Karen and Jon at his age."

Virginia's round face was troubled. "Connie, do you think?" She couldn't finish her question.

"I don't know." I wiped my eyes. "Steve's taking him to the ophthalmologist tomorrow. I...I just can't bear that dear little boy going down with Batten Disease. Pray for strength."

Hands reached out to touch me. Friends stood behind me. "You're here, Lord Jesus," Virginia began. "You love Davey, and You love Connie."

Each person offered a prayer for strength and healing. Miriam ended, "Now, Lord, pour Your peace into Connie's wounded spirit. May she trust You to hold her son. In Jesus' name, Amen."

The next morning, Davey wriggled as I wiped grape juice off his face. "When I get back from the eye doctor's, do I have to go to kindergarten?"

"Yes, honey."

"Why do I have to go to the eye doctor anyway?" The question stung my heart.

"He's just going to peek into your eyes to find out why you haven't been seeing some of those words on the blackboard," I explained.

"Maybe I'll have to wear glasses."

"I hope so," I answered unthinkingly.

"You do? Well, I don't!" he replied indignantly. "What'll the other kids think?"

While the two were gone, I kept busy, trying to push back grief and anxiety. On the porch, I shook the dust from scatter rugs and turned the cushions on the old settee. How many years had my parents' maple settee seen action in a Castor home? Twenty at least. Karen had slept on it after a seizure. Jon and Rick were listening to a story on it when I first discovered Jon's failing sight. Now, I grabbed *Living Light*, the same devotional my dad had read to his family back in Brewer, Maine in the '30's.[9] "Pity me, O Lord, for I am weak...I am upset and disturbed...In Your kindness, save me." (Psalm 6.2, TLB) I prayed the words in anguish.

Outside, the car door slammed. Davey burst into the kitchen waving a lollipop, full of news about his visit to Dr. Davis. "I don't need glasses, Mom!" He dashed into the playroom to line up his matchbox cars. Hardly daring to ask, I looked at Steve's face and knew the truth.

"We can't be sure, Connie," Steve told me in a flat voice. "The retinal scars don't show yet, but there's no other explanation for Davey's loss of sight. The doctor thinks it's the beginning of Batten Disease." There wasn't much to say as we clung to each other.

Davey was off to school, Steve left for the office, and the house was quiet again. I wanted to pray, but all that came out was a cry of despair. "My God, it just doesn't make any sense! Not Davey, our special one!" I knelt by the settee, pounding the cushions in anger and helplessness. Weren't two damaged children enough? What more could we learn in the loss of our little son?

Memories flooded my mind—the church bells ringing on the day he was born; the comfort of returning home from seeing Karen in the hospital to kicking, crowing baby Davey; and the puckish smile and quick hugs that endeared him now to each of us. I told God all this that day as I knelt by the old settee. When I was finished, my questions echoed in the silence.

Should we tell the children? Not until we get a definite diagnosis from Dr. Davis, Steve and I decided. The second examination revealed nothing new. The doctor firmly told us there could be only one reason for our son's 20/200 vision: the beginning of Batten Disease.

Soon after, Rick cornered his father early one Sunday morning. "Dad, why has Davey been getting eye exams? Has he got the same thing Karen and Jon have?" I heard his sobs all the way downstairs when Steve gave him the answer. The two brothers, blond and alike temperamentally, enjoyed a close relationship.

"Connie, we'd better talk this out as a family," Steve advised. "Let's stay home from church." It was a subdued group who met in the living room. Jon was away on a wrestling tournament, leaving us free to talk. But what to do with Davey? Snuggling in Miriam's lap as the two rocked in the old black needlepoint rocker, he quickly fell asleep. "I guess you know why we're all here," Steve began hesitantly.

Miriam was the first to speak. "I've kind of suspected that Davey had the disease ever since those eye exams." She looked at her sleeping brother. "But I can't stand to think of his going blind or...or...changing." Her voice was strained as her eyes filled with tears. "I just want to enjoy him the way he is right now."

Rick shared angry feelings. "Why does God allow two good kids like Jon and Davey to have such a thing?" he demanded to know. "Why not me?

I just don't get it." His fist punched the cushion. Anger and sorrow clouded his face.

Steve told about the depression of dragging through his office work. "It's a heavy load on me no matter what I'm doing."

As honestly as I could, I described my feeling of anger and the questions plaguing me. "I believed that because God sent him at the time Karen was dying that he was a special gift. I was sure he'd be safe from Batten Disease," I started to cry. "I just can't believe…this beautiful little boy has it!"

I held up Carother's book *Power in Praise*.[10] "I want to praise God even in the middle of this sorrow, but I can't seem to do it," I leaned back, feeling helpless.

Cathy in simple faith invited the Holy Spirit into our desolate circle. "Well, let's pray."

And that's what we did. Gathered around Miriam and the sleeping child and with arms holding each other, we began to pray. Rick was first. "Oh God, help my little brother to grow up to play football and baseball." His voice broke.

"And help him to see as well as I do," Cathy continued.

"Thank you, God, for Davey just the way he is right now. Help us to take good care of him," Miriam voiced her gratitude.

The Holy Spirit moved among us. "Thank you for his neat smile," I added.

"And for Davey's hugs," Rick said.

"Thank you that You are with him no matter what happens," Steve prayed.

"Be with J.P. in the tournament," Cathy asked. "Lord, maybe he could just pin one wrestler?"

We laughed. "We just place Davey in Your loving arms. Hold him close to Your heart," I asked the Father. "We trust You and love You, Lord. In Jesus' name we pray, Amen."

Cathy added a P.S. "Okay, Lord, we don't have to worry anymore 'cause You're taking care of him." At that moment, a presence of love united us and surrounded us, lifting the load of grief. We looked at each other through the tears.

"I don't know what happened," Miriam exclaimed, "But I sure feel better." Davey woke up, stretched, and said, "I'm hungry. How 'bout a PBJ?"

FIFTEEN
AGAWAM OASIS

Amidst the ebb and flow of both the storms and calm in the Castor family, Agawam was our one sure place of renewal. Ron Eckler, a Webster teacher cohort of Steve, and Harriet, his wife, had graciously invited us over the years to use their Canadian lodge. For at least two weeks, we'd vacation there during the summer. In the summer of 1975, with our station wagon packed to the hilt with children, groceries, and suitcases, we drove past Toronto into the wilds of Ontario. A dirt road took us to the camp store and dock on the shores of Kawagama Lake.

The "Queen Mary," I dubbed the big boat with a powerful motor that awaited us. Life jackets buckled, boxes and suitcases stashed in the back, and "Let's go, Dad" from Rick—we were on our way across the lake to Agawam. Spray in my face, wind in my hair, I began shedding tensions from home.

"There it is, the boathouse!" Cathy shouted.

"I'll help you dock, Dad," Miriam nimbly jumped to weathered boards, securing the rope.

"Listen!" Jon ordered us. For a moment, we sat still. The gentle lap of waves against the rocky shoreline, sigh of wind in the hemlocks, and a cardinal's call—we joined Jon in the sounds of Agawam.

We trudged up the hill as we lugged our cargo. I stopped and let go of my suitcase to breathe in the essence of the place. "What do you smell, Jon?" Like beagles with their noses to the wind, we sniffed the air.

"Something sweet," Jon reported.

"Yup, honeysuckle," I said.

"Trees—evergreens."

"You're right!"

"And the ground," Jon concluded.

"It's the moist earth!" I agreed. My eyes surveyed the old lodge built in 1897. Shadows on the chinked logs contrasted the sunlight on the mossy roof. White birches stood out against dark green pine and hemlock trees.

Steve unlocked the heavy plank front door. We walked into the twenty-four square foot living room with its ten light-filled windows. Mexican Indian rugs and artifacts decorated the walls and floor. Cushioned red-wood furniture centered around the big stone fireplace. The other side of the room, with desk, table, chairs, and sideboard looked out over the lake. "Smells like Agawam, alright," Jon grinned, "Wood smoke!"

Rick gazed longingly at a sizeable mounted trout over the cabinet. "Yup, this is my year for catching the Grandfather," he declared, plopping his new fishing rod in the corner.

"Cathy, remember when you were little, how scared you were of Old Joe?" Miriam teased her sister. She was pointing to a morose-looking moose head on the far wall. From its enormous antlers hung a camp lantern.

"Well, I'm not scared of him!" Davey boasted.

"Is the deer head still here?" Jon inquired.

"Come here and give him a pat," his dad gave him a boost for a muzz-ley welcome.

Davey took off down the hall, head tilted to see with peripheral vision. "This is my room," he called. Two wings ran off the living room, one housing three large bedrooms and a bath, the other a bright roomy kitchen.

Miriam staked out the girls' territory. "The front room is ours, Cathy."

"The shelves are for my stuff," her sister asserted.

"Hey, Jon, grab your duffle bag, and let's go down to the Tacklebox." Rick linked an arm through his brother's. Off they hiked to the remodeled icehouse with two sets of bunk beds. Fishnets studded with weights and hooks festooned the paneled walls. Rick set up a tape player on the dresser for Jon to listen to his favorite talking books. Currently, it was "The Cross and the Switchblade."

At Agawam, propane gas ran the stove and refrigerator; a small motor pumped the water from the lake, and a generator manufactured electricity for our fierce nocturnal anagram bouts. "Make sure it's cranked up for tonight." I ordered Steve, the self-proclaimed champion. "I plan to skunk you."

"We're playing, too," Rick and Miriam chimed in.

After supper, we sat out on the screened side porch to watch the sunset over the lake. Mauve, peach, and fiery orange splashed the horizon. Miriam described it to Jon. "God is an amazing artist," she concluded. I read aloud Psalm 19.1-3, "'The heavens declare the glory of God; the skies proclaim the work of his hands. Day after day they pour forth speech; night after night they display knowledge. There is no speech or language where their voice is not heard.'" (NIV) Each of us offered a prayer of thanksgiving.

The next morning at breakfast, Jon brought up the subject of water-skiing. Rick and the girls were eager to get started, too. "Think I can get up this year, Dad?" A knot of fear settled in my stomach. What if he had a seizure in the water? At age seventeen, he was having them more frequently.

I later voiced my concern to Steve. "It's always a risk," he admitted. "But Jon loves the thrill of bouncing over the lake. I don't want to take that from him."

I reluctantly fastened his life jacket, pointed his skis in the right direction, and yelled, "Gun it!" to his dad. On the third try, we all screamed "Yahoo!" when he stood up. He was wobbly at first but then straight and tall. Plumes of spray caught the sunlight as he sliced his trail on the water. Afterward, wrapped in a towel, Jon was exuberant. "I did it! I did it!" he gloated.

The next day, we boated over to where Bear Lake joined Kawagama. The kids were like seals in the falls that shot them down smooth mossy rocks into quiet waters. Jon had just zoomed out and was starting to swim back to shore. He suddenly disappeared under the water. A seizure! Steve and Rick dove in. Steve kept Jon's head above water while Rick held on to his thrashing body. His face was blue, his breathing ragged as he lay on his stomach.

"From now on, let's make sure Jon wears a lifejacket," Steve tersely advised. "If we hadn't been right there, he could have drowned." Jon coughed up water as color returned to his face.

It was a subdued family that returned to Agawam. "Could Jon die?" Davey asked me. "I was scared."

"We'll take good care of him, honey," I assured my youngest son. Wrapped warmly on the sofa, Jon slept the rest of the afternoon, but as

Steve was helping him into the kitchen for supper, he went limp in his dad's arms.

"Come quick! Jon's having another seizure!" Steve called. Rick ran to help, carrying him to the sofa.

This one lasted longer than usual as spasm after spasm jerked his body. Breath was cut off. I looked around the circle of worried faces. Cathy cried; Davey stood behind me. At last, loud gulping gasps brought relief to me. Their brother's strange noises and mottled blue skin frightened the children. Jon then sank into a deep sleep.

"I'm worried, Steve," I confessed later. "I'm afraid he could go into stasis, you know, seizure after seizure."

"Out here, what could we do?" Steve was concerned.

"Let's up his Dilantin and Pheno before bedtime," I suggested. "We'll keep him in the living room."

"I'll be right beside him," Rick offered. "Mom, Dad, you both need a good night's sleep." He knelt down beside his sleeping brother; we joined him. "Lord Jesus, take care of my brother, Jon." Tears flowed among us. "You know how much I love him."

All of us except Rick and Jon slept soundly that night. "I think something was backfiring in that brain of his," Rick reported next morning. "He was restless and a little crazy in his muttering. No seizures, though."

"I call that love in action, your vigil with Jon all night." I hugged my sixteen-year-old son. The bond between them was strong.

That morning, Rick fished the channel between peninsulas. Soon, there was a strong tug, and he began to reel in the line. "Wow!" he yelled, "I think I snagged a huge one!" We cheered from the shore. Rick landed a big bass and prepared it for lunch. It was the most tender and sweetest, fresh fillet of the season.

"A reward from the Lord," his father pronounced solemnly.

Jon was alert and eager to participate in Agawam activities for the remaining ten days of our vacation. Once again, he rode the waves on water skis. Afternoons, he listened to "The Sword and the Switchblade" in the tackle house. We talked about the story. "Wow, Mom," he was excited. "Jesus can really change people's lives!"

Each of us had our little triumphs. Rick actually hooked battle-scarred old grandfather trout and threw him back. "Too tough and old to eat," he decided.

"You have a soft heart, Rick," his dad noted.

Cathy, Miriam, and I sketched and watercolored scenes around Agawam. The log wall in the kitchen blossomed into an art gallery. In fact, after the boys caught the urge, it became a contest. Davey and Jon collected bits of moss, nuts, leaves and flowers and made tactile collages with Miriam's help. Everybody won a prize. "I'll make you popcorn," judge Steve promised.

Chilly nights found us playing board games by a roaring fire in the old stone fireplace. Steve surprised us budding artists with a batch of fudge. Popcorn and cocoa tasted good as Rick took on Jon, using his special checkerboard. Miriam and her dad played serious chess. My Chinese checker prowess was challenged by Cathy. Finally, I beat the anagram king by one word.

The evening before our return to Elba, I studied those faces glowing in the firelight. Like jewels, I stored them in my memory bank. Miriam, with her expressive eyes, tilted nose, and lips prone to smile, was lovely. She had returned from France after a year of studying in Paris. She was our college scholar.

Jon reminded me of Karen, the same thatch of chestnut hair and freckles sprinkled over his turned-up nose. He and Rick had the protruding Castor ears. He was excited about seeing Gerald again and getting back on the wrestling team at School for the Blind.

Rick was blond and handsome, his hair longer now. His wild sense of humor kept us laughing. Industrious, he had earned himself a dirt bike by working in the potato fields of Elba.

Cathy was a teenager with a face like an angel. Wavy blond hair and big blue eyes made her beautiful. A budding artist, she loved to draw and paint.

Davey's cloud of soft bright hair and long-lashed blue eyes were still irresistible to all of us. His sight was diminished. In the fall, he would begin third grade at School for the Blind. At times, a wistful sadness shadowed his face. I sensed he was making a connection between himself and

Jon. Being different was hard for Davey. In my heart, he was God's special gift, entrusted to His care.

Steve, the father, was pensive now. There was a far-away look on his face. How he loved his children and nurtured their talents! But how little we knew each other. The gulf between us saddened me.

For this place, Agawam, imbued with memories of good times, redolent with chimney smoke and piney air, I offered thanks to God. The generosity of Ron and Harriet Eckler reflected their awareness of our family's special needs. The future was uncertain, but the present shimmered with life.

SIXTEEN
GRADUATION

A challenge that would stretch my creativity and understanding to the limit arrived one January afternoon via a phone call. On the other end of the line, Glen Thompson, superintendent of the School for the Blind, made an offer. "Would you consider teaching English in high school and social studies in middle school? Your experience with your own blind children has prepared you."

Dumbfounded, I replied. "I don't even know Braille."

"A lot of our students can type. Some are partially sighted," he countered. "And we'll provide an assistant who will read Braille homework and tests for you."

"You must have substitutes who are better qualified than I am."

"To tell the truth, since Marcia Jones decided to take maternity leave, we've run through quite a few teachers."

"Why haven't they worked out?"

Mr. Thompson cleared his throat and then hesitated before speaking. "I'll be honest. The last one opened the homeroom door and was doused with water. Another left after finding a snake in her desk drawer," he explained. "Those kids are devilishly ingenious. And I'll have to admit, both teachers were humdrum."

I laughed. "So, actually you're looking for someone to capture their interest. I'll think it over and call you back. I'll need to talk it over with the family."

"Do it, Connie," Steve encouraged me. "You've done subbing before with some pretty tough characters. I'll give you extra help around supper time." Cathy and Rick agreed to pitch in as well.

Jon's reaction clinched the decision. "Yikes! You'll be my English teacher, Mom! We haven't done anything except fool around since Mrs. Jones left."

• • • • • • • • • • • • • • •

Mr. Thompson and I sat down together to work out the details. "I'd like to do *Rock Opera Tommy* with the English classes," I announced, "If anything can catch their attention, it will be a deaf, dumb, and blind pinball wizard. I'll expurgate a few songs that aren't appropriate."[11]

The superintendent smiled. "What's your rationale for choosing 'Tommy'?" he asked.

"I believe a profoundly handicapped hero presented in their kind of music will get the kids talking and writing about their feelings," I ventured.

Mr. Thompson gave me the reins. "They are yours for the next five months! Don't forget, I'm here to help."

The classroom was devoid of any signs of life. Steve and Miriam, who was on break from college, helped me make it homey. They lugged in a big green shag rug for one corner and moved bookcases to block it off. I found cushions that I could use as backrests in a storage room. A stereo record player and speakers, donated by one of the students, were set up. With plants in the windows and bright colors on the bulletin board, room 205 was ready for business.

I knelt by the bed on Monday morning, my first day of school. "Lord," I prayed, "please love these students through me. Show me how to teach 'Tommy.' I'm asking You to bring about a miracle of communication. In Jesus' name."

Jon had arranged for my own personal bodyguard. "Gerald told the guys he'd crunch 'em if they tried any tricks on you, Mom," he assured me, so as I climbed the stairs in Severne Hall to room 205, excitement surged through me. I was beginning an adventure. On my desk were a shiny red apple and a small bouquet of mums. "Welcome, Connie, great to have you on board," the card read. The smell of furniture polish (yes, we'd cleaned everything), the cozy corner ready for action, and the American flag—I felt welling up in me a surge of gratitude. It was good to be back in home-room, saying, "I pledge allegiance ..."

"Tommy" was an immediate hit. Students sat on the rug or cushions, bouncing to the rhythm of the overture. "Keep your ears open for signs of rejection," I had instructed them. They listened intently, some taking notes on their Braille writers, others on a pad. Dick Trimble, the history teacher next door, popped his head in, making the "O.K." signal with his thumb and finger.

Since all four English classes were small, from six to eight in number, everyone had time to share in discussion. Charles, an albino boy with a thatch of silvery hair and damaged pink eyes, was perceptive. "Tommy felt rejected by his stepfather," he observed. "I know how much that hurts."

"When have you wanted to crawl into a shell?" I asked the rest of the class.

Margaret, a pretty dark-haired girl spoke. "Once at my cousin's party, the kids ignored me because I am blind." Her face was pensive. "It was like I was invisible."

Jon added, "I felt that way when Rick would run off with his friends and leave me behind."

Each day, we listened for twenty minutes and then talked about the dominant themes raised in the rock opera. What's it like to be bullied? Why would anyone take drugs? How does it feel to be blind in a sighted world?

The Christmas song was poignant, describing how normal children peer around the corner at the tree while Tommy remains lost in his isolated world.

I asked students to identify what Tommy really wanted and needed. Margaret, who had a clear sweet voice, sang the recurrent motif, "See me, feel me, touch me, heal me."[12] Tears were in her sightless eyes. "Tommy was so lonely, all boxed in," she explained. "He needed somebody to break down the wall and see him as a human being."

"Yes, and understand his feelings," Gerald added.

"And give him a big hug," Charles said.

"Thank you for sharing your insights," I was moved by their depth of emotion. "You express yourselves with feeling, almost like a poem. Here's your assignment. Write a poem about something that spoke to you in 'Tommy.' On Monday, you may read it to us if you'd like. It doesn't have to rhyme. Just express your feelings."

There were a few groans. "At a poetry reading, there are usually refreshments," I enticed the budding poets. "How about some Pepsi and chocolate chip cookies?"

At home, Saturday morning Jon was discouraged. "I can't write a poem, Mom. I just don't know how."

"Come here and sit down," I invited him beside me on the settee. I had become more aware in class of his academic decline. Despite limitations, however, Jon's outlook on life was still positive. "What would you like to write about? I'll help you," I offered.

"I can hear and talk," my son said. "Tommy couldn't even do that."

"Do you want to think about what's good in your life?" I prodded him. From his naturally thankful heart came a poem that took form as he spoke:

"Building my fort and capturing the girls, that's fun.
And I love the outdoors and feeling the sun.
Having Gerald for my best friend at school,
And a brother like Rick, that's cool."

Jon was grinning proudly as he taped his creative effort on the bulletin board. Each member of the English classes eagerly shared his or her first attempts at writing poetry. As we munched cookies and sipped Pepsi, we listened to and affirmed the outpouring of personal feelings. The bulletin board was alive with offerings that came from each heart.

Two weeks later, we played the final song from "Tommy." When the mirror was smashed, Tommy had been healed, able to speak, see, and hear for the first time. After listening to the finale, Jon declared, "That's a song to Jesus."

Charles agreed, "Who else could help us climb those mountains every day?"

The WHO would be surprised at their conclusion, but I concurred. "Amen, thank you, Lord," I prayed silently.

After the gripping experience of "Tommy," we faced the reality of preparing for Regents exams. Each week, it was four days of studying and grilling, but Fridays were for music and poetry. Most of my students made it through the grueling week of Regents and some did it with flying colors.

Jon's I.Q., however, had dropped to eighty-five. I was heartened to see how flexible his teachers were. Each prepared a unique exam for him, given verbally with his answers recorded on tape. He was promoted with the rest of his peers to the senior class of 1976.

Over the past year, Batten Disease and seizure medication had affected Jon's coordination. Nevertheless, Gerald encouraged Jon to keep going to wrestling practice. The two, heavyweight sectional champion and a lightweight who had never won a match, would work on moves on their bedroom floor. "You can do it, man." Gerald clapped his huge hand on Jon's back.

One match was memorable. Returning home with his number one fan, his father, Jon burst into the kitchen highly excited. "Hey, Mom, he was like spaghetti in my hands!" he exulted. Ahead by points in the third round, he had out-wrestled his opponent until the very end. One mistake, and he found himself pinned. No matter. His coach and teammates rose to their feet, cheering and clapping for their feisty wrestler who had almost won that day. Gerald was happy for his friend. "I told ya!" A smile like sunshine lit up his face.

Years later, Cathy, in a letter to Jon, reminisced about her brother's spirit: "I remember how proud you were to be a member of the wrestling team. I didn't like to watch you wrestle, seeing you struggle against your opponent with all your might—and then so often get pinned. But you had a different attitude. 'I almost pinned him,' you'd say. Or 'I was on top of him three-fourths of the period.' You always saw the good, you did, not the defeats."

The following spring, as graduation quickly approached, the class of '76 buzzed with anticipation. "Here we come, Toronto!" Charles cheered when I saw him in Severne Hall. I had arrived for a meeting to decide whether or not Jon was able to go on the senior trip. His balance was wobbly; his seizures more frequent; and his cognitive ability continually declining. Somehow, he was blithely unaware of the changes.

"Toronto, here I come." He had made the class chant his personal mantra.

In the superintendent's office, concern charged the atmosphere. My five-month stint as substitute teacher had put me on a first name basis with the faculty. Glen Thompson was sitting at the conference table with the class advisor Dick Trimble, school nurse, and psychologist. I had grabbed Gerald's arm and brought him along for support. Although a junior, Jon's guardian angel spoke on his behalf. "My buddy J.P. had better be included. Since first grade, he's been part of us here."

"I know, Gerald, but we have to think of Jon's safety." Glen Thompson rebutted. "Edna, how frequent have his seizures been?" He turned to the school nurse.

"Two last week. None so far this week," she replied.

"How about the balance problem?" I asked. "Gerald has been escorting Jon to classes."

Dick Trimble joined in. His shock of blond hair and lively blue eyes reminded me of Rick. "I say we hire a one-to-one aide for Jon. Seizures are manageable," he pled his cause. "And when you think about what lies ahead for this courageous kid," his voice was husky, "he deserves the fun of our trip to Toronto."

The consensus was, "Yes, let's do it!"

The next Friday, Jon was helped aboard the bus by Tim, a college student, his personal assistant who knew him from church. Steve and I yelled goodbye and then joined hands in a prayer for his safety. Interestingly, I didn't worry about my son over the weekend. A deep-seated peace assured me that he was in good hands.

Sunday evening, the bus rumbled around the circular drive to the entrance of Severne Hall. I could hardly wait to see Jon. The first one out with Tim's help, Jon wore a visor cap and waved a Toronto flag. His face was alight with a radiant smile. "Man, what a blast!" he exclaimed. "I did everything!"

Tim was laughing. "Including roller-skating and eating everybody's leftover chicken!"

"Jon was the life of the party," Dick Trimble filled us in. "He was the first to try something new."

"Like the bumper cars," Margaret chimed in.

"No seizures," Tim told me privately.

"Thank you all for making possible a trip that Jon will always remember." Steve and I were grateful.

On June 24, 1976, the day of Jon's graduation, the Castor family occupied a row of seats in the auditorium. The first chord of "Pomp and Circumstance" brought the audience to its feet. First in line was Jonathan Paul Castor, in his blue gown and tasseled cap, marching down the aisle on the arm of Glen Thompson. On stage, he stood up tall and proud to receive his hard-earned diploma. The most exciting moment of all was the announcement during awards. "To Jon Castor, we give the Sportsmanship Award for his commitment to the wrestling team and for his courageous spirit against all odds." Tears flowed among the family as cheers and clapping accompanied Jon's journey, with Mr. Trimble at his side, to receive the engraved award—never a win but always the sturdy buoyant spirit that said "next time."

After a reception in the cafeteria, we celebrated at home our son's amazing accomplishment. He was the first Batten child to earn an academic degree. Not only that, but the School for the Blind had given him an entire shelf of history books. A leak in the library roof had dribbled water on the collection. Only slightly damaged, the books in Braille were later mounted in bookcases on a wall in Jon's bedroom. He could still read and enjoy our country's past. "That's what you get for being a history fan, Jon," Rick teased his brother.

Jon grabbed a volume at random, traced the title with his right-hand fingers. "The Civil War, Volume One," he read with proper dignity. "Want me to read to you, Rick?"

SEVENTEEN
BLIZZARD OF '77

Snow had begun softly falling that morning. At noon, swirling clouds of flakes hissed against the windowpanes. We were living in Springville where Steve was assistant superintendent. After bidding farewell to the blue mansion in Elba, we had acquired a modest old home on East Avenue with a wrap-around screened-in porch as its decisive feature.

"Hey, Mom, take a look!" Rick called from the living room. "Have you ever seen anything like that?" A lip of snow was dipping off the porch roof. We stepped out on the veranda to better view nature's sculpture.

"This storm is a big one," I shivered. So far, clear plastic panels had protected the floor, but now gusts of wind pushed against the screens. "O Lord, I pray You will bring Steve safely home." It was a silent petition.

"Aunt Connie," Andy yelled, "Listen to this weather advisory." He was with us for the school year while my sister recuperated from a back problem. We joined him on the sofa.

"There is a severe blizzard in the Buffalo area. The thruway and major highways are closed because of zero visibility. Conditions are extremely dangerous." The announcer sounded ominous. Like a mother hen, I wanted my brood around me in this storm. Davey was safe at School for the Blind, and Miriam was in her dorm at William Smith College in Geneva.

Cathy, in her red flannel pajamas, was just emerging from a long winter's nap. With no school, she'd slept in. "Can you believe what's going on out there?" she exclaimed.

"Your dad is out in this treacherous blizzard," I told her. "Let's ask God for his safe return." I grabbed a hand on either side, and we lifted Steve up in a circle of prayer.

The front door flew open. Steve's jacket and hood were caked with snow, and his face was red. "I need you guys to shovel," his voice was hoarse. "The car's stuck halfway into the road." With strong, young muscles at work, snow flew faster than it fell. The boys kept shoveling as Steve gunned the motor and tires spun. At last, in a spray of white, the station wagon crunched down the driveway into the garage.

It was a hungry exhausted crew who devoured a platter full of subs and bowls of steaming chicken noodle soup. All through the night, the wind howled as blankets of snow covered the landscape. Even into the next day the storm continued. The blizzard of '77 had buried our mailbox, and the porch snow lip joined a drift, obliterating the corner of our house. Pictures flashed on TV of submerged cars being extracted from ten-foot drifts.

"Skiing will be great once Kissing Bridge and Holiday Valley are groomed again," Rick predicted.

"We'll have a blast," Cathy joined in. "Maybe, we can teach Andy to ski."

"Can I go with you?" Jon asked.

Steve and Rick exchanged questioning glances. At the end of the last season, Jon had often taken a tumble. The sheltered workshop had him in a wheelchair. My stomach knotted at the thought of his skiing an intermediate slope.

"Dad, let's give Jon a chance," Rick later requested. "I'll ski right beside him. This will most likely be his last time."

The following week on a sunny Saturday morning, four pairs of skis were strapped on the station wagon. Andy went along to keep Jon company in the lodge while Cathy, Rick, and their dad tackled the expert slopes. Jon was more aware of his limitations now. "I'm sure gonna try," he declared stoutly. "Coach Gugel always said, 'You don't try, you do.'"

"We'll do it together," Rick promised.

"Just one good run for Jon," I prayed as the wagon drove away. At the Kissing Bridge lodge, Steve's brother Dick and his clan joined them.

That evening, a tired group of skiers sat around the fireplace, sipping hot chocolate and reminiscing. Jon was quiet in the easy chair near the fire, cozy in his red striped flannel pajamas. His hands were unsteady, so I helped hold the cup of cocoa. "Did you make it down the hill?" I asked him.

"Sure did," he asserted. "Fell a couple of times but Rick helped me up. Uncle Dick sat by me at lunch. He said I'm a trooper."

"Jon's a trooper alright," Rick affirmed his brother. "I'd say he had two good runs."

"I was just too tired after that," Jon's voice was low. "I won't be skiing anymore." It was a young man's face I saw there in the firelight—a glint of tears in his eyes, a smattering of freckles across his nose and cheeks, a bit of stubble on his chin, thick chestnut hair, and a mouth usually ready to smile. A handsome lad he was!

"Andy?" he called to his cousin.

"Yes, J.P."

"I want you to have my skis."

Andy crouched down beside his cousin's chair and put an arm around him. He was having trouble speaking. "Are you sure, Jon?"

"I'm not able to keep my balance anymore," he stated as a matter of fact. "Now, it's your turn."

This was a passage for my son. No complaints as Batten Disease stripped him of the sport he loved. Simple acceptance as he blessed Andy with his ski gear. The tears said it hurt, but Jon's generous spirit made it a beautiful offering.

In May, the reality of the disease hit home. One night, Andy knocked on the door of our bedroom. "Jon's having a seizure," he reported, his voice shaky. It was a hard one. Jon had fallen out of bed and was still thrashing as we knelt beside him. He slept peacefully through the rest of the night.

"He's having another one," Rick yelled as he and Andy held him at seven A.M. Within the following two hours, Jon's body had been wracked by five convulsions.

Steve had gone to the office. "Let's get Jon to the emergency room," I ordered. As I looked at his limp body and mottled blue face, I was terrified. There was no sign of response. Was this the end? Frantically, I called the office, but Steve was not there.

"I'll take care of him, Mom." Rick picked up his brother and carried him over his shoulder. We laid him in the back of my car. Thank God, the hospital was only a block away.

A Valium drip kept Jon seizure-free for the rest of the day. I sat beside my son's bed acutely aware of the ugliness of this disease that was killing his brain cells and threatening his very life. I felt weak, like water poured out. "O Lord Jesus," I prayed. "Two sons—how can I go through this?" Davey was ten years old now and just a week had past since he had experienced his first seizure.

I held Jon's manly hand and felt the rough spots on it. How he loved sanding wood and helping put together planters at the workshop! How proud he was of his check for $5.00! Just this Saturday, we had planned to sandpaper an old dresser that I had stripped down to bare wood. So willing he was, so eager to contribute what little strength he had left!

Now, I looked at his face peaceful in sleep. His eyelids fluttered and opened. I squeezed his hand. "Hi, Jon."

"Hi, Mom."

"I love you, Jon."

"Love you, Mom."

Inwardly, I told myself, "Nothing can erode your spirit, Jon Castor. You are God's child. Nothing can separate us!"

• • • • • • • • • • • • • • • •

It was the summer of '77. Rick had graduated from high school and was looking for direction. Upstairs in the master bedroom father and son were sprawled on the bed. I sat in the easy chair by the window. Steve asked the crucial question. "What do you want to do with you life, Rick?"

"What are my options?" Rick countered.

"There's college," I ventured, knowing this was touchy territory.

"Not now. I'm tired of school. I want something outdoors and active."

"Work on a construction crew?" Steve queried.

"I don't think that's what I'm looking for."

"Where do you see yourself as needing to grow?" I asked.

"I'm pretty far from the Lord. I sure need to grow spiritually."

Something clicked with Steve. He bolted upright in bed and shot a question at his son. "Remember the last letter from Highland Christian Mission in Papua New Guinea? They're looking for workmen who'll keep the buildings repaired."

Rick looked interested. "Tell me more."

Steve unfolded the newsletter. "There are pigs to corral, horses to train, latrines to be dug, and buildings, new and old, to work on. 'We need strong young men who'll accept the challenge,'" Steve read.

"This sounds like something I'd enjoy doing," Rick responded.

Contacts were made with the mission's representatives in Albany. Rick would need to raise $250 a month. Our pastor suggested a "Rock-a-thon" with sponsors for each rocker. One Friday all over the fellowship hall, church families and friends rocked and rocked and rocked. Pledges amounted to over $1,000.

Jon was Rick's most generous supporter. Every month, he received a check from Social Security for $138. "I'll give $100 every month, Rick," he offered.

"Jon, that's too much." Rick was astonished at the enormity of the gift. "Mom, what do you think?"

"Jon, can you get along on $38 a month?" I asked.

"Sure. Rick's gonna be a missionary for the Lord, and I want to help him."

Rick hugged his brother. "I accept gladly!" he agreed.

Later I observed, "This is something Jon would love to do—if he were able—to go as a missionary."

"It's kind of like I'm going instead of him." Rick had tears in his eyes.

There were tangles of red tape to wade through as we waited for the final stamp of approval from Papua New Guinea. With passport and financial support ready, Rick was packing to go.

"Are you really sure about being a missionary in New Guinea?" I asked. The implications of losing the presence of my vibrant buoyant son were dawning on me. Steve was more and more absent. Rick's strong love for Jon had given me strength as his brother grew weaker.

"I believe God's got something to teach me at Highland Christian Mission." His voice was firm. "I'm doing the right thing."

The whole family was there to say goodbye and watch his plane take off for the West Coast. "I'm going to miss him," Jon said.

Cathy was crying. "He's so much fun."

Davey was afraid. "Do you think he could be killed over there?"

"God's taking care of him," Steve assured him.

"And all of us, too," I added.

EIGHTEEN
A GLIMPSE

"They want me! I'm their choice!" Steve had put down the phone, looking both dazed and elated.

I'd been anxiously hovering and listening. "Congratulations! Steve Castor, superintendent of schools at Geneseo!" I hugged him. "Doesn't that have a ring to it?"

"And listen to this. There's the possibility of renting a house right across the street from the school."

"Somebody's taking care of us!" I exclaimed. "Let's make an appointment to see it."

On a sunny May morning in 1978, we drove down a lane to the country estate of John and Sheila Chanler. On both sides of the pathway, a peach tree and wisteria bush were in full bloom. A sweep of lush green lawn, tall maples, and a horse barn created a gracious setting for the stately old colonial home.

The owner was awaiting us. "Mr. and Mrs. Castor?" A petite pretty woman said as she shook our hands.

"Connie and Steve," I said. "Thank you, Mrs. Chanler, for taking time to give us a tour."

"Call me Sheila," she replied, unlocking the front door.

"Grandfather clock would fit perfectly at the bottom of the stairs," Steve noted as we entered the hall. The living room wallpaper of horses in hunting scenes revealed the owner's interest. It was a large light-filled room with a fireplace. A double door opened to a den with its wall of shelves. The screened porch would be delightful on a summer's evening.

The dining room, with four windows and gold leaf touches on the walls, was inviting. "I can just see the clan gathered here for Thanksgiving," I murmured.

"Look! There's a downstairs bedroom for Jon," Steve exclaimed. "With a bathroom." The kitchen was old-fashioned but adequate, and five bedrooms upstairs were ample space for our family.

I nudged Steve. "How much do you suppose rent is for a gorgeous home like this?" I whispered.

Steve cleared his throat and turned to the owner. "Sheila, we really like this house, but we're wondering if we could afford the rent."

She smiled. "In about five years, John and I plan to renovate the place and move out here from our townhouse. Since my father's death, the homestead has stood empty," she explained. "I've been looking for the right family to live here in the meantime. I was thinking $300 a month for rent. How does that sound to you?"

Steve and I exchanged a look of surprise. "Very reasonable," Steve responded. "We promise to take good care of your country home. Our family antiques will be in their element here."

By the end of June, we were settled into our new location. It was difficult for Jon to leave behind his friends at the sheltered workshop in Springville. Batten Disease was increasingly limiting the simplest activities. His speech was slurred, and walking required help. Nights were restless. Incidents of agitated nightmares and falling out of bed prompted Steve and me to take turns sleeping in his room.

Structure to Jon's days was re-established when the sheltered workshop in Warsaw agreed to include our son. Every weekday morning, I'd turn the shower on. "Jon, time to scrub," I'd announce.

"Okay, Mom," he grinned. Sitting on a stool, he washed his belly while I sudsed the rest of him. We'd sing together "Jesus Loves Me" and laugh when he splashed me in the face. Memories of scrubbing a small chubby boy, and his making waves with his brother in the bathtub were bittersweet.

Jon didn't like Depends. "No!" he shouted, his fist flying as I ducked and fastened the velcro on the adult-sized diapers.

"Just for work, Jon."

"Okay, Mom." On good days, he could feed himself. Sometimes, his hand would shake with tremors, and then he would let me help.

Cathy, at sixteen, warmed my heart with her love for Jon. She wrote a letter to her oldest brother: "The times that are most special to me are those spent together in Geneseo. My admiration for you grew as I saw you leave each morning for work at the sheltered workshop and then return home exhausted and sometimes unable to walk. But you stuck with it, J.P. And that paycheck you'd earn every once in a while would all be worth it— even if it was only $3.00. Your face beamed when you showed us your check.

"After work, Mom and I would set you up on the couch with a cup of warm tea and play Rick's tapes from Papua New Guinea. The words of your brother on those tapes really reached you someplace deep inside, Jon. So often, your eyes would fill with tears as you listened. I grew closer to you then, as I began to understand your hidden sensitivity. You allowed me to care for you in a new way as you let down your defenses and accepted help from me."

How we missed Rick! Letters and tapes were our lifeline. He wrote in vivid detail about the bumpy muddy trip in an ancient truck from Goroka, New Guinea, to Highland Christian Mission. Waiting for him around Lake Galilee (actually a pond) and singing a loud welcome were students and teachers of the mission school. His first project was moving an old latrine and building a new one. "P-e-e-ew!" was our reaction.

Indeed, Rick had a knack for reaching Jon's spirit by speaking directly to him. "Hello, J.P., this is your brother Rick. How's my main man?"

"Good," Jon replied, a big grin on his face.

"Guess what flew into my tent last night?"

"What?"

"A huge moth as big as a bat!"

"Wow!"

"When I was trying to shoo it out, it landed on my head!" Jon chortled. "Are you laughing, J.P.?"

"Yeah."

"Well, I wasn't laughing. I was yelling!" Rick always included a colorful incident addressed to Jon, his biggest financial supporter.

One afternoon, I returned home from visiting a friend to find Cathy sitting in the den beside her sleeping brother. Hunched over with her face in her hands, she was the picture of dejection. "Tell me what's the matter, Cathy," I demanded.

There were tears in her eyes as she spoke. "I stayed after school today to work on my painting in the art room. I looked at the clock. It was four o'clock. I had forgotten about being here when the van returned with Jon at three-thirty."

My chest felt tight. "What… what happened?"

"I ran home as fast as I could," she continued. "I looked everywhere, but no sign of Jon, except for a tipped-over chair in the dining room. Then, I noticed the cellar door open."

"Oh, no!"

"I turned on the light and saw him at the bottom of the stairs."

"Was he hurt?" I glanced over at Jon's bruised cheek.

"You know how he moans when he's in pain, Mom. 'Oooo. Aaah. Oooo. Aaah.' I was scared because he wasn't moving."

"Think it could have been a seizure?"

"No, he was alert. I helped J.P. up. What a job!" Cathy sighed. "He took one step at a time with me right behind him. I was praying all the way up the stairs. A couple of times, I thought we were both going down."

"Good job, Cathy!" It was a Herculean task for a slender girl.

"Thanks, Mom," she looked relieved. "Somehow, I got him into the wheelchair and onto the sofa."

I knelt down beside my sleeping son. His face was peaceful, his thick hair soft. *Oh, Jon, what a struggle each day is for you,* I thought, stroking his hand. *I wonder how long we can keep you at home.*

In December, the director of the workshop informed me of a staff decision. "Jon is failing, Mrs. Castor," his voice was kind but firm. "Both mentally and physically, he is too impaired to benefit from our program."

Jon's utter exhaustion after work was proof. "Thank you for all you've done for him," I replied. "That little paycheck meant a lot to him." The daily program for my son had provided me time for leading a women's group at church and for banner making. Where would I find space to grow spiritually?

Fear and a sense of helplessness engulfed me like a tidal wave. Davey would soon be home for Christmas vacation. A call from Mr. Legouri, psychologist at School for the Blind, had worried me. Seething anger over his limitations had erupted in my youngest son. After throwing a pool ball at a classmate (he missed, thank God), Dave had to be forcibly restrained.

Just the previous night, Jon had kicked the covers off his bed and lunged at me. Steve remained distant, sometimes not coming home until late at night. "Oh, Lord, how can I handle these two hurting angry sons?" I wailed. Paraphrasing the words of the psalmist in Psalm 6.2-3, I prayed, "Pity me, O, LORD, for I am weak. Heal me…for I am upset and disturbed. My mind is filled with apprehension and gloom. Oh, restore me soon."

Cathy found me weeping and listened to my pain. Later, she gave me a scripture verse calligraphied on a slip of paper:

When I said, 'My foot is slipping,
Your love, O Lord, supported me.
When anxiety was great within me,
Your consolation brought joy to my soul. (Psalm 94.18–19, NIV)

On a practical level, Cathy volunteered to help evenings. Her gentle touch with Jon brought out the best in him. She wrote to her brother, "Bedtime was a special time, as I helped you get your pajamas on, then tuck you in. We'd pray together that familiar prayer: 'Jesus tender shepherd hear me, bless Thy little lamb tonight.' You'd say those words so clearly. I loved tucking you in, helping you feel warm and cozy and secure for the night."

Periods of confusion and aggression became more frequent, so nights in the twin bed next to Jon took their toll. Seizures, along with incontinence, occurred during the wee hours of the morning. I felt, as I had with Karen, on the edge of burnout.

Steve and I talked to healthcare specialists about possible placement. A public health nurse came to evaluate Jon's disability. "Your son certainly qualifies for long term care," she concluded. We sent an application to the county infirmary on the outskirts of town. Clean and quiet, it was accessible for visits, but it was, oh, so sterile.

On a cold morning in January, the phone rang. "We have an opening for your son," the social worker said. "You must have him here within twenty-four hours because we have a waiting list, you know."

I dragged out the big brown striped suitcase we'd taken to School for the Blind when Jon started first grade. He was aware of the commotion as dresser drawers flew open. Miriam was there to help as we packed six pajamas, twelve briefs, and assorted pull-on jersey pants and tops. "Hope we've got enough socks," I groused. A tape player was included.

"Let's keep Rick's tapes," Cathy advised. "They'll get lost at the nursing home. We'll listen when we visit."

"Mom, am I going to school?" The words Jon spoke were clear and stung like a dart.

Karen asking that same question about Newark flashed in my mind. What could I say? This was the county infirmary. Miriam diverted her brother. "Try this game, Jon. You'll have lots of new stuff where you're going."

"School?" he asked again. Miriam and I looked at each other as tears welled up. I left the room.

"I feel terrible sending him there," I cried. "It's so cold and impersonal." Miriam put her arms around me.

"Me, too," she said. "But Mom, you're worn down. Caring for two boys with Batten Disease could put you over the edge." Miriam understood the tension. She was working with learning disabled children in Rochester. "I've put together a box of things to help the activity director work with Jon."

I sat down next to my son on the den sofa to answer his question. "You're going to a place kind of like school. There'll be games and activities for you to do. Every afternoon Cathy, Dad, or I will come to visit. On weekends Mim [Miriam] might stop by to see you."

Later, a train of burden-bearing Castors trailed Steve and Jon into the county infirmary. The nurse at the station dubiously eyed our collection. "My goodness," she sputtered, "I don't know where we'll put all this stuff. He only has half a room."

Jon sat slumped in his wheelchair and listened. "School?" he asked. By now, we were settling him into a room near the nurse's station. Across the hall, a tall thin man, probably in his forties, watched the new arrival with keen interest.

Miriam introduced herself. He shook her outstretched hand. "I'm Vincent. I've been in this place too long." Bitterness clouded his face. "I wouldn't allow a dog to live here."

"Sounds like you're feeling down," Miriam retorted. "If you get to know my brother, he'll cheer you up. Come on over and meet him. He's blind and really needs a friend."

Vincent's glowering eyes softened as he told Jon his name and took his hand. "Hi, Man," Jon replied. It was the beginning of friendship for the two.

The empty room back home felt almost like a death. The irrepressible vital person who had lived there was forced into a nursing home by an ugly disease. Or was it I who forced him? David, the sprite with golden hair and laughing eyes, was changing into an angry adolescent who fought Batten tooth and nail. As I stood in the doorway of Jon's silent room, I sighed. "Lord God, I need to hear from You. I need a word of encouragement."

It came unexpectedly while Steve and I listened to a concert by the Rochester Philharmonic in the college auditorium. During a Haydn symphony, one theme was repeated by different parts of the orchestra almost as if they were talking to each other.

I found myself caught up in a vision of Heaven. Banks of angels and archangels sang "Jesus is Lord" to the melody of the Haydn theme. Small choirs of children answered. "Jesus is Lord." Groups of believers joined in, and at the far end of the majestic choir, a pure white light washed everyone in brightness. I knew it was Jesus.

While the singing continued, our whole family played in vivid green grass. The day was dazzlingly sunny, the sky bluer than ordinary, and flowers literally glowed with color. Karen came toward us, a lovely slender girl with freckles and shiny long hair with bangs. She was alert and seeing. She grabbed Miriam's hand as the two did a Scottish dance.

J.P. and David, big muscular hunks, played football in a wild tussle with Rick. They all exuded health and vitality and could see perfectly. Steve and I sat on a bank watching, full of contentment and free of anxiety. Cathy, with blond hair flying, joined Karen and Miriam's dance. The finale was pure childlike pleasure: all of us rolled and turned somersaults down hills of soft green grass.

In my innermost being, I knew that because Jesus is our risen Lord and Savior, this delightful vision would become reality. Beyond the present suffering, Jesus was preparing a place of unimaginable glory and beauty for all of us.

NINETEEN
CELEBRATION AND DESPAIR

It was the day of the wedding, August 18, 1979. In just two hours, Miriam was marrying Joe Schill in the living room of the Chanler homestead. "It's still drizzling out there," I sputtered as we moved chairs from the lawn to tight rows inside. My frazzled self surveyed sparkling windows and immaculate woodwork that we obtained at a cost. The scrub team, Cathy and her sister Miriam, had seethed when I pointed out a streak and sent them back with Windex.

A carrot cake in tiers and garnished with daisies graced the dining room table. Quiches, salads, and fresh fruit had been prepared by the Methodist Ladies' Circles to serve from the screened porch.

Showered and dressed in my mother-of-the-bride long chiffon gown, I stopped by the bride's bedroom. Miriam had moved back to her own homey nook in the old house. Now, she sat rocking in an antique Castor chair. Wearing a simple off-the-shoulder white eyelet dress (made by me), she was beautiful. Her thick sun-touched brown hair was wreathed in a band of daisies. I noted her tranquil face as she looked out the window. Turned up nose and blue-green eyes, there was still that pixie look about her. I broke the silence. "You're so peaceful, Mim." Being with her, I had begun to let go of the jitters.

"It's going to be a beautiful wedding and a great afternoon, Mom," she predicted. "The drizzle will stop, and we'll be out on the lawn dancing."

At four P.M., my father, who was in his 70's, and newly ordained sister Miriam waited in white robes in the living room with Joe the groom. Joe's steady blue eyes lit up as he caught a glimpse of his bride. A hush fell over the crowd as the melody of "Simple Gifts" on classical guitar filled the room. Cathy and cousin Kari, bridesmaids in blue-sprigged eyelet, walked slowly in from the dining room. Then came the bride smiling with her eyes focused on her man.

On the front row beside me sat Jon, hunched over and silent in his wheelchair. Dave, grinning beside his dad, was in his element. A party animal, he knew this was going to be one wingding of a celebration.

I listened as the vows were spoken, a modern version of those Steve and I had voiced at our wedding twenty-eight years before. "To have and to hold from this day forward, for better or for worse, for richer, for poorer, in sickness and in health, to love and to cherish 'til death do us part." I glanced over at Steve, wondering where in our marriage the promise "to cherish" had gone. Our vows had been severely tested, almost to the breaking point. *O Lord, grant these two Your love to share with each other*, I silently prayed.

After the ceremony, a ray of sun shone through the mist and drizzle. A fresh breeze carried music of the string band as guests kicked their heels in folk dances. David, his long hair flying, grabbed his sister's hand, and together they whirled amidst a circle of other dancers.

Andy, Jon's faithful friend, knelt beside his cousin's wheelchair and offered him a bite of quiche. No response. "Aunt Connie, I can't believe how much J.P. has changed." My nephew's hazel eyes were troubled. "He's so thin. Don't they feed him in the nursing home?"

Andy had pinpointed a deep concern—Jon's decline. I pushed it back into the recesses of my mind as the party continued.

The evening star twinkled above the horizon as Japanese lanterns cast soft light upon the trees and around the porch. The band played a waltz, and Miriam and Joe held each other for the last dance.

Alone on the porch that evening, I thanked God for a day of joy and celebration. Joe and Miriam would soon pack their belongings and head for Alaska, fulfilling their dream to explore the Yukon wilds. My kids were in transition. Cathy was preparing for her freshman year at Grove City College in Pennsylvania. Rick would soon be home from Papua New Guniea to search for work as a builder. Dave in puberty and fired-up by Batten Disease frequently experienced mood swings. Today, it was the exuberance of the wedding that fueled him, but tomorrow, it might be anger erupting in violence.

The transition for Jon was demeaning—a slow erosion of basic abilities. The first few months at the nursing home had been peaceful. One of

Cathy's letters to her brother revealed her experience with him: "It was so hard to see you move into the Geneseo Infirmary. I hated seeing you in a hospital setting, but you accepted it. For you, it was like a new school or a new place to work. Your acceptance helped me accept it, Jon.

"I treasure those days of visiting you there, wheeling you out to the patio for a game of ball or to the chapel for some prayer time together. Your prayers were so simple, so beautiful. 'I love the Lord; I love my family.' I always left that place refreshed, a little sad sometimes, but with my mind tuned into the Lord.

"The two weeks before leaving for college, I was really appreciating you, Jon. I didn't know if you'd still be there or not the next time I returned home. I sat by your bedside as you gently touched my hands, exploring them with yours. You touched my hair and felt how long it was. You even touched my braces and wondered what on earth they were. Remember the sundae I brought you? You ate the spoon as well as the ice cream. I loved those days I spent with you, Jon, talking, praying, reading, and playing. What a friend and brother you were!"

Sunday afternoons, watching the Buffalo Bills play football were companionable family times for Jon. Propped up in a recliner and with a bowl of popcorn by his side, J.P. talked to the team. If they let their opponents make a touchdown, he bellowed, "You dumb dumbs!" If the Bills scored, he yelled, "Go, dumb dumbs!" We gave him a warm wooly lamb that he snuggled in his recliner.

After church, Steve had been his son's chauffeur to and from the infirmary. One Sunday, he found Jon bedridden and unable to respond. He had resisted efforts to get him up and dressed. "We'll just let him be," Steve decided.

When I stopped by later for a visit, Vincent, Jon's friend across the hall, intercepted me. "I'm worried about Jon. He's not eating."

"What's causing the change?" I asked anxiously.

"I think he's depressed. He sits for hours tied to a chair. Staff pretty much ignore him."

"Vince, thanks for keeping an eye on him. He needs a watchful friend like you."

I found Jon in bed, curled in a fetal position. He was crying. "How are you, Jon?" I asked.

"Bad."

"Where do you hurt?"

"Bad." Small sounds like sighs made me think he was in pain. The tears were quiet. No sobs. The contrast to his sunny self of the past weeks wrenched my mother's heart. I looked under the sheet. Thin legs and concave stomach reminded me of Karen. Beside his bed, I sat rubbing his head and back. A tape from Rick stirred a response.

"Guess who's coming home to see you, Jon?"

"Rick." A flicker of a smile touched his lips. My son fell into a peaceful sleep, listening to his brother's voice.

At the nurse's desk, I stopped to express my concerns. "How do you help Jon eat?" I asked. "He's very thin. I'm worried about his getting nourishment."

"Mrs. Castor, he refuses food. There's nothing we can do." The nurse was defensive.

"How about a supplemental feeding of Ensure between meals?" I suggested.

"I'll let our nutritionist know your wishes," she replied.

Rick returned home in January of 1980, tan, trim, and eager to talk about his adventures in the Highlands. Pictures spread out on the dining room table caught the flavor of life at Highland Christian Mission. Especially winsome were close-ups of the nationals, brown faces with smiling eyes and wide grins. "You should hear them sing, Connie! And climb? I swear they have suction cups on their feet, right up the sheer face of the mountain barefoot!"

Rick described a rare genetic neurological disease called kuru that plagued the bush people. "They call it 'the laughing sickness,'" he explained. "I saw a few people demented and crippled by it. Reminded me of Batten's."

Rick came back with new abilities. An itinerant Australian master carpenter had volunteered his services to the mission for a year. With my son as apprentice, the two had built a new dorm. Now, Rick was eager to find work with a local contractor.

More important, Rick's faith had grown strong and sure. In the beginning of his second year, Dave and Cathy Hicks sent word that their ship *The Logos* would be docking in Lei, a city on the New Guinea coast. His Aunt

Cathy (Steve's sister) and her husband were missionaries with Operation Mobilization.

The two made the arduous trip all the way to Highland Christian Mission to spend time with their nephew. It was obvious that he needed a change of scenery after months without a break, so he traveled back with them to their ship. Cathy and Dave challenged Rick to surrender his whole being to God. "Alone in my stateroom I met Jesus. I heard His voice calling my name," he told us. "He turned my life around."

Everyone at the mission saw the difference when Rick returned. Friendship knows no cultural boundaries, he learned. Bilake, a student, and Walaga, a national worker, were among his close friends.

"My very best friend is my brother Jon," Rick announced as he walked into the room at the infirmary. "How about a hug!"

The two brothers reunited in a way that deepened Rick's commitment to care for Jon. The changes were not a surprise. "I'm just glad he's still alive," Rick said.

A move to Bath, New York, was brewing after a brief two and a half years in Geneseo. Steve began his duties as the superintendent of schools in January of 1981, commuting during the winter months.

In the meantime, a builder known in Geneseo for his excellence hired Rick. "Dutch is tough, but I'm learning a lot," he reported.

It wasn't long before Rick was settled into his own apartment, but he still always made time for his brother. He wrote about these memories in a letter to Jon: "Sometimes, I'd walk into the infirmary tired and uptight from a hassle-filled day on the job. It's funny how a framing miscalculation can blot out the beauty of the universe. Yes, here would come your beaten, downtrodden Rock. I must confess there were days when I came out of a sense of duty, not love. You'd be there, hands folded behind your head, big smile on your face, clear eyes roving back and forth, and spider legs crossed in a contemplative pose. In that moment upon entering your room, the meaningless drudgery to which my spirit had succumbed would be lifted.

"Your smile had a beautiful effect on me, J.P. I'd often think in those times, 'What on earth could he be smiling about?' You'd help me realize where that smile came from. Your family's love always registered with you.

Your spirit was faithful to respond with an 'I love you' or 'I love everybody.' When all else was stripped away, love remained."

In May, we moved into a rambling ranch house atop Burton Street hill, our new home in Bath. Wide windows overlooked a picturesque village scene. Centenary United Methodist Church welcomed our family with open arms. The Tuesday morning prayer and praise group became my base of support. How powerful is the bond of Christian love! In each of our moves, I had discovered a core of people whose prayers and practical caring lifted my spirit. God only knows how much I needed spiritual backing. There were times when the ravages of Batten Disease in Jon seemed more than I could bear, so keeping a journal helped me express my feelings.

In an entry dated January 4, 1982, I wrote: "Jon, God's child over the years, has uniquely, bravely, uncomplainingly accepted his limitations. How often when he had stumbled and fallen, he made nothing of it! Now, the removal by Batten's of even simple abilities is more than he can endure. He bites and kicks and pounds. He covers his face with a pillow and wraps the cord of the call button around his neck. His actions cry out, 'Get me out of here!' When he's too weak to hold his body up, they tie him in a vest to the chair. He becomes angry and violent at being strapped in.

"Lord Jesus, Jon is truly Your child. He has come to a breaking point. This is more than his weak body and mind can stand. You know the hurt and frustration this young man is feeling because You experienced such unspeakable agony on the cross. I commend his spirit to You, in Christ's name. Amen."

At this time, Rick was an island of mercy to his brother. Rick's strength and love could always penetrate the darkness of dementia. Jon was able to respond, "I love Rick...love, love, love." Rick kept holding him like a baby in wonderful unconditional love.

Several weeks later, a call from the head nurse in Geneseo frightened me. "Jon's not doing well. Please come immediately." Since Steve was away, it was comforting to have my sister Marti with me. As we stood by the bed, Marti cried. She had loved her nephew since his toddler days in Evanston. I hardly recognized my son. His face was swollen like a balloon ready to burst.

"What, what has happened to cause this?" I demanded to know.

"It may be a medication problem," the nurse informed me. "The doctor put him on a new seizure prescription that reacted with Phenobarbital."

"Thank you for your honesty." I could hear the concern in her voice. "But how could this happen?"

"As soon as I checked with our pharmacist, we stopped the Phenobarbital," she explained. "I think you'll soon see an improvement in Jon's condition."

On the way home, Marti, a registered nurse herself, helped me make a decision. "Do everything you can to transfer Jon to the nursing home in Bath."

"Marti, the first thing I did when we moved was to call admissions at Steuben County Infirmary."

"Any luck?"

"Long waiting list. Placement between healthcare facilities is rare." I sighed, knowing I had given up too soon. "But you're right. We'll contact anyone who can help with a transfer."

Steve personally delivered an application to the Steuben County Infirmary, explaining the urgency of Jon's situation. Local officials listened with compassion. The prayer and praise group at church went into action by asking God to intervene.

We yearned to have our son close enough for daily visits. Rick had been carrying a heavy load. "Lord, it's time for Steve and me as parents to be with Jon during the time he has left," I told God. "You're the one who can make it happen."

The phone rang early one February morning. "Mrs. Castor, we have a bed open for your son. We've contacted the other facility. They're willing to transport him here by ambulance around eleven A.M." I wept tears of relief and gratitude.

"I'll take the rest of the day off," Steve offered when I called him at the office. "We can help pack his things."

In his room at Geneseo, we emptied drawers and carried boxes to the station wagon. When an aide washed and dressed Jon, I was appalled at his emaciated body. Steve put his arm around Jon's thin shoulders. "You're going to a new place near our house," he reassured him. "I'm going to see you every day."

"And I'll be over at lunch time," I promised.

Jon was quiet as he was lifted from the bed to the gurney. We stopped at the nurse's station on the way out. "This is a good move for your son," the head nurse sympathetically said. "He needs his parents."

Outside, it was a sunny frosty morning with a chilly nip in the air. Jon, in his hooded jacket and tucked in with blankets, was snug. His unseeing eyes were open as if his clouded mind tried to understand the whirl of a new journey. I sat beside him in the ambulance, my hand on his shoulder. "O Lord, You are working out each step of the way for Your beloved child, Jon," I prayed. "Just one request. Please give him someone to love him at Steuben County Infirmary." Soon, Jon's eyes closed in sleep. I sensed again that underneath it all were those everlasting arms, holding us both.

TWENTY
CHALLENGED

Above the din, I yelled, "Are you ready for this?" The head nurse on south one exchanged uneasy glances with a young nursing assistant. The ambulance crew wheeled my son down the hall to his new room in Steuben County Infirmary. Growls and roars ricocheted off the walls. Thrashing legs and pounding fists gave a clear message. Jon was a human tornado.

"Mary Jo, he's all yours," the nurse gave an encouraging hug to her aide whose reaction surprised me.

"You just wait and see," the blond woman's blue eyes flashed. "Look how thin this young man is! I'll get some meat on his bones!"

Wow, she sees J.P. as a challenge! I thought gratefully. Jim McAllister, the physician's assistant, attempted to get Jon's vital signs. A flashback of my son's strong muscular arms in contrast to his present puny body wrenched my heart, and Mary Jo saw my tears.

"Mrs. Castor," she looked straight at me, her hands gripping my elbows. "I'm going to work with Jon to understand where that anger is coming from," she promised. "You'll see a change."

On the drive home, I felt a deep inner peace. "O Lord," I prayed, "You cleared the way for Jon to be close by. Thank you for providing an angel who really cares about him." In Bonnie, Jim, and Mary Jo, I sensed compassion for my hurting son. Could their care reach him beyond the devastation of Batten Disease? "With You, God, all things are possible."

Once back home, we settled into a routine. At eleven-thirty A.M., I took a lunch break from my job at church to be with my son. Now, on a warm spring morning in late May, I wheeled Jon out to the patio. Maureen Galatio, activity director, was working with residents to prepare soil in a raised bed for growing a garden. I had come early to explore possibilities.

"Feel how warm the dirt is, Jon." She guided his hand to sense its moist texture.

I *hope he doesn't try to eat it*, I thought nervously.

"Smell the manure I mixed in with it." Something stirred in Jon's memory. He sifted the rich soil through his fingers and sniffed the pungent air.

"Good," he pronounced.

"Let's start a garden, just for you," Maureen encouraged him. "Hold out your hand." Into his palm, she dropped nasturtium seeds. "Now, we'll make some holes together." A smile lit up his face as she poked his pointer finger into the loam. "Let's see if we can plant a big fat seed in each one." Gently, she guided his hand along the row. "We'll cover 'em up and see what happens, maybe next week."

"Flowers," Jon said clearly.

Mary Jo arrived with a tray of food. "Hey, Goose, have you been digging in the dirt?" She laughed, scrubbing his hands with a sudsy cloth. "Chicken for lunch today, your favorite." The patties were lightly browned. "He does better with ground food," she explained, slipping a bib around his neck.

"Please give me a lesson in helping him eat," I requested. "You have the magic touch, Mary Jo."

Jon had gained fifteen pounds in three months. The physician's assistant fine-tuned his medicines so that seizures and agitation were rare. There was an aliveness in Jon's face now as Mary Jo took the time to feed him, conversing with him as he ate.

Frequent visits from us, his parents, contributed to Jon's sense of well-being. In recollection of this time, Steve wrote: "How often, as words started to fail him, Jon would tell us, 'You're a good father, (or mother, or brother, or sister.) I love you.' No matter how discouraging the day may have been at school, leaving me feeling no good or not loveable, a conversation with Jonathan would give me a new perspective on my life and its meaning. He'd begin with a warm smile as I entered his room. 'Jonathan, what are you smiling about?'

"'I'm glad,' was his usual response.

"'Glad? What are you glad about?'

"'You.'

"'I would feign surprise. 'Me? Why are you glad about me?'

"'You're good.'

"'Oh, Jon, I'm not so good. Why do you say that?'

"'I love you.'"

The bond between father and son affirmed them both.

Finding a chair that could contain Jon's active body was a challenge to staff and to his family. He'd shake the screws loose in an ordinary wheel-chair. A recliner on wheels couldn't hold him because he'd flip those long skinny legs over the side. "Let's try him on the floor," Bonnie ventured. "He needs space to move around."

In a nook by the nurse's station, a foam pad was spread out, topped by a quilt from home. A gentle wrestling match with Rick, a back massage from Miriam, or listening to James Brown soul music with Dave—this was a place for fun and comfort.

One steamy afternoon in July, I wheeled Jon down the hall to the patio. Whom should I meet but the director of nurses from his former health care facility! She was attending a workshop on Alzheimer's at the infirmary. She stopped us. "Jon Castor, I can't believe my eyes!" she exclaimed. There were thirty pounds on his formerly gaunt frame and a smile of contentment on his face. "What's made the difference?" she asked.

"Tender loving care," I replied. *And an angel or two along the way*, I said to myself as we settled in the shade of the veranda by the patio. Edging the flagstone, red geraniums, tall blue delphiniums, purple and pink petunias, and deep gold marigolds bobbed in the breeze. "Let's check your nasturtiums, Jon." I said. On one end of the raised bed next to tall tomato plants, yellow and orange blossoms nestled among verdant greenery. I guided his hand through the leaves and helped him pick a bouquet for Mary Jo.

Today, my son was peaceful. He lifted the blooms close to his eyes as if trying to see them, and then he inhaled their tangy fragrance. "Flowers," he said proudly. My bittersweet yearning that Jon could see the glorious colors gave way to gratitude for the love surrounding him. Recalling the words of the psalm, I inserted my son's name:

> "When I said, 'Jonathan is slipping,'
> Your love, O Lord, supported him.

When anxiety was great within him,
Your consolation brought joy to his soul." (Psalm 94.18–19, NIV)

•   •   •   •   •   •   •   •   •   •   •   •   •

"Bonnie, do you think the Castor clan could take over the solarium on Jon's birthday?" I asked the head nurse. After the long snowy winter, the family was ready to party.

"Sure. I'll clear it with the administrator," she agreed.

Jon's twenty-fifth on April 1, 1983, would be a celebration to remember. All of us were aware that time was short for J.P. There had been incidents of a very slow heartbeat; Batten Disease was affecting the brain stem.

Miriam and Joe had returned home from Alaska; Cathy made a special trip from Grove City; and Rick and Dave were in charge of the one-and-only game—wheelchair football. Since Jon would be the goalie in the middle of the solarium, the ball was fuzzy and well padded.

While I spread out refreshments on a safe corner table, each member of the clan commandeered a wheelchair. Whizzing around the room, catching passes and blocking runs, teams cheered and taunted each other as Jonathan chortled. Rick scored the first touchdown.

After the game, Jon quietly held the football, his meager supply of strength depleted. A tradition in the family was to say "thank you" to God for something we loved about the birthday kid. Staff joined us in a circle around Jon.

"Thank you for my brother," Dave prayed. "I love him."

"Thank you for his wonderful care and for his peace," I added.

"For Jon's smile and courage."

"God, Jon's a gift. Thank you."

"Thank you, Lord, for Jon's good year."

"Time for cake!" young Dave reminded us. Jon couldn't see the lighted candles, but he heard us belt out "Happy Birthday to you!" He knew he was loved.

•   •   •   •   •   •   •   •   •   •   •   •   •

While the family vacationed at Agawam the following summer, Steve returned home to rebuild a school budget that had been voted down. On Monday morning, a phone call from the infirmary informed him that Jon's heart was faltering. "Please come immediately. I don't think your son is going to make it." Jim, the physician's assistant worriedly explained.

For two days, Steve sat by his bedside as Jon's breathing and heart would stop and then be started again by a small seizure. "I felt a sense of terrible helplessness and grief," Steve recalled. "How could I get word to the family in the wilds of Canada?"

Amazingly, Jon's heart clicked back into normal rhythm; he could smile again. Jim gave Steve the go-ahead to travel to Agawam.

After this incident, Jon often refused food. The return of weight loss and agitation were hard to bear. Mittens on his hands, fleece around his heels, and padded guardrails protected him from bruises. Somehow, Mary Jo still knew how to penetrate the fog of dementia with her cheerful, "How's my Goose today? Come on, let's see a smile!"

First, Jon pursed his lips but then he let out a loud Bronx cheer. "You're mad, aren't you?" she'd ask.

"Mad," he echoed.

"I'd be mad, too, in your shoes," she rubbed his head. "You're still my Goose, you know."

Then came the slow sweet smile that said love could always reach Jon's spirit. After he had fallen asleep, I asked Mary Jo a question. "Remember that first day, how roaring angry Jon was?"

"How could I forget!"

"You promised to find out the root of his fury," I reminded her.

"It's complicated, Connie," she hesitated.

"Go on. I'm interested."

"Well, beyond the backfiring of a brain damaged by Batten Disease are the memories of a strong young man who loved to build a fort and wrestle and ski," her voice was husky.

"Add to that malnutrition and neglect," I continued. "Rick said his brother was starving before he came here."

"Wouldn't you be angry, Connie?" Mary Jo's eyes brimmed over with tears. She was feeling Jon's pain. "I gave him permission to vent his anger. I told him I understood."

"You affirmed my son as a human being," I was grateful. "That's when he began to eat! How can I ever thank you for building him up—body, mind, and spirit?" We sat quietly beside the young man asleep in his bed. "This will be his last Christmas, Mary Jo," I said. A little tree twinkled in the window while its festive colors belied the sorrow in my heart. I was thankful for the privacy of a single room.

"Connie, when Jon dies, for us on staff it will be like losing a member of the family." Tears spilled over. "I still catch glimpses of the spunky, funny person Goose is," she continued. "Let's enjoy each day we have with him."

I took her words to heart as I wrote in my journal: "I am sitting here by Jon's bed, singing a wordless lullaby as I cradle his head and shoulders. Indeed, feelings come back from my young motherhood when almost in ecstasy I nursed him, dressed him, watched the dimple in his cheek, the mischievous turn of his cocky head, the bright blue eyes full of joy.

"Now I look at his twenty-five-year-old face, peaceful in sleep. The curve of the cheeks, the tilt of his nose, the Castor sticking-out ears, the mop of chestnut hair, his hands, infant-like, folded on his chest—Jon is beautiful to me. They tell me he's been chuckling and laughing. I thank God for the gift of this pure son, now back in infancy.

"Today, I put my eyes close to his; place my cheek on his; and feel the slow pulse of life. More deeply, I sense the holy essence of my son. His goodness and patience and usual joy in the midst of such limitations speak to me of Jesus living in him. His mind is clogged, body weak, the long thin legs useless, and eyes sightless—but what about Jon's clear, loving, laughing spirit?

"Sometimes, I long for this boy who was intelligent, handsome, and courageous to be able to experience life normally. What an outstanding young man he would be had the genes been right! Yet I wonder if the purity would have survived the stress of growing up in this confused world?

"All I know is that Jon is perfect in that inner core. He loves me as I am in some primal way. The awful barriers that make loving so difficult are absent. To come here and cuddle him, to talk our funny language, to feed him and to say 'I love you, Jon'—it's restorative.

"Thank you, Lord Jesus, for this special son sleeping in innocence. Thank you for living inside him, Your Spirit in his reaching out to me. You are holding him in life or death. Amen."

TWENTY-ONE
INTO THE LIGHT

The sanctuary was hushed. Organ chimes were softly playing "O Little Town of Bethlehem." In silence, we awaited the coming of the Christ child. The pastor invited us to partake of communion at the altar when we were ready.

I breathed in the beauty of this holy place. Twinkling lights danced among the branches of a tall Douglas fir. White and gold chrismons, symbols of Christ, hung on its boughs. A candelabra glowed behind the altar. I longed for the peace promised by the angels to infiltrate my spirit.

Kneeling at the rail with Steve beside me, I held a small cup of grape juice. The second beatitude, words from the Sunday school lesson, echoed in my mind. "How happy are those who know what sorrow means for they shall be given courage and comfort." Like towering surf, waves of impending loss broke over me.

"Lord Jesus, I haven't the strength in myself to endure the death of another child," I prayed. Steve reached for my hand. Through a blur of tears, I saw the anguish in his face. Now, another arm embraced me. Rick had joined us at the altar. What had God the Father felt when He gave His only son to a hurting world two thousand years ago? I knew God understood our pain. Jesus was walking beside us in our sorrow.

Rick, Steve, and I stood up, hugged each other, and then joined our church family encircling the sanctuary. Each face was lighted by an individual candle as we sang,

> "Silent night, holy night
> Wondrous star, lend thy light.
> With the angels let us sing
> Alleluia to our King."
> Christ the Savior is born, Christ the Savior is born."[13]

The day after Christmas, there was a flurry of activity around the dining room table. "Hey, who took the scissors?"

"Please pass me the tape."

"Don't hog that whole roll of wrapping paper!"

"Where'd the ribbon go?"

Everybody was wrapping a present for Jon. Cathy was now married to Mark Collier. Together, they worked on a big teddy bear. Rick was engaged to Mary. They stuck a bow on a cassette holder full of tapes. Miriam helped young Dave package a sweatsuit. Steve wrapped paper around a boom box while I slapped on the tape. Everybody had contributed to the new cassette collection. Jon especially appreciated praise songs. "And some soul music," Dave added, tossing one last James Brown recording in the piled-up laundry basket.

The solarium was festively decked in garlands, wreaths, and a Christmas tree. Mary Jo and crew had wheeled Jon's bed into the middle of the room. "Tone it down, gang," I requested before entering. "We don't want to overwhelm J.P." Nobody paid any attention to me.

"Merry Christmas! How 'bout a hug?"

"How's my main man, J.P.?"

"Jon, open my present first!"

Jon beamed, chortling. Mary Jo had him dressed in red and green. To see our family love reflected in his face was Jon's gift to us. "My Christmas goose!" Mary Jo exclaimed. "You are all his lifeline!" She pointed toward a table full of holiday goodies. "Help yourselves to cookies and punch."

Jon wasn't the only one excited. The party animal young Dave was exuberant, too. He hoisted his sister Miriam into his arms and twirled her around. "Proving his strength," Steve noted. Cathy sat quietly beside her bedridden brother, holding his hand and stroking his shaggy hair.

"It's tough giving this guy a haircut," Mary Jo apologized.

Rick sat on the other side of the bed. "How's J.P. doing?" he asked.

"Lately, he's been perky," Mary Jo replied. "Every day I've been telling him about your coming for Christmas."

"I've missed him," Rick was rueful. "After seeing him daily in Geneseo, I slacked off."

"You were right there when he needed you," I chimed in. "Now, it's our turn."

"Come on, gang, let's gather 'round and sing Jon some carols," Steve corralled the family. First "Jingle Bells" had us rockin' and rollin'. Then quieter, the old familiar songs of Christmas reminded us of what the season was all about.

We sang:

> "How silently, how silently the wondrous gift is given,
> So God imparts to human hearts the wonders of His Heaven.
> No ear may hear His coming, but in this world of sin,
> Where meek souls will receive Him still,
> The dear Christ enters in."[14]

"Look, Mom, Jon understands," Cathy noticed his wet eyes. She bent down close. "You know about Jesus coming at Christmas, don't you, J.P.?"

"God loves," he answered clearly.

• • • • • • • • • • • • • • •

It would be under different circumstances that the family gathered around Jon again. A phone call from Bonnie Linnahan, the head nurse, brought Steve and me to his bedside early one morning in February. Before we left home, we had called the children.

When we entered the room, we were alarmed to see how chalk white he was. Bonnie was taking his pulse. Her usually smiling face was drawn in a frown of concern. "Sometimes, Jon's heart stops for twenty seconds at a time. He quits breathing, and then seizure activity jump-starts it again." Her voice shook as she spoke. As we watched, Jon's face became flushed. He reared up, gasping for air.

"I hope Rick and Mim make it in time," I mumbled, afraid. I knew my son's condition was serious. Steve had witnessed the chain-stokes breathing back in August, but it was a shock to me to see his struggle.

I respected the strength in Steve as he held Jonathan through the spasms. Rick arrived and sat on the other side of his brother. Two strong arms supported my son. Miriam and I clutched each other in fear during those moments when his heart would stop, once for thirty seconds. Then, his body would shake, and blood rushed to his head. "Come on, you two," Rick scolded us. "Shape up!"

"Look!" Miriam was concentrating on her brother's face. "Jon's trying to give us the Bronx cheer!" Sure enough, he puckered up his lips and sputtered out a loud one.

"Goose, are you mad?" Mary Jo asked.

"Mad," Jon replied faintly.

Somehow, my son's feisty response in his fight to keep going calmed our anxiety. Jim McAllister arrived to take vital signs. "How long can this go on?" Steve asked.

"The brainstem regulates heartbeat and breathing," the physician's assistant explained. "Batten Disease has damaged its function. Jon's blood pressure is very low. I don't know… " his voice trailed off.

At noon, Bonnie poked her head in the door. "Somebody has brought you lunch," she announced. "I'll take over. You need a break." In the solarium, a friend from Bible study group had spread a feast—homemade vegetable beef soup, chicken salad sandwiches, apples, and cookies. Lunch was an oasis of normalcy, and we were hungry. Several friends from church stopped by to pray with us.

During the afternoon hours, I begged God to release Jon from his struggle to live. Around four o'clock, the answer came in a surprising way when he began to breathe normally. Bonnie took his pulse. "It's a nice regular sixty," she said. Color returned to his face, and a little smile gave us hope.

"Who do you love, Jon?" Steve asked his son.

"My father and my mother," he replied weakly.

"How about your brother Rick?" his sibling teased.

Jon puckered up for another Bronx cheer.

"That's my goose!" Mary Jo exulted. We laughed, enjoying a brief interlude of hilarity. "Go on home and get some rest. Jon's ready for some supper and a good night's sleep."

The next afternoon, I found Jim listening intently to a rattle in my son's chest. His face was flushed and his eyes half open. "Aspiration pneumonia," the physician's assistant explained. "At lunch, Jon had a seizure while an aide was feeding him. He ingested ice cream directly into his lungs."

"This morning he seemed so much better. What does this mean?" I asked frightened.

Jim looked away. "The truth?" he questioned.

Dread knotted my stomach. "Yes."

"Within the next twenty-four hours, he'll spike a high fever which will take his life."

"I thought it would be his heart!" I objected, incredulous.

"His heartbeat is fast but regular. I'm sorry. There's nothing I can do for him medically."

Mary Jo stood beside me with an arm around me. Her eyes were filled with tears. "We'll do everything to make him comfortable, Connie. I'll leave you two alone."

I lay my head on the pillow and my hand over his heart. "Jon, I thought your tough can-do spirit had licked the odds one more time," I told him. "Now this!" I kissed the smooth skin along his temple. "I want to tell you how much I love you, J.P. It won't be long until you leave your sick body. You'll be with Jesus."

I began to weep. I cherished even this tenuous thread of life. "Jon, I love your generous heart, your accepting spirit. Just yesterday you said you loved your father and your mother. How can I let you go?" Those strong hands that had sanded boards and built a fort were lying peacefully crossed on his chest. His hair smelled sweet. They must have bathed him last night. The gaunt face and half-closed eyes reminded me of how much this truly good young man had suffered.

"It's time for you to be with Jesus, Jon." At that moment, I released him into the Father's hands. I read aloud the Lord's comforting words to His disciples from John 14.1-3: "'Do not let your hearts be troubled. Trust in God; trust also in me. In my Father's house are many rooms; if it were not so, I would have told you. I am going there to prepare a place for you. And if I go and prepare a place for you, I will come back and take you to be with me that you also may be where I am.'" (NIV)

Steve and I sat together and sometimes alone with our son. His lungs became more congested and his temperature slowly climbed. On February 29th, we were home at suppertime getting a bite to eat when the phone rang. It was Bonnie. "Jon's fever has spiked at 107°. We're bathing him in cold water, trying to get it down. You'd better come right away."

At the bottom of the stairs going up to South One, we paused for prayer. "God help us," I cried.

"And take our dear Jon into Your presence," Steve whispered. Each step I climbed felt as if twenty-pound weights were tied to my legs. Slowly, we walked to Jon's room. Mary Jo was crying in the hall. "Is he...?" I asked.

"Just now..."

We opened the door. A few involuntary movements and then the stillness of death. With brimming eyes, Bonnie covered the thin blue body with a sheet. She closed his eyes. "I'm so sorry...We did all we could," she wept.

The smallness of what was Jon and the absence of life—the loss was overpowering. As bereft parents, we held each other and sobbed. Then out in the hall, we huddled with Mary Jo, Bonnie, and Jim while our tears mingled. "Thank you, thank you for all your care and love and for the good years our son had here." Once again, we stood beside the bed to say goodbye, shocked to see the thin mottled bird-like body that had once been Jon.

Late that night on quiet Burton Street, a hearse pulled up in front of the house. "I need some papers signed," the driver mumbled apologetically. It was the most desolate feeling in the world as Steve and I watched the vehicle holding Jon's body drive down the hill into the night.

• • • • • • • • • • • • • •

On the Sunday of Jonathan Paul Castor's memorial service, banners hung by the altar. One proclaimed "He Lives," another, "Nothing can separate us from the love of God." I respected the courage and deep love of my children who honored their brother that day.

"As I look back, I remember special times that Jon and I spent together in Springville," Miriam shared. "Daily rides on the tandem bicycle were highlights for both of us. Though he could barely walk, he surely knew how to pedal. After a teetering take-off, we would tear down the block, with Jon yelling behind me, 'Faster, Olds, faster!' Little choice did I have as we surged forward. In silent ecstasy, we shared the thrill of the wind in our hair, our lungs sucking in the cool air. Our hearts pounded with a steady strong pulse. How Jon cherished his strength! How he reveled in his health, challenging the fate of that inevitable disease and death!"

The choir sang a song that we had often listened to by Jon's bedside:

"A time will come for singing
when all your tears are shed,
when sorrow's chains are broken,
and broken hearts shall mend.
The deaf will hear your singing
when silent tongues are freed.
The lame will join your dancing
when blind eyes learn to see."

The last paragraph of Cathy's letter to her brother touched me deeply. It was hard for her to read it. She wrote, "I saw you last Christmas, surrounded by the whole family in a bed full of presents. I ache to see you again, Jonathan, to see your beautiful face with its thick brown hair and sparkling eyes. I am missing you so badly. Yet I hold onto the realization that I will see you again. And you won't be bound to that bed. You will run to greet me, maybe even pick me up and swing me around in the air as you see your grown-up sister for the first time."

Rick helped me catch a glimpse of Jon's new life: "What's it like to be saturated with the Light of one you have worshipped for a lifetime, Jon? Here I am rejoicing in your eternal adventure, praising the Creator, knowing someday I'll join you. Then, I'll be whole, like you are. I can imagine your eyes, perfect and clear, and a smile radiating beauty that now I can only experience in fragmented memories. Yes, J.P., you are in the light of the Lord. I'm glad you led the way."

Something healing was going on within my spirit as I listened to the words of my children. Beyond the sorrow, I pictured Jon now in the light of God's presence, seeing with new eyes. I sensed the deep joy of knowing he is bathed in love and beauty and peace.

• • • • • • • • • • • • • •

In the weeks following Jon's death, on one level, I knew that my son was at peace in God's presence. Another part of me, however, was vulnerable to disturbing flashbacks. I'd suddenly awaken from a sound sleep seeing that thin blue body still and cold. That desolate picture would appear before my eyes while in church or taking a walk.

One spring morning, I sat on the back patio in tears. "O God, I can't take it anymore. I don't want to remember Jon this way. Heal my damaged mind." I sat in stillness and expectancy before the Creator.

In my mind's eye came a scene of beauty. From a sphere of shimmering light tumbled a stream of sparkling crystal clear water. Deep green grass and wild flowers edged the river. Suddenly, at my feet was my dead child. "Pick him up and place him in the water," a voice commanded.

Surprised at how light the body was, I waded into the stream and dipped the lifeless form into the healing waters.

Before my eyes, my son stood tall and whole. His blue eyes sparkled; his face glowed with health; and his body was strong and muscular. Jon's face was turned toward the light as he raised his arms in praise. Then, he turned to look directly at me. "This is who I really am," he seemed to say. Since the vision, I have never had a flashback. I see his face, radiant with eternal life.

But in all these things we overwhelmingly conquer through Him who loved us. For I am convinced that neither death, nor life, nor angels, nor principalities, nor things present, nor things to come, nor powers, nor height, nor depth, nor any other created thing, shall be able to separate us from the love of God, which is in Christ Jesus our Lord."

PART III

DAVID

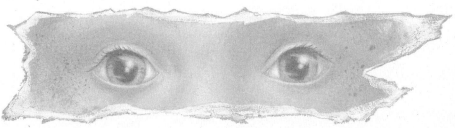

TWENTY-TWO
A FAMILY DIVIDED

In the swirl of events shaping our lives, there comes a moment of decision that is pivotal. The implications are far-reaching. In white-hot anger from a wounded spirit, I forged a change of direction that would affect not only my life but that of each member of my family.

Travel back in time to a July morning in 1973 when I sat at the kitchen table in the old blue house. I was grappling with the choice of leaving my husband. The marriage had been violated, its foundation shattered. The situation was no longer viable.

My sister Miriam, visiting from Maryland, encouraged me to call a Rochester lawyer. My hand shook as I dialed the number. Busy signal. "Here I am, forty-four years old, and I don't even know how to drive!" I sputtered. "What about transportation to the law office?"

"Connie, I'm not returning to D.C. until I provide the help you need right now." Miriam covered my hand with hers. "I'll get you there. Try again."

"Clark and Murphy Law Firm," the voice was impersonal. "Yes, we handle separation agreements. Can you come for a three o'clock appointment tomorrow afternoon? Here's the information we'll need." I grabbed a pencil and jotted down a list.

After hanging up the receiver, I collapsed into a chair. "I can't believe I'm doing this… " A deep breath calmed my pounding heart. "But I'm just not able to live with Steve anymore."

"Connie, you're making the right decision," Miriam concurred.

I looked into my youngest sister's hazel eyes. I saw compassion and strength. She provided stability and wisdom in the midst of turmoil.

The lawyer, a kindly older man, was surprisingly understanding as I explained my financial needs, including $10,000 for a downpayment on a house. "I've never even written a check," I confessed. "Steve has always taken care of the finances."

"You'll learn fast, Mrs. Castor." Mr. Murphy shook my hand. "I'll contact your husband's lawyer as soon as we write up the agreement and you approve it. I'm sure there'll be no problem in getting his signature."

"You're planning to buy a house?" Miriam asked surprised on the drive home.

"Yep, I'd like to find a small bungalow in Webster," I replied. "Davey and Cathy will be coming with me. Three bedrooms and space for the boys on weekends would be nice. With Jon at School for the Blind and Rick in sports at Elba, it makes sense for them to stay put."

"I see that nesting gleam in your eye already," she teased.

That night, the fall-out of leaving the marriage hit with full force. How could I tell the children? Timidly, I knocked on the door of Cathy's bedroom. "Come in, Mom," she invited me. Papered in a miniature red print with white tieback curtains, it was a cozy place. My daughter was propped up on pillows in her four-poster bed, listening to music. At age eleven, her long blond hair and tranquil face revealed emerging beauty. How dare I break her heart!

She looked up at me, anxiety clouding her eyes. "You've been crying, Mom! What's the matter?"

"I saw a lawyer today," I blurted out. "I need time away from your father."

"You mean a divorce?" she asked incredulously. "I knew that you and Dad were having trouble, but…but…" She burst into tears.

"This is a separation to give me a chance to heal. I'm really hurting." I could hardly continue. "I'm looking for a house in Webster."

"I don't want to move. All my friends are in Elba." She buried her face in a pillow and sobbed. Praying silently, I knelt beside her with my hand on her shoulder. A picture flashed in my mind of a lighthouse built on a rocky shore. Huge breakers were slamming against the rocks. In a small boat, I was in turbulent waters, wanting desperately the guiding light of the Lord Jesus to bring me into quiet harbor. O *Lord Jesus*, I pled, *Open the way for the children and me to be safe in You.*

Cathy was calmer now. "You have to do this, Mom." It was partly a statement of fact and partly a question. "Can't you work it out with Dad?"

"The problem is too deep and painful. Right now, I need a place to think and…" I couldn't find words. "I know this is a terrible shock to you, honey."

"I always thought we were the perfect family, living in this old house, having fun, loving each other…" Her voice trailed off. "What's Davey going to think about this?"

Actually, Davey's six-year-old trust and innocence protected him as he absorbed the news. It was several days later that he sat on my lap in the old black needlepoint rocker and talked. In the meantime, I had contacted a realtor in Webster and looked at just the right bungalow for us. Its big attraction was a swimming pool in the back yard. Davey was full of questions.

"Can I go swimming? Any kids around my age? Will I see Dad, Rick, and Jon?" I reassured him on all three counts.

Rick was angry when I broached the subject. "You mean you're leaving Jon and me? You and Dad—I've heard you arguing. Other times you've gone for help, Mom. Remember that counselor guy you were seeing?"

"This is different, Rick," I countered. "There's a very deep wound in me. Being away from your father will help it heal. You and Jon can come every other weekend to visit us in Webster."

"I just don't get it!" His fist hit the table.

Jon was quiet. "I'm going to miss you, Mom," he said, his eyes full of tears.

My heart was heavy as I knelt beside the bed that night. "O Jesus, You loved the broken and the weak while You were here on earth. I place Rick and Jon in Your strong hands while I am away. In Your name, Amen."

Less than three weeks had passed when a caravan of trailers and my daughter Miriam's car pulled into Kircher Park. The house was small with a spacious light-filled kitchen, two bedrooms upstairs, two down, and a family room with fireplace in the basement. Steve's brother Dick gave me a hug after unloading the last box in the living room. "This will be a great place for you and the children." His backing cheered me. As plans for the separation had unfolded, I was amazed by the love and concern among family and friends.

Now, I faced the gargantuan task of unpacking a pyramid of boxes. "Hey, Mom, let's go swimming!" Two half-naked children clad in bathing suits pressed their noses against the screen door while Miriam, my oldest daughter, was helping me in the moving process.

"Good idea, you guys!" Miriam agreed. "Come on, Mom, get your suit, and let's take a plunge! We'll unpack later."

"I'll help," Cathy promised.

"Me, too," Davey echoed.

Under the back steps, he had found an inner tube. His sister grabbed an inflated pad, "Left here just for us," Miriam concluded. Two children from up the street joined us. On a hot August afternoon, the cool water soothed our tired muscles. Sparkles of sunlight in the splash of a dive refreshed my spirit. Excited chatter of young ones getting acquainted foreshadowed friendships for Cathy and Davey. I flashed back to the lighthouse, and for this moment, I let go of resentment and worry. I savored the safe harbor the Lord had provided.

• • • • • • • • • • • • • • • •

It took us a week to settle into our home on Kircher Park. Carpet and curtains were already in place. Furniture transported from the old blue house graciously fit small rooms. Cathy and Miriam dug into boxes and filled the big wall of shelves in the kitchen pantry. Davey settled his toys in a nook off of the living room.

"I love this sunporch," Miriam declared, staking out her space. We made up a daybed and placed her dresser out there. Crisp white cottage curtains added light and privacy and hominess. At eighteen, she was aware of the circumstances catapulting us into relocating. "I'm backing you all the way, Mom," she promised. In the fall, she was headed for William Smith College in Geneva. "It's not far. I'll need some weekends home."

I knew the nesting instinct was a buffer from the anger and hurt lying just under the surface. Right now, all I could say was "Thank you, God, for caring for us."

I made a list of things to do as a new resident of Webster. First on the agenda was to contact the school district and enroll the children in first and sixth grades. Mrs. Collins, David's teacher, invited me to her classroom. "I haven't got my driver's license yet. Would you mind picking me up?" I asked hesitantly.

Out in the driveway sat my bright orange 1970 Datsun station wagon, a terrifying challenge. "You're just learning to drive?" There was a hint of disbelief in the teacher's voice.

"I must learn before my daughter leaves for college," I explained. "She takes me out evenings. We're not a good combination."

She laughed. "You'll do fine. Probably someone outside your family would be more patient." I made a mental note to call a friend's spouse who was a former driving instructor.

In the classroom, big colorful posters of autumn in New York hung on one wall, opening up vistas of beauty. "Just a reminder to the children of our Creator's gifts," she commented. "I change them with the season." A reading corner was cozy with rug, cushions, and a huge stuffed bear. "This is Poo, our class mascot."

"Tell me about your son's special needs," Mrs. Collins asked.

"His sight is pretty good right now, 20/200," I informed her. "He can see large print books and is eager to read. The Association for the Blind in Rochester will provide books and magnifiers as needed." I gave her the telephone number.

"His sight will become less during the year?" she asked.

"It will decrease. That's the sad part and the challenge." My voice broke. A flashback to Karen's loss in second grade was vivid. "I hope he'll be able to finish first grade here."

I saw sympathy and then a glint of determination in the teacher's gray eyes. "I'll do everything I can to help David feel he belongs here in our class." I sensed her keen mind planning ahead. "I have an excellent aide who'll work with me on providing tactile stuff and lively tapes."

"Yes, his hearing and touch will grow more acute. I saw that with Karen and Jon." She had been informed about the diagnosis of Batten Disease. "There's one concern I worry about," I continued.

"I think I know what that is," Mrs. Collin's direct gaze revealed understanding. "How will the other children treat your son?"

"Yes. Karen used to come home crying, feeling left out and confused with no friends," I explained.

"Well, there's Someone much bigger than you and I who's caring for David." She pointed to a picture on her desk of Jesus with the children.

"Thanks for that reminder, Mrs. Collins." I returned home with a deep sense of peace about my son's first grade teacher.

Cathy's reaction to the initial week of school wasn't hard to decipher as she picked at her meatballs and spaghetti Friday evening. "I feel like an outsider, Mom." Tears spilled over. "Everybody knows each other. I miss my friends in Elba."

I reached for her hand, feeling a slow knife of guilt turning in my stomach. It was I who was putting her through this. "Honey, I'm sorry. But how about your teacher? Do you like him?"

Her face lit up. "Mr. Guderian's a riot! Guess what our project is for science—making a hot air balloon!" I sent up a silent "thank you" for a man aware of Cathy's pain. Later, he nurtured her gift for writing poetry and for expressing her feelings through art.

One fall afternoon, Cathy excitedly burst open the front door. Her arm was around her little brother who clutched a big print picture book. "Listen to this! Davey can read!"

My son's blond hair stood on end, an exclamation point to the proud smile on his face. "Ready?" he asked, opening the story of *Big Brown Bear*. "It was time for brown bear to wake up," he began. Dave's voice was full of expression as he shared with us his first adventure in reading. "Mrs. Collins says she's proud of me," he exclaimed. "Poo Bear sat right next to me in class."

"We're proud of you, too!" I hugged him. "Let's go to the library soon so that you can choose your own books to bring home." The Association for the Blind made sure a good variety was available.

The orange Datsun daily challenged me. For Miriam, teaching me to drive was torture. Out on back roads at twilight, I shook with fear and self-doubt. Could klutzy middle-aged me ever learn to put in the clutch or shift, steer and park?

"No, Mom!" Miriam had reached the end of her rope. We were parked sideways on a manicured lawn one evening. "Turn left on the next street," she had instructed. In the darkness, I had mistaken a driveway for a road and had somehow landed on the grass. "Get out right now!" she commanded. "I'll get us out of here before someone yells at us!" I felt like a dumb kid.

The next day, I took Mrs. Collin's advice and called my friend's husband, a driving instructor. He agreed to work with me in the daylight on weekends. "I'll have you tooling along in no time!" he promised. Calmly, he reviewed the basics, teaching me to use my rearview and side mirrors. Driving in traffic scared me, but John's reassuring presence and step-by-step instruction successfully gave me confidence. Several weeks later, after I had parallel parked five times in a row, he announced, "You're ready for your driving test, Connie."

"I'm shaking in my boots!" I shared my fears with the ladies in the Bible study group. "The test is eleven A.M. next Thursday." My friends gathered around me and prayed for peace and a clear mind. With a sense of adventure and God's presence, I passed with flying colors. A week later, I tucked my driver's license into my wallet. "Thank you, Lord," I prayed. "In Your strength, I made it over a huge hurdle."

The other challenge was taking care of finances. With $550.00 to work with, I sat down at my desk each month with a heavy sense of responsibility. Making out my first check was an important step away from dependence upon Steve. Extra income from occasional substitute teaching helped.

One afternoon a big wind blew off the storm door on the porch. There was no extra money in the bank to buy a new one. "Lord Jesus, You know the need," I turned to my unseen partner. "I trust You to provide for us." The next day $50.00 arrived, tucked in a note. "I thought you could use this," it read. No name. Prickles of awe ran down my back. Cathy and Davey were watching wide-eyed as I waved the check in a gleeful dance. "Wow, Mom," Cathy was excited. "God's really taking care of us!" We joined hands in a prayer of thanksgiving.

Something good was going on inside my daughter, a lifting of her spirit. One evening after tucking Davey into bed, I had stopped by her room. She was sitting in a rocking chair reading her youth edition Bible. "Honey, I see a change in you. What's making the difference?" I asked.

"C'mon in and sit down," Cathy invited me. I perched on her bed. "Remember how insecure I was? I felt as if my whole world was turned upside down after you and Dad split."

"Me, too."

"Well, in the Bible, it told me just where to turn when I was feeling down. Like the psalm I'm reading right now. 'I will say of the LORD, "He is my refuge and my fortress, my God, in whom I trust."'" Cathy read aloud. "'You will not fear the terror of night, nor the arrow that flies by day.'" (Psalm 91.2, 5; NIV)

"God is speaking to you through His Word," I observed.

"Yep, I feel safe now. He's right here with me." That evening in the quiet of Cathy's bedroom, mother and daughter shared Scripture and the comfort of the Father walking with us on a difficult journey.

TWENTY-THREE
RETURN TO ELBA

Shivering in the biting chill of November, I stood on the porch steps. One hand waving from a back window of Steve's station wagon returned my goodbye. Cathy and Davey were on their way with their dad for a weekend in Elba. Now, I opened the front door and listened. The ticking of a clock and the wind rattling windowpanes were sounds of loneliness. With "poor me" feelings nibbling at my spirit, I wanted to run from this isolation. Other Saturdays, I had anxiously crammed the time with friends for lunch or an overnight with a college classmate, but this day, the dam holding back the anguish and hurt of my severed marriage was about to give way.

"Be still and know that I am God" (Psalm 46.10) had leapt at me that morning in my devotional book. "But Lord, I'm afraid," I countered the challenge.

Afraid of what?

To face myself and the whirlwind of emotions around this separation.

What else are you afraid of?

Davey's nightmares and his failing eyesight.

Even though you walk through the valley of the shadow of death, Jesus was speaking to me, *You will fear no evil, for I am with you.* I knew that in the stillness of my empty house it was time to face my inner self.

Out on the sunporch, I had made myself at home in Miriam's nook. A fresh notebook for journaling, my Bible, my favorite C. S. Lewis books, and a photo album were stacked on the end table.

I clicked on the space heater and settled back into pillows on the daybed. "The Spirit of truth…will guide you into all truth," I read in John 16.13 (NIV). I sat quietly, trusting the Spirit to direct my thoughts. I was transported back in time to Corea, Maine, where I, an eight-year old, fished with Papa. I smelled the creosote, briny fish, and the salty tang in the air. I heard the gulls crying and the waves sloshing against the wharf. The wind parted my hair and the spool of line was rough in my hands as I waited for a flounder to nibble. A sense of well-being and sheer fun engulfed me.

I could also see my father, who wore a blue beret and knickers and who sat in a folding chair as he intently peered at the lighthouse. With German crayons, Papa made the scene come alive on his artist's pad. Whitewashed stones of the old tower, shadowed saltbox house, profusion of light in the foreground, and cloud-swept sky—he captured them all. In the meantime, I climbed rocks and picked blueberries from scrubby bushes, drinking in the breeze, warm sun, and blue ocean.

It was evening in my mind's eye. I pictured myself being tucked into the brass bed upstairs in the coastal farmhouse we rented. Mama sat on the bed, asking about my day and saying "Jesus Tender Shepherd" with me.

The next day, my brother Buddy, baby sister Martha, Mama, Papa, and I headed for Bar Harbor in the Model T. In a sheltered rocky cleft, Papa built a fire to roast corn and hot dogs. Buddy and I threw dried seaweed on the flames, laughing as it snapped and popped. Nimbly, we jumped from rock to rock as lithe little children, free and joyous.

Later, looking down into mysterious Thunderhole, a deep vortex of water swirling and crashing below me, I was afraid. Papa's firm hands on my shoulder reassured me. Those same strong arms had held me during my baptism. With tears of gratitude, I felt unspeakably blessed to have parents who loved me, affirmed me, and guided me toward the Lord Jesus.

Remember who you are, Connie, remember your heritage, the Spirit was saying. Looking into the thunderhole of emotions around the decision to leave Steve, I felt the Father's everlasting arms holding me.

First of all, I laid out before the Lord my feelings of guilt. Which were false and which were real? Steve's choices and actions had closed the door on a marriage relationship. It felt right to be away from him. I refused to feel guilty about that.

But not being there to mother Rick and Jon gnawed at my conscience. The boys considered their alternate weekend visits a holiday. Rick, the troubadour, attracted Kircher Park girls by singing impromptu humorous ballads. At fourteen, his buoyant funny self was vulnerable to peer pressure. I knew he was smoking. Rick, Miriam, and Jon had gone through confirmation classes the year before. Greg, the youth pastor, told me later. "Never before have I had a class like that. Big questions from Rick and your daughter. They were a challenge." I knew Rick needed the steady support and guidance of his mom.

And Jon? Out of the three, he had decided to join the church as a sturdy believer. Steve and Rick attended all his wrestling matches and cheered him on. During weekend visits, Jon would fill me in on his "almost" pins and adventures with his strong roommate, Gerald. Recently, he had asked me, "Mom, when are you coming back? I miss you after school." His face was sad. "You know how we used to sit around the kitchen table, Cathy, Rick, Davey, and me. You always had chocolate chip cookies in the jar and asked us about our day." Jon's honest question had touched a deep chord in me.

Then, there was Davey. He needed a dad to discipline him. I was too soft with him. Ever since visits to the eye doctor back in kindergarten, I sensed that he had connected his loss of sight with Jon's. There were nights when his sleep was disturbed. "Help me! Help me!" He cried out. I held him until he stopped trembling.

An incident the week before had jolted me into the reality of his diminishing vision. In the field to the back of our house, the neighbor kids with Cathy and Davey had trampled a labyrinth of paths in the tall grass. After supper, "hide 'n' seek" was a favorite game. Scrunched down out in the field one evening, Davey waited to be found. Somehow in the scramble of children, he was overlooked. Cathy came home without her little brother. "He's not here?" she asked surprised. "I thought Davey was with Billy."

"It's dark and I'm worried," I fretted. Flashlight in hand, Cathy and I trudged along the paths, searching.

To our right came the sound of sobbing. We found our lost boy hunched over in the grass. With our arms around him, we pulled him up, his face swollen and wet. "I was afraid nobody would ever find me," Davey was calming down. "At first, I tried to find the path, but I kept falling down. I hate not being able to see."

"I'm sorry, Davey," Cathy hugged her little brother. "I won't let this happen again."

After prayers that night, I tucked a warm blanket snuggly around his body. His tousled blond hair was still damp from a bath. "Mom, am I going to be blind like Jon?" I looked into my son's wide blue eyes fringed with long lashes.

A *face like an angel*, I thought, *snub nose, expressive mouth that likes to smile and those typical Castor sticking-out ears*. His question wrenched my heart. How could I answer? "You are David Mark Castor, your own special self. God is taking very good care of you."

"Boy, I was scared out there. I couldn't see anything."

"Cathy and I couldn't either, but we found you with our flashlight." Content, he snuggled down for a peaceful sleep.

The Bible lay open on my lap as I returned from haunting images of my boys. "O God, show me the way to love my sons," I prayed. I turned to a verse in Jeremiah 31.3-4 (NIV). "'I have loved you with an everlasting love,'" the Lord spoke to me in His Word. "'I have drawn you with loving kindness. I will build you up again, and you will be rebuilt.'"

As I ended my first Saturday of reflection and prayer, I thought, *Aha, a light is dawning! Today, the Lord reminded me of the foundation of my faith as a child, the heritage of love from my parents.* These weekends alone with God would be times of rebuilding my hurting, needy self. I placed my sons in God's hands.

• • • • • • • • • • • • •

Six months had passed. Reams of journal pages later, I sat thinking out by the pool the first weekend in August. The children were with Steve. I was troubled as I re-read the note from Mrs. Collins, Davey's first grade teacher: "Because of David's increasing loss of vision, he is not able to see large print books. Through tapes, tactile art projects, and reading aloud, the aide and I have kept his bright mind engaged in learning. We have enjoyed having your son in first grade. New York State School for the Blind in Batavia is our recommendation as he enters second grade. It is equipped to handle David's needs. I wish him God's blessings, and you, too, Mrs. Castor."

I sat taking inventory of my situation. David and Jon would both be at School for the Blind. Rick was entrenched in football and basketball at Elba. Miriam would be returning to college. *It will be just Cathy and me here in Webster*, I thought. *It's time I go back to the old blue house and take care of my children.*

Impossible! There was the matter of pride in asking Steve if he would consider my return. Our lives had been totally separate over the past year. There had been no indication that he wanted me around the homestead. His interests were elsewhere. I needed to soak this decision in prayer.

The underlying direction from God was clear. *Your job is to care for your children and quit judging your husband. I have been rebuilding you. My strength will be yours as you return to Elba.*

But dare I risk asking Steve? My stomach knotted at the thought. Besides, I loved my peaceful life at Kircher Park. Cathy and I were close as we laughed and cried, sharing our ups and downs together.

"I like it here," she had commented after a Marco Polo game in the pool. "I have a lot more fun with my friends at Webster than the kids in Elba. I wouldn't want to go back."

For myself, I was attending a lively church and was part of a woman's Bible study that nurtured my spirit. In the fall, I'd have to begin work on my master's degree in order to teach high school English. A career? My head spun as I took a brisk walk around the block.

That evening, I leafed through *The Business of Heaven* by my favorite author, C. S. Lewis.[15] Through a devotional reading, Jesus spoke directly to me. "No person can reach absolute reality except through Me. Try to retain your own life, and you will be inevitably ruined. Give yourself away and you will be saved. If anything whatever is keeping you from God and Me, throw it away. If you put yourself first, you will be last. Come to Me, every-one who is carrying a heavy load. I will set that right. Your sins, all of them, are wiped out. I can do that. I am Rebirth; I am Life! And finally, do not be afraid. I have overcome the whole universe."

In silence, I considered the implications of letting go of pride and fear, the barriers keeping me from obeying God's directive. I wanted LIFE. I gave my heavy load to Christ.

The phone rang. It was Steve asking about arrangements for bringing Cathy and David home. My heart began to pound. My throat tightened. This was the moment.

"Steve, I'm making an offer," I began.

"An offer?" he sounded cautious.

"Yes, I would like to return home before school begins."

Dead silence on the other end of the line. His breathing sounded as ragged as mine. Finally he spoke, "May I ask why?"

"I want to take care of the children. Our kids need a mother and father they can depend on," I croaked. Another silence.

"I'll have to think this one over," Steve ended the conversation curtly. "I'll be in touch."

Two weeks later as I fussed and fumed about the first day of school fast approaching, Steve opened the door a crack. "Let's get together with all the children for a picnic at Letchworth Park," he challenged me. "They should have a say in this decision."

I broached the subject with my daughter. "All of us at Letchworth? Are you thinking of getting back together with Dad?" Cathy demanded an answer. "I was just getting settled in Webster, and you drag me back to Elba!" She was not in my shaky corner.

Steve brought steaks. I made salad and a cake. Miriam toted in a cooler of ice and pop. We held hands around the table as we thanked God for our picnic. "Hey, it's been a long time since all of us said grace together!" Jon exclaimed.

Steve announced, "Your mother and I are thinking about…" he hesitated, "about living together again. She made an offer to return home."

I was sitting next to Jon. He turned to me, and his eyes brimmed with tears. "Oh, Mom, every night I have been praying you'd come back." He put his arm around me and squeezed hard. Jon's tears of joy and fervent prayers were the confirmation I needed.

Miriam cornered me behind a tree. "Mom, is this what you really want to do? Is it the right thing for you?"

"Honey, the right thing for me is to take care of my children," I replied. "The Lord's been working with me this past year, making me stronger."

"I hope you know what you're doing!" she sounded dubious, but the decision was made.

After three teachers rented the Kircher Park bungalow, into the driveway of the old blue mansion the first week in September pulled a caravan of trailers and my orange Datsun. It didn't take long to put the furniture back in order, but finding my place in a patriarchal household was difficult. Steve's headquarters were the den, and I had the master bedroom upstairs. It was an uneasy alliance.

I stopped by Cathy's bedroom one evening. She was crying. "Cathy, tell me what's the matter." She pulled away from me.

"You've forgotten about me ever since we moved back here," she looked up at me reproachfully, her eyes smudged.

She was right. Frantically cleaning and settling in, I had neglected our nightly chats at bedtime.

"I'm sorry, honey. I've just been going nuts around here," I admitted. "I miss our quiet times together and sitting by that pool."

"I miss my friends back in Webster." Tears were flowing again. "It really hurts to leave them." A wave of nostalgia swept over me as I recalled our peaceful little home. I knew what she was feeling.

"Is there anything good about being back in the old blue house?" I asked.

"Yep, Jon." A smile slowly lit up her face. "He keeps saying, 'Cathy, I'm glad you're home!' He even hugs me."

"And Rick's happy, too," I noted. "When I filled the cookie jar, and we all sat around the table talking, he said, 'It feels like home now!'"

"I'm kind of worried about Davey, though," Cathy said. "He really misses Billy."

"It's hard for him to get used to this house. His sight's going fast." I sighed. "And being at School for the Blind will remind him of his handicap. "

"Mom, it isn't easy coming back. Just don't be too busy to spend time with your youngest daughter!"

"I promise. Pray for me, Cathy," I requested as I gave her a goodnight hug.

TWENTY-FOUR
WOUNDED SPIRIT

"**D**avid Castor, I'm glad to meet you," Steve LeGouri held out his hand. Like a frightened animal, the seven-year-old boy drew back. My husband and I had transported our son to the New York State School for the Blind for preliminary tests and introductions before the first week of classes. "I can see! I don't belong here," he objected. "This is a school for blind kids. I'm not blind!" We exchanged uneasy glances.

"Hey, you're a fighter; I bet you're smart, too." The tall lanky man looked at our scowling son with compassion. "There's something in my office I'd like you to see, David. Come in and take a look." He touched the boy's shoulder. "How about a Coke?" The two disappeared behind a door labeled "School Psychologist."

While we waited, Steve and I recalled Karen's excitement about settling into Knight Hall. "She blossomed after a miserable time in second grade," I recounted.

"And Jon," Steve remembered, "A little guy named Moses made him feel welcomed right away. He loved it here and still does."

"David's a different story," I sighed. "I think he knew he had Batten Disease the first time you took him to the eye doctor."

"He's in fierce denial," Steve's brow was furrowed with worry. "I wonder how staff will handle him." We paced the hall, stopped at the cafeteria for a cup of coffee, and sat down to wait.

Finally, the door opened. Dave was grinning, jauntily wearing a Buffalo Bills cap. "You should see the bunch of hats Mr. LeGouri has in there. He let me pick out my own."

"Dave, can I tell your mom and dad about the test you took?"

"Sure."

"Your son measured high on the Otis I.Q. test, one of the highest I've recorded in this school."

"Wow!" I exclaimed.

"I'm not surprised," his father responded.

He turned to David. "Do you want to tell your parents what you decided about coming to this school?"

"Well, first of all, I told Mr. LeGouri I don't want to learn Braille."

The psychologist smiled. "I agreed. We have many ways of learning around here."

"Then he talked about kids who needed help from someone like me who can see," David continued.

"Don't forget what I said about your sharp mind!"

"Yeah, he said I was smart enough to work on hard arithmetic, but what I'd really like are ski lessons this winter at Bristol Mountain," Dave added. "That's where Rick and Mim and Jon learned to ski. Remember?"

He's appealing to my son's strengths, I thought.

His dad gave his son a hug. "That's right! You're seven now. It won't be long until you're hitting the slopes with us."

That winter, skiing became Dave's passion. Taking Jon's place among the family ski bums, he tackled the hard slopes at Swain and Kissing Bridge. "Right to one o'clock. Left to ten o'clock or quick left to nine o'clock," he followed directions and the sound of his father's voice.

The darkening of his vision was a mute subject. Wrestling, a sport for "blind kids," didn't interest Dave. Steadfastly, he stuck to his guns about not learning Braille. Typing, however, he enjoyed. Mobility training, he refused. "I don't need a cane. I can see just fine!"

In Springville, one hot summer evening, I tucked ten-year-old Dave into the daybed on the screened front porch. Sultry June weather made the upstairs stuffy. It had been a full day for my son. Andy, his cousin, had worked with him at building a jump for their bikes in the nearby woods.

"You should have seen him, Aunt Connie!" Andy regaled us with their feats of derring-do. "He was one brave dude, sailing over the bump into the air! Didn't even wipe out!"

I knelt down beside Dave to say "Jesus Tender Shepherd" with him. "I'm proud of you, honey," I told him. "Skiing in the winter, biking in the summer, you're great at sports."

"Tomorrow Andy's taking me fishing." He turned over, yawned, and fell asleep.

"Lord, bless the two cousins," I prayed silently, "And help them to land a big one."

On a cot in another corner of the porch, I welcomed a breeze stirring leaves in the maple tree and cooling my damp skin. I clicked out the light. I was just drifting into sleep when something awakened me. The daybed was shaking. I ran to Dave and laid him on his side. A gran mal seizure racked his body. The awful familiarity of gasping for air and of a blue-tinged face wrenched my spirit. The bed was wet. How could I explain this to Davey? He was too smart not to know that Batten Disease was making inroads.

Andy was there to help as we lifted him to my bed and changed Dave and the bottom sheet. The daybed had been protected with a rubber mat. Andy, rubbing his chin, stood staring at his younger cousin, who was deep in post-seizure sleep. "Damned disease!" Angry tears streaked his freckled cheeks. "I hate it! Young Dave doesn't need this!"

Our youngest was being backed into a corner emotionally by the disorder. His blindness was limiting movement and, therefore, causing falls and bruises. The anticonvulsant drugs affected his energy. Nightmares were terrifying to all of us. "No, no! I hate God!" David would awaken trembling with fear and screaming. That summer a camp for visually impaired children in Vermont involved him in team sports. Steve had hesitantly left him there. How would he relate to other children? A phone call alarmed us. "Your son had two seizures today," the counselor reported. "He's not happy here, very irritable."

"Should I come and get him?" Steve asked.

"No, I'd like to work with Dave," the young man replied. "Maybe, he'll talk to me." When Dave returned, he was withdrawn in sullen anger and had little to say about camp.

Steve wrote about his son's despair: "It had been a bad day for David, talking back to his mother and being generally obnoxious to the family. When he was particularly insolent, I finally gave him a spanking and sent him to his room. He refused to go, so I helped him up the stairs with a few well-placed swats. He was crying uncontrollably. 'David, what's gotten into you?' I asked. 'You don't usually act like this!'

"'Dad, what's going to become of me?' he sobbed. And suddenly, like a curtain going up on a nightmare, I had a glimpse into David's private hell. He was already almost totally blind. He was aware that his brother Jonathan sat in a wheelchair, unable to walk. He knew his sister had died at fifteen. I couldn't do anything else but take him in my arms, hold him, and weep with him.

"We talked about Batten Disease and about what lay ahead. I told him, 'No matter what happens, Dave, we'll be in it together.'

"He put his arms around me and said, 'Don't worry, Dad. It will be okay.' In that moment of unforgettable father-son closeness, my son was thinking of my pain more than his own.

"It wasn't okay," Steve continued the story. "Shortly after that conversation, David attempted to kill himself by jumping out of a moving car. His nightmares intensified when he'd wake up screaming, 'The devil is trying to get me!'

"For his own safety, he was placed in West Seneca Children's Psychiatric Hospital where they gave him drugs to reduce anxiety. I remember driving up there after work. He enjoyed playing a board game called Mastermind. He loved it because he could beat me regularly. And I wasn't letting him win. His mind was still keen, alert, analytical." Steve's presence as a caring father was important to his son.

The next few years at School for the Blind were stormy for David. Like an anchor amidst his mood swings, Steve LeGouri was there for him. Listening, drawing out the reasons behind his feelings, and working with teachers, he cared deeply for this troubled child.

"Dave carries an enormous load of anger," LeGouri explained. He had come to our home in Geneseo to discuss the situation. I needed the warmth of the fireside to quell the cold fear clutching my spirit. "Frankly, the house parents can't handle him in the dorm. We've decided to try David as a day student."

"You mean he'll live here at home?" I asked.

LeGouri heard the anguish in my voice. "Connie, I know this is very difficult for both you and Steve."

The father's shoulders slumped. "We're barely making it through weekends," his voice cracked. "Combine Batten Disease with puberty...it's..."

"Explosive!" LeGouri finished his sentence. "He'll be in school during the day. Our van will provide transportation. Keep in mind that it may be for your son's best interest to return to West Seneca."

The idea seemed almost inviting, yet I knew our parental responsibilities. This was his home. "Do you have any advice about how to handle him?" I questioned.

"Let him listen to his favorite songs," the psychologist suggested. "Somehow, the Beatles connect with David's feelings."

"How about the heavy metal rock he sometimes plays? I hate it, especially when he cranks it up!"

"It gets his anger out. He needs the outlet."

I was acutely uncomfortable with this kind of music as therapy. The words and the dissonance felt like evil insinuating itself into our home. "Oh, God, where are You?" My spirit cried out. "Have mercy on my son."

Four weeks later, I sat in the den with my Bible open on my lap. "Then Jesus told them," I read in John 12.35 (NIV), "'You are going to have the light just a little while longer. Walk while you have the light, before darkness overtakes you.'" The darkness had descended on David and was about to envelop me. Full of anxiety and tension, and bearing the brunt of my son's anger, I felt as if I were being sucked into the maelstrom of despair. Memories of the past month with Dave reeled through my mind like snippets of a movie.

I had asked him to turn down the rock and roll. He growled, "No." A rotten confrontation resulted. I felt like killing him.

His sexuality was running rampant as well. When Rick found him in bed with my undies, he blew up at his brother and then later apologized. Coming off the bus one Friday, Dave grabbed my arm. "I made up a poem. Wanna hear it?" He recited a ditty, full of dirty words and sexual exploits. *Steve LeGouri, how do I handle this one*? I thought.

Later on the sofa in the den, he called for me. "Come and listen, Mom." I sat close to Dave, his hand on my arm, as his favorite Beatles' songs were playing. One plaintive ballad described a blackbird with broken wings and sunken blind eyes, singing a lonely song in the dark of night—a song of longed-for freedom. There were tears in Dave's eyes and mine, too, as we shared the sadness.

An incident after supper revealed how close to the breaking point we as parents were. Dave had grabbed half an angel food cake, crumpling it to bits as he stuffed it in his mouth. "You're an animal!" I screamed. He became a snarling obnoxious creature.

"Go into the den and sit with your dad," Rick ordered. Dave curled up in the gold easy chair and hyperventilated.

"Put on your shoes and socks, David," Steve ordered. He refused. Rick and I were horrified as the confrontation escalated into a violent spanking with a belt on bare buttocks. In the process, Dave screamed unbelievable obscenities and curses at his father. Steve, too, was out of control.

As I relived the kaleidoscope of events, I cried out to God. "Where are You in the darkness? Is there any hope for my anguished son? Any hope for us who react with fury to his anger?" I turned in my Bible to Jesus' words at the beginning of his ministry:

>"*The Spirit of the Lord is on me,*
>
>*Because he has anointed me to preach good news to the poor.*
>
>*He has sent me to proclaim freedom for the prisoners*
>
>*And recovery of sight for the blind,*
>
>*To release the oppressed,*
>
>*To proclaim the year of the Lord's favor.*" (*Luke* 4.18-19, NIV)

In response, I wrote in my journal: "I am carrying an intolerable burden, the sense that this child has been given more than he can carry. There lies Jon—crippled, inarticulate, helpless, and retarded—a very mirror of David's future. Dave's sight is gone; his hands tremble; seizures strike suddenly; speech is slurred; he's beginning to stagger; and learning is slow. All are signs that he is deteriorating faster than his brother. Surely, he is bruised, a captive, a blind child sorely in need of a Savior and the Good News.

"David is truly a tragic figure," my journal continued. "How can God bring any good out of this? How will Christ's light penetrate the darkness that snuffs out hope? My fragile son is unable to pray or open the door to Jesus. I must love him enough to lift him into His presence. How did Jesus cast out demons? 'Be quiet! Get out of him,' he commanded in Luke 4.35 (NIV) That's what David needs now. O Lord Jesus, come in authority and power to wrestle the darkness out of him."

I was alone with David one Saturday afternoon. I was aware of how my screaming at him had fanned the flames of anger. Maybe, we could sit on the sofa, and I could read a psalm to him. Dave would have none of that. Perched on a kitchen stool, he muttered threats, punctuated by his favorite nasty word.

"Junk, junk, everything and everybody is junk, especially me," he repeated like a mantra. Meaningless non-life gripped his soul.

In David's hands was a carved cane that Rick had brought back from New Guinea. Slowly, he began swinging it, whacking the woodwork. He moved toward the breakfast table. "Dishes smash'em," he roared. His eyes glowered with hate. "Mom, Mom, where's Mom?" As he clobbered the table and called my name, a shiver of fear crawled down my back. I needed help.

I grabbed the phone and called the police. "My son's out of control," I reported breathlessly. "Could you send someone who can talk to a crazy twelve-year-old?" I gave the address and backed away from the flailing weapon.

The doorbell rang. A young officer listened to the necessary details and observed the situation. "David Mark Castor," he spoke with authority. "Put down that cane right now. I'm a policeman!"

My son recognized the power of the law. "A cop? Wow!" A big grin spread across his face as he dropped the stick. Maybe, he was important after all!

Bill stood beside him, gently questioning the troubled boy. "Why are you so angry, Dave?"

"Because I heard Dad and Mom talking about sending me away."

"Away?"

"Yeah, to West Seneca, a place for crazy kids."

"That really makes you mad—and sad, doesn't it?"

"Yeah, I'm nothin', and I'm no good!" Then, my son began to sob, his hunched shoulders shaking.

Bill, the young officer, stood quietly with his arm around the boy. I stroked my son's blond spiky hair until crying subsided.

"Hey, Dave, how about a ride in the squad car?"

A smile broke through the tears, "Yeah, man! A ride! Let's go!" Half an hour later the two returned. "Mom, he even let me try the siren!" How grateful I was for Bill's caring for my hurting son!

On March 10, 1979, Steve Castor and Steve LeGouri drove David to West Seneca just two years after his first stay. There was a curious emptiness inside me, a sense of failure and deprivation in not being able to care for the boy.

When Steve returned, the family gathered around the coffee table in the den to share our feelings. "I'm sorry," Cathy began. "I'm such a wimp that I haven't been around much."

"I felt helpless," Rick added. "Nothing I could do or say reached Dave."

"My yelling sure didn't help," I admitted.

Steve had trouble speaking. "I lost it when I spanked him," he confessed. "I think he's in the right place for now."

We all needed a rest, we agreed. I lit the tall white candle on the table, to me a symbol of the Light that penetrates the darkness. Holding hands, we joined in prayer for our absent ones—Jon at the nursing home and David in West Seneca.

A call from Steve LeGouri brought reassuring news that Dave had dropped his tough stance and was bright-eyed and cooperative at the psychiatric center. Was a flicker of hope beginning to glow in the night?

TWENTY-FIVE

THE HEALING WORD

It was Thanksgiving Day, 1979, and the dining room in the Geneseo homestead erupted with laughter and conversation. Family, thirty-two strong, gathered around a string of tables to celebrate our blessings. Cathy Hicks, Steve's youngest sister, sat next to her nephew. "Wild Young Dave, huh?" she teased him. "That's what they call you. How come?"

"Sometimes I'm mad. Sometimes I'm sad," he explained. "Right now I'm glad."

"That's a poem," his aunt noted. "So, what's making you happy today?"

"You," he chortled. "Try my hat on." He laughingly plopped his Buffalo Bills cap on her curly hair. Suddenly, the cap was like a hot potato, circulating around the table.

"My turn, my turn!" cousins squealed.

Loving the attention, he yelled, "Who stole my cap? Yuk, it's greasy!" It had landed on the turkey.

All day long, Aunt Cathy and her nephew were inseparable. A Bible open on Cathy's lap, sometimes they talked in a quiet nook. She and her husband Dave had dedicated their lives to mission work with an organization called Operation Mobilization. Their visit to Rick in Papua New Guniea had been a catalyst for his spiritual growth. On leave after a voyage on the *Logos*, the mission ship, they were soon to work at mission headquarters in Atlanta. Hope stirred in me as I watched the bond between Aunt Cathy and Dave strengthen.

That evening, Cathy saw the dark side when Dave refused to get ready for bed. His face twisted in rage as he hurled foul language at anyone who tried to intervene. "I think it's demonic," Cathy ventured later. "Would you consider deliverance, Connie? My friend Judy and I could come to work with you and Steve to lift the evil oppression Dave's under."

A week later, the two sat in the living room beside a blazing hearth with David and us, his parents. Judy was blessed with a beautiful voice. She softly sang, "Jesus Loves Me" to our son. Cathy asked, "Do you believe that Jesus loves you, Dave?"

I looked at the boy's face. His head was bowed in dejection, and tears dropped on his folded hands. "Do you know that Jesus loves you?" his aunt repeated the question.

"No," his voice was barely audible. "He made me blind; he made me have seizures." I drew in my breath, surprised. David was facing his disease.

Cathy, Judy, Steve, and I laid hands on him. Each of us prayed for Dave's deliverance, and we ended in the Lord's prayer. He was quiet and respectful. I sensed his spirit was open and searching for help.

Later, after tucking him in, we talked. "It's an age-old question that's haunting him," Steve noted. "There's enough of that good mind left to ask, 'Where does evil come from?'"

Cathy was in deep thought. Judy chimed in, "I didn't sense demonic activity tonight."

"When Dave was a little guy," I added, "He had a simple childlike faith in God, his heavenly Father."

Cathy spoke, "What terrible torment for him now to believe that his Father God has deliberately afflicted him with this vile disease! He's suffering from a deep festering wound of the spirit." On our knees, we beseeched the Lord God in Jesus' name to reveal His love to David in a very real way.

Reverend Len Sweet, minister at the United Methodist Church in Geneseo, helped pave the path. As a professor and provost at Colgate Rochester Divinity School as well as a well-known author, his time was precious. As our son's pastor, he ministered to this hurting boy. After a visit in David's room, he shared his insights with us. "This young man is keenly aware of the changes in his mind and body because of Batten Disease." Len's brown eyes darkened with concern. "Part of him is yearning for God's comfort in the midst of suffering."

"I was surprised he wanted to come to your confirmation class," I interjected. "I told him maybe next year. He's too volatile now."

"Of course he's volatile," Len's eyes flashed. "How can he believe in a God whom he believes is killing him with this disorder?"

"I'm having questions myself," Steve admitted.

"This is beyond us," our pastor concluded. "I will pray with you right now for wisdom and guidance." With an arm around each of us, Len Sweet's deep voice lifted our son in earnest supplication for God's intervention.

A phone call from Cathy Hicks further illuminated the path of direction for David. "Connie, there's a new version of the Bible out. A friend let me listen to John's Gospel." Her voice sounded excited. "It's part of a Bible translation done on audio tape with music and dialogue. It's simple, direct, and lively! I have a feeling Wild Young Dave might go for it!"

"Wow! Maybe you're right!" Her enthusiasm was contagious.

"We want to give the New Testament to him as a combination Christmas and birthday present. We missed his thirteenth in August."

"You two are missionaries. This must be expensive!"

"God is providing a way. We've been soaking our very special nephew in prayer. This may be His answer."

The package arrived in time for Christmas, gaily wrapped and waiting under the tree. "Here's a gift for you from someone special," his dad announced at present opening. He read the card. "Dave, this package is God speaking to you from His Word. With love and prayers, Aunt Cathy and Uncle Dave."

That afternoon we took turns as we stretched out with pillows on the den floor and listened with Dave as he began his journey into the New Testament. Beautiful music introduced the scenes in Matthew 5.3. Animated dialogue, the sounds of everyday life in Palestine, and the commanding voice of Jesus made the Gospel come alive. Dave was entranced.

Jesus teaching the Sermon on the Mount caught his attention. "Humble men are very fortunate," Jesus told them, "for the Kingdom of Heaven is given to them. Those who mourn are fortunate! for they shall be comforted. The meek and lowly are fortunate! for the whole wide world belongs to them." (TLB)

"Mom, that's Jesus talking," he told me. Over and over again, he rewound the tape and listened to the Beatitudes. Jesus' healing lame and blind people were Dave's favorite stories. Christ's agony on the cross brought tears and a question: "Why did He have to die?"

"Jesus carried all the bad things like sickness, sadness, and meanness on the cross to save us from evil," I told him.

After the holiday and Dave's return to school, a phone call from Steve LeGouri encouraged us. "Listening to those Bible tapes has calmed David," he reported.

There was one morning during Easter vacation that is forever etched in my memory. Dave was lying on the breakfast room rug with a pillow under his chest as his chin rested on his hand. Morning sun bathed his body in light, blond hair glowing. The cassette player was on the floor in front of him. Alert, intense eagerness played on his face. I was ironing nearby and listening with my son. "Mom, hear this! Come here!"

I unplugged the iron and curled up beside him. Paul's words in 1 Corinthians 15 spoke to both of us: "Our earthly bodies which die and decay are different from the bodies we shall have when we come back to life again, for they will never die. The bodies we have now embarrass us, for they become sick and die; but they will be full of glory when we come back to life again. Yes, they are weak, dying bodies now, but when we live again, they shall be full of strength." (1 Corinthians 15.42-43, TLB) He pressed the stop button and turned to face me. "Guess what! I'm going to have a new body!" He turned the tape on again. "Listen!" he ordered.

"Every human has a body just like Adam's, made of dust, but all who become Christ's will have the same kind of body as His—a body from heaven." Again, he stopped the tape. "God's gonna give me a body just like Jesus. Did you hear that?" David's face was radiant. The light of hope shined in his blind eyes. Even his Castor sticking-out ears lit up.

He switched on the tape. "When this happens, then at last the scripture will come true, 'Death is swallowed up in victory.' O death, where is your victory? O Grave, where is your sting…How we thank God for all this! It is He who makes us victorious through Jesus Christ our Lord!" Another pause. Tears sparkled like diamonds in Dave's blue eyes. "Mom, Jesus loves me. I love the Lord," he solemnly announced.

The tape switched on again. With my arm around him, I rested beside my son savoring the miraculous moment. Day after day, God's Word had been entering Davey's broken heart as a balm to bitterness. The wound, so ugly and crippling, was healing. Today, he saw beyond Batten Disease to eternal life with Jesus.

I called Len Sweet to share the good news. "What a wonderful God we have!" he exclaimed with a deep hearty laugh. "How simple and how beautiful! Healing for Dave came though listening to God's Word."

In June of 1981, we made the move to Bath. Dave traveled home on weekends from summer school in Batavia, and he looked forward to splash parties in the pool with Miriam and Rick. I'd take him shopping, sometimes in a wheelchair. Girl's voices riveted his attention. "Hi, chick," he called while offering a hand to shake.

Bible tapes were still his main focus, reassuring him that God loved Wild Young Dave. After the anguish of the past, we were deeply grateful for the center of peace in our son.

This sense of well-being continued and prepared the way for the most exciting adventure of Wild Young Dave's life. My daughter Miriam and her husband Joe were experiencing the rugged beauty of Alaska and loving their weekend forays into the wilderness. In February 1981, a phone call from Miriam almost unhinged me. "Mom, Joe and I have a great idea!" She was calling from Anchorage but sounded as though she was right next door. "Cousin Matt is planning a trip to Alaska in May." A pause. I braced myself for what might come next. "Matt's willing to fly Dave out with him."

I sat down stunned. "You mean take him out of school for six weeks…and be totally responsible for him?"

"'Way back when he was five and we found out Davey had the beginning of Batten's, I made a promise." Her voice quavered. This was important to my daughter.

"What was it, Mim?"

"I promised to share as much beauty with my little brother as a lifetime could hold, no matter how much or how little time we'd have. Now's the opportunity, while he's still aware. We want to take him on some wildlife expeditions around here." I heard urgency in her voice.

"He is much more stable now, and a change in meds has helped his balance," I conceded, bracketing objections. "But what about school?"

Miriam had done her homework. "I've already visited a center for kids with physical and mental impairment. They're willing to enroll him on a temporary basis," she explained. "Is Dave around? I want to talk to him!"

I handed the phone to my son who had been eavesdropping. "Alaska! Me? Yeah, man! I want to come!"

"Hey, how about earning some money?" I challenged my son. "You could put it toward your airfare."

"How?" he asked excited.

"There are all kinds of things to do around this house!" By scrubbing counters and the bathroom, washing dishes, and cleaning his room, Dave gradually accumulated $40.38 toward his flight to Alaska.

In May, the day before Dave's big departure, I dragged the huge purple suitcase down from the attic. Into it, we crammed everything from boots to his cassette player. Hefting the bulging suitcase, I staggered to the front porch. Too excited to have slept much, Dave climbed into a big station wagon with some young missionaries. They were giving him a ride to Washington D.C. to meet cousin Matt. As we waved goodbye, Steve and I wondered what kind of adventures awaited this eager boy.

Matt called from Anchorage two days later. "We made it, Aunt Connie! Young Dave scared me half to death when he had a seizure in the bathtub at my grandmother's house. But he's fine now!"

"Love it here, Mom. We're going to track down a moose tomorrow," Dave's voice was full of joy.

"We're having a blast," Miriam chimed in. "We've got some wild adventures planned."

"Just don't forget his meds—and I'll be praying for you," I sounded like a clucking mother hen.

Miriam captured the wilderness flavor of the Alaskan expedition when she wrote: "We did weekend journeys with Dave and me huddled in sleeping bags in the back of the pick-up while I described each sight enthusiastically…eagles, moose, and grizzlies. Camping at Mount McKinley was the best. One afternoon, we were hiking up a mountain trail, and Dave whispered, 'Hey, what's that noise?' I hadn't heard it. Sure enough, as we rounded the bend, we encountered a whole herd of dall sheep. It was their rhythmic breathing that he had heard. That was the closest I had ever come to another species in the wild.

"Our last day in Alaska was spent on the Kenai River. Dave was strapped into the bow seat with a crew of us, paddles in hand. What a day that was, exhilaration from the wild eddies and glacial water which inevitably splashed in! It must have felt like a roller coaster for Dave, especially in the bow.

"I am so thrilled to have shared that day with him. He could see the cow moose with her calf and the bald eagle in her nest along the river as clearly, if not more so, than we sighted passengers.

"I say this because, as Dave regressed over the next few years, he continued to be able to articulate each and every species we "saw" together that spring. I swear, they were some of the last words he was able to speak before the disease stripped him completely of his expressive language."

Miriam flew home with Dave around the middle of June. How could I ever adequately express my gratitude for the unique adventure she had given her youngest brother? The first thing Dave pulled out of the suitcase was a box of souvenirs: a silver moose on a cord, a grizzly's tooth, a rock from the river they rafted, wolf calls and scary grunts recorded on a tape, and an eagle's feather. As he recounted adventures in staccato sentences, I was amazed at how much Dave had learned and absorbed. The experience gave him a healthy sense of himself. Miriam and Joe had affirmed his remaining strength and engaged his mind through on-the-spot action in the wilderness.

"I'm really proud of my brother," Miriam gave him a hug. "He's an outdoor man, strong in his legs and tough in white-water."

Another part of Dave, namely his spirit, was also being nourished. Pat Crippen, the youth Sunday school teacher, welcomed him into a class at Centenary United Methodist Church. "I didn't quite know what to do when he raised his hand and said, 'The Lord,'" she laughed. "But he made the class interesting. The other kids accepted him."

Pastor Wendell Minnigh asked Dave a question one Sunday after church. "Dave, do you love the Lord?"

"Sure do."

"You're my 'Amen' corner, you know." Pastor was referring to Dave's occasional comments during the sermon of "That's right," or "The Lord." "Would you like to join Centenary?"

"Yes! When?"

"After you and I talk about your faith in God and our church."

Later Wendell observed, "Connie, your son has a very real faith in Jesus Christ. He shared some favorite scripture on his New Testament tapes. It's time for him to become a member."

On a warm Sunday morning in spring, Pastor Minnigh announced, "Today, David Castor is joining our fellowship." Steve brought his son to the altar. "You may kneel, Dave." Pastor's hand rested on his blond head. Clear "I do's" followed each question in the ritual. David listened to the last one. "Do you promise, according to the grace given you, to live a Christian life and always remain a faithful member of Christ's holy church?"

Sunshine poured through the bright colors of sanctuary windows, resting on Young Dave as he knelt at the altar rail. In that holy moment, I praised God as the shepherd brought His lamb into the fold.

David raised his hand and solemnly declared, "The Lord."

TWENTY-SIX
WORSHIPPING IN THE STORM

To each of my Batten children, God has provided "angels," agents of light and mercy in what could be a desolate journey. Joyce through her friendship enriched Karen's life at Newark Developmental Center. Mary Jo had worked and laughed with Jon at Steuben County Infirmary, putting meat on his bones and a smile on his face.

David Gray, unbeknown to him or to me, was being honed by the whetstone of Knight Hall to be David Castor's special caregiver. In 1979, his initial assignment was to work with multiple handicapped blind children. He earned his stripes caring for the toughest kids.

Three years later, David Gray graduated to the upper level in Knight Hall to care for younger, normal blind kids, except one, a small six-year-old, a head-banger recently admitted. "Kojak was his name," Gray recounted. "After a whiff of gas, I bent down to check his pants. Wham! Kojak's head connected with mine like a sledge hammer!" The blow sent Gray to the hospital with a fractured scull. Partial loss of hearing and a groggy memory resulted. Undaunted, the aide returned to New York State School for the Blind two months later for his most challenging assignment yet.

At age fifteen, Wild Young Dave was living up to his name. Edgy and demanding, he was a trial for teachers and house parents. "I've got a tough one for you," the school nurse dared Gray one evening. "You've no doubt heard of David Castor, very difficult to handle. You're needed now at Hamilton Hall to take him for meds and settle him for the night."

Gray described the first encounter. "Devilish eyes, a big watch on a rope around his neck, and a cock-eyed cap perched on his head—I knew this kid was different."

The boy spoke in a staccato outburst, pulling on the aide's arm. "Nose! Nose! Nose!"

"What does he want?" Gray wondered. "A tissue?" We passed one to Dave.

"Yeah!" He honked loudly and handed the Kleenex back. "Eat it!"

"Mercy, what now?"

"Eat it!"

"I'll save it for dessert later." Wild Young Dave broke into uproarious laughter. The two had hit it off!

"Would you like to work with David Castor on a regular basis?" Nurse Flo Contadorio queried Gray later. It was obvious he knew how to handle their volatile resident.

"Yes, full-time on the three to eleven shift with no relief from other aides."

"He's a handful. Are you sure?"

"Yes, I'm sure, and I'll tell you why. David Castor is a Christian. I am, too. Besides, he's a lot of fun."

"Wait until you listen for hours to his Bible tapes," the nurse warned.

Gray discovered that Young Dave would tolerate no interruptions. If someone popped in after school, he stopped the cassette, rewound it, and listened again from the beginning. The words registered on a deep level. "Lord, Lord," he would pray, pointing upward, or "Heart, heart," a hand on his chest.

"I respect the way he meditated on the New Testament," David Gray commented. "Sometimes, he'd ask, 'Hear that? Hear that?' For me, a person with a mending scull, this was a great way to absorb Scripture."

Intrigued by notes sent home with Dave's laundry, I wanted to meet my son's new mentor. Here was someone fascinated by the kid's personality, who appreciated his feisty spirit. "So, tell me how you handle Young Dave when he's agitated," I requested. While my son took an after-school nap, David Gray and I were getting acquainted in the living room of Hamilton Hall.

"It's as if his battery is overcharged when he sits there roaring and pounding his wheelchair tray," the aide noted. "I never take it personally. It's Batten Disease making his brain backfire."

"So, what do you do?" I was interested. As the disease progressed, I needed options.

"I get him down on the floor, and we wrestle it out," Gray explained. "After he's had a frustrating day in the classroom, this seems to work."

"How about at night?" I questioned. "That's when he gets ornery."

"A bubble bath calms him right away. The sound of water running into the tub diverts the yelling into anticipation." The aide laughed. "Just give him a sponge, and he scrubs himself, the bathtub, and the walls. After a bath, he enjoys listening to his tapes."

I looked at David Gray. Sideburns framed a round face. Wiry hair behind a receding hairline emphasized expressive eyebrows. Twinkling brown eyes under horned-rim glasses and a longish pointed nose, accented by a moustache, gave him a gnome-like visage. I noted his small mouth, prone to smile, and the hint of a double chin. Gray's arms were strong and muscular. A round belly and short legs completed the picture. His voice was raspy and full of emotion, which gave him the gift of telling a story vividly. His face reflected his feelings. I knew I had met an honest, caring person.

While my son continued napping, I prodded his caregiver for more details. "Tell me about your adventure in the rain," I urged. "You mentioned in a note that the raincoat had been put to use."

One afternoon, thunder boomed and rain splashed against the windows of Hamilton Hall. Young Dave was excited. "Outside! Let's go!" he commanded. Gray knew the reason for urgency. Hanging on a peg in the closet was a brand new green raincoat sent from home. On the floor sat shiny black rubbers. "Outside! Let's go!" The order was repeated.

"But it's pouring out there," Gray objected. "I don't have a raincoat."

"Don't care."

This will be an adventure, the aide thought ruefully as he helped his charge into watertight gear.

"See? See?" Young Dave proudly stretched out his arms and chortled with glee under a green hood. The aide strapped him into the wheelchair, and out they rolled into the elements.

With the rumble of thunder and with rain pelting his new coat, Young Dave lifted his face and raised his hands to Heaven. The deluge felt like a baptism.

"The Lord, the Lord," he spoke in awe.

"Where? Where?" Gray asked, soaked to the bone.

"Right here!"

"I felt as if I were on holy ground," the aide concluded the story. "I have never felt closer to God than that afternoon as Young Dave worshipped in the storm."

After my son awoke, he announced. "Hungry. I'm hungry."

"I'll treat you both to pizza," I offered. It would give me a chance to see the two interacting.

As we sat in the booth, I noticed table manners were improving. "Here's your napkin, Young Dave. Remember, small bites."

The only thing that interrupted concentrated chewing was the sound of a young female voice. "Chick, Chick! Hi, Chick!" he called.

"Hey, Young Dave, tell me what you do for fun with your friend Dave Gray," I requested.

"Motorcycle ride," he grinned. "Me on the back." I must have looked surprised. "I got permission from Flo Contadorio," Gray quickly explained. "Dave was a proud dude to wear a helmet. He sat behind me with his big arms around my middle. At ten miles an hour, we circled the grounds."

"Fun!" Young Dave added.

Later, when his teacher heard about it, she scolded Gray. "You must be nuts. What if he had a seizure?"

"What do you think, Connie?" the caregiver asked me.

"The Castor clan goes for adventure, in spite of the risk," I approved. "Teaching our blind boys to ski is an example." That evening, I knelt beside my son's bed in Hamilton Hall, my heart full of thanksgiving. This angel in his life saw the zesty, sometimes prickly part of Dave and rejoiced in his unique personality.

"Here I am getting paid to fellowship with this kid, sing with him 'I've got the joy, joy, joy, down in my heart,' and listen to Scripture on his tapes. He's helping me grow in my faith," Gray explained.

Not everyone on staff viewed David Castor with understanding. One of his teachers believed he should be placed in a nursing home. Dave sensed the disapproval and resisted. Part of him was still fighting Batten Disease. Gray overheard the teacher lecturing Dave one day: "I am the boss, and you do what I want you to do!"

"God is the boss," my son declared.

• • • • • • • • • • • • • • •

David Gray posed a question to his wife Esther. "How can we help nurture this young man's faith?"

"Let's bring him to prayer meeting," she ventured.

"First, come and meet him. See what you think," her husband requested. Wild Young Dave roared with agitation the first time Esther visited him. She backed off, afraid. Gradually, her gentle touch won him over. He'd hold her hand and trace the long nails with his fingers.

"I think it's time," she told Gray. "Bring Young Dave home for dinner next Wednesday."

"Yes, you are free to take him off campus anytime you'd like," Flo Contadorio agreed. Dave's face lit up, and his eyes sparkled as he headed for the Gray household in Elba. While Esther worked on a chicken dinner, Young Dave grabbed a dishcloth and scrubbed the counters and refrigerator. *Dare we take our boy with us tonight*? they wondered.

Entering church reached back to something deep inside Young Dave. Sitting straight in his chair with hands folded, he looked like a saint. The Grays were surprised when he stood up to sing hymns and belted out the words in his monotone. Once, the pastor announced a favorite, "Standing on the Promises." "We'll stay seated for this one," he added. But not Dave! Up he rose, staying firmly on his feet until the final "Amen."

"I tugged on him, but he wouldn't budge," his caregiver reported.

The pastor laughed when the Grays apologized later. "Look at the words. Dave was standing on the promises!" With a grin, the boy reached out to rub the minister's brush cut. "The way I look at it, this young man's a blessing."

Esther remembered the evening she took Dave downstairs to pray with the ladies. During the quiet, he became restless. When he threw back his head, his body jerked, and with a crash, his chair collapsed. He landed in the lap of the lady in back of them. Nevertheless, the Baptist ladies accepted their unpredictable guest and included him in their prayers.

A weekend at home in Bath was memorable for both sunshine and shadows. It was a bright fall morning in 1983. Friends had offered us the use of their summer home on Keuka Lake. Miriam was with us, caring for

Dave while Steve and I paddled a canoe along the shoreline. Willow branches swayed in a gentle breeze, golden tendrils touching lawns. Maples blazed orange and red against an azure sky. The splash of water as our paddles dipped into the lake, the warm sun on my back, and the companionable silence between Steve and me brought healing to my spirit.

When it was Miriam's turn in the canoe, my son and I sat beside the lake listening. "What do you hear, Dave?" I asked.

"Airplane," he pointed upward. "Motorboat, too." He opened his blind eyes wide as if to see it. A crow cawed nearby. He laughed and imitated the raucous call.

I found some pebbles. "Think I can skip this one?" He felt the smooth flat stone.

"Nope." Dave was right. Kerplunk. Finally, a double hop made me feel like a kid again. Dave threw stones, listening for the splash.

When Miriam and Steve returned, we spread a tablecloth on the trestle table for a picnic lunch. "Hot dogs, yum." Dave was enjoying the menu.

"Mom, look, his head is twisting to one side." Miriam was worried.

"I'll lay him down on a blanket." Steve placed his son on his side and sat beside him. It was a different kind of seizure. As legs thrashed and arms moved, his eyes were wide open. "Help me," he cried. The jerking limbs continued. Now, he was hyperventilating, face pale and still conscious. "Help me." Dave's plea broke my heart. Must this beautiful day end like this?

"Let's get him in the station wagon to the emergency room." Steve's voice was terse. Thank God Dr. Huang, Dave's pediatrician, was on call. As Dave lay on the gurney, his breathing was rough and fast; his face was turning blue. Finally, the valium drip began to take effect, and the thrashing stopped. Breathing became regular.

I stroked his damp blond hair and touched the slow pulse beating in Dave's temple. The blue tinge around his eyes reminded me of Jon, so frail now. Two strong sons cut down by the unstoppable inroads of Batten Disease!

"We'll keep him overnight just to make sure he's okay," Dr. Huang decided. "I'll talk with the neurologist about his meds."

"Wanna go home." Dave was aware.

"He'll do better in his own bed," I intervened. "This kid can be a handful."

"Your choice. I'm right down the road if you need me." Dr. Huang was also a Burton Street resident.

Later at home, I had a fire crackling in the fireplace. Dave curled up on a quilt by the hearth with his cassette player beside him. "New body tape, Mom," he requested. I fast-forwarded the tape to 1 Corinthians 15, his favorite chapter. With a pillow under my head, I snuggled beside him. Content to feel the warmth of his mother holding him, Dave rested peacefully. "Hear that? Listen, Mom."

"In the same way, our earthly bodies which die and decay are different from the bodies we shall have when we come back to life again, for they will never die." (TLB) He pushed the pause button.

"The Lord," Dave said.

"You believe that, don't you?"

"Yup, God's gonna give me a new body." I treasured that sentence, a long one for my son. The promise was our touchstone in the months that followed.

TWENTY-SEVEN
THE WEIGHT OF GRIEF

Around the dining room table, the family gathered for a clan confer-ence. It was Friday evening, just two days since Jon's death. Grief hung in the air like gray damp fog. There had been "the bustle in the house" of sending out invitations to the memorial service. Emily Dickinson's quat-rain adorned the front page in my daughter Miriam's calligraphy:

"This world is not conclusion.
A sequel stands beyond,
Invisible as music,
But positive as sound."[16]

Rick read it aloud. Would Young Dave see it that way for his brother? He posed the question, "How do we tell him about Jon's death?"

"Maybe listening to his favorite scripture might help," I ventured. "This is Dave's lifeline, knowing he'll have a new body."

"But will he understand that for Jon?" Cathy asked. Newly married, she and Mark sat close. He had a protective arm around his wife.

"I'm concerned about what Jon's dying will do to his fragile hold on sanity." Steve's face was somber.

"He's been fighting Batten's fiercely," Miriam added. "The message will be: 'The disease won.'" Finally, the family bowed in prayer and asked for wisdom and direction.

Saturday morning after breakfast, we met in the den. David sat in the recliner. Early sun warmed us all as Steve knelt before his son. He gently took Dave's hand. "Jon's in Heaven with Jesus now," he said. There was no response. "Next time you see him, Dave, he'll have a new body."

"My tapes, listen," he demanded. The words from 1 Corinthians were like a refreshing drink of water to our thirsty souls. "For our earthly bod-ies, the ones that we have now that can die, must be transformed into heavenly bodies that cannot perish but will live forever... Death is swallowed up in victory!… How we thank God for all this! It is He who makes us victorious through Jesus Christ our Lord." (1 Corinthians 15.53-54, 57; TLB)

Yes, Jon was absent, but oh, the glory for him now! Around the circle, sorrow and gratitude intermingled. It would be awhile before the youngest realized that his older brother was dead.

Todd and Wendy, a couple from church who knew how to handle Dave, stayed with him Sunday afternoon during the memorial service. "No mention of Jon," Todd reported. Friends and family packed the Burton Street ranch after the service. Aunts, uncles, and cousins hugged Dave and made him laugh. He basked in their attention.

I wrote a note to David Gray and tucked it in the clean laundry bag. "Please let us know how Dave is coping with Jon's death." As the van drove away, I had an uneasy sense of a volcano about to erupt.

A call the next day confirmed my intuition. "Anger is breaking out again," Gray filled me in. "They called me early to help Young Dave. Just once he mentioned his brother and said 'Jon's in Heaven' and he pointed up."

Next, Steve LeGouri took the phone. I felt a knot of anxiety grabbing my stomach. "Please come and get David." I could hear the frustration in his voice. "His anger is violent, more than the staff can control."

"How are we supposed to handle him at home?"

"Right now, I'd recommend placing him in Elmira Psychiatric Center," came the reply.

I was shocked. "He's that bad?"

"Yes, I'm afraid David might hurt himself. Jon's death has sent him over the edge. I'll make arrangements."

Two days later, I sat in the reception room of the psychiatric center. Once again, I felt pain spiraling down into despair. Since West Seneca, there had been four good years. Now what? An attendant brought David to my side and seated him in a chair. His eyes were wide and staring. Shoulders hunched, his left arm trembled, and he mumbled incoherently. There was no sign of recognition.

The facility was drab and sterile, whereas West Seneca had been full of bright colors and designs. This place was for adults.

Dave was in a padded room with one cot and nothing else. As I held my son's shaking hand, I resolved to get him released soon. Prayer circles at church rallied. Friends backed us in petitioning God for our son's healing.

In a week, Wild Young Dave was home again. It was a roller-coaster ride of sudden mood changes. Saturday morning, we were awakened to the sound of loud pounding on his bedroom walls. Rick and Miriam, on hand to help, stuck their heads out from doors. "Bathroom! Bathroom!" Steve helped his son down the hall. Dave muttered threats, punctuated by his favorite expletive. Fury transformed his face into a mask of hatred.

On the way back to his room, Dave's fist landed a solid blow on his father's shoulder. Steve smashed him to the floor. Miriam, watching, hurtled down the hall to pull her dad off her brother. She clawed at the seething tangle of arms and legs. "Let me handle this!" Steve roared. I was crying helpless tears. Rick catapulted out of his room. Through brute strength, he yanked Miriam and Steve off of Dave, lifted his brother from the floor, and held the sobbing boy. "Jon, Jon, Jon," he cried.

At the crucial moment, an angel of mercy arrived on the scene. Chas Griffen, our counselor friend, had come early before leading a retreat at church. Over the years, he had guided our family through troubled waters. At Jon's memorial service, he had picked up signs of a family in crisis. "Before the retreat, I'll be available for a family counseling session," he promised.

It was a battered group he'd walked in on that day. "Let's talk," Chas ordered. Dave, with an extra Phenobarb, was sleeping soundly. Downstairs in the family room, we each had a turn to vent our whirlwind of feelings. Chas skillfully guided us to own our emotions and actions. No laying blame on others. "You as a family have reached the breaking point. It's time you placed David in a facility that is equipped to care for him." Chas was firm.

"But nobody will take him," I wailed. "School for the Blind can't. Craig refused, saying he doesn't fit the developmental criteria. Monroe Community Hospital said the same thing."

"Craig opened the door a crack," Steve interrupted. "I'm willing to take him there and leave him. They have to accept emergency situations. Pack up his clothes, Connie. I'll drive him over this afternoon."

When Steve, Chas, Miriam, and Rick left for the retreat, Dave was still in a deep exhausted sleep. I descended the cellar stairs to a job I dreaded. I would have to open two big boxes of Jon's things to augment Dave's wardrobe. I pulled the flaps open and pulled out a favorite teddy bear. From deep inside, a music box began to play, "Somewhere My Love." I smelled the familiar aroma of Lysol and baby powder. Suddenly, I was there in his room, cradling Jon's head, crooning a mother's wordless love and feeling the warmth of his body. A sound like keening rose from my innermost being. "Somewhere My Love" was the dirge for the unfinished lives of my Batten children. For Karen, cut off so young. For Jon, my beloved son. For David, whom, in desperation, we were abandoning.

Steve returned at noon. "I'll come with you," I offered as we stacked suitcases into the station wagon.

"I'm driving Young Dave myself," he demurred. "We need time together." I looked into a face darkened with agony. Lunch was quiet. Dave took his medicine willingly and was hungry for macaroni and cheese and a hot dog.

"Going for a ride, Dad?" he asked as Steve zipped up his jacket. The early morning brawl was forgotten.

"Steve, all of us at the retreat will be praying as you travel to Sonyea," I promised. A forty-mile trip, driving could be dangerous with Young Dave's mood swings. A *turn in a sad journey*, I thought as the station wagon disappeared down the hill.

Entering the circle of friends at church, I was bathed in sheer love. Some gathered around me, laying hands on my head and shoulders as they lifted Steve, Dave, and the family in prayer. Later, with Chas, we delved into the parable of the Good Samaritan, a story of healing on many levels.

Steve joined the retreat for supper in the fellowship hall. "Your prayers kept David in the car. It was a rough ride," he informed us. "He tried to unbuckle his seat belt. The last ten miles I held onto him with one hand and steered with the other." He paused and continued in a breaking voice. "As we started out, there was a moment when I think he heard me say, 'I love you!'"

We listened to the rest of the story. Craig staff had accepted this roaring new resident. With expertise, they gave Dave a shot that quieted him.

Encouraging about permanent placement, they talked about getting him back to School for the Blind as a day student.

After the retreat had ended, Chas brought the family together. "So, how in the world are you?" he asked.

"Numb," I answered.

"Feeling guilty but relieved," Steve replied.

"I've got some stuff to work through," Miriam looked at her dad.

"Me, too," Rick said. "Mostly, I feel sad for Young Dave. He'd really been enjoying life before Jon died."

"Let's huddle," Chas directed. Clasping hands, we came closer. "You are precious people. Jon's death and Dave's breakdown have stretched you to the limit. Please don't blame anyone. You are each grieving. Support each other and listen to each other. Our Lord is a healing Savior."

My first visit to Craig conjured up pictures of Newark—the grunts and cries, deformed limbs, and some residents curled in fetal position. Tony, at thirty years old, had a body the size of a six-year-old, except for a very large head. I touched his spastic hand and said hello. He responded with a slow, sweet smile. Charlie, who had Down Syndrome, was always happy. When I offered my hand, he pumped my arm and exclaimed "Hi! Hi! Hi!" Gradually, Dave was adjusting. Family visits made all the difference.

Miriam, who lived nearby, described time spent with her brother: "Impossible now were rides up the big bad Burton Hill on the red tandem bike when Dave had peddled with every ounce of strength he still had. Now excursions were less vigorous. I piled him out of the wheelchair into my crazy Spitfire convertible. I had a time trying to keep his head in the car because he loved the wind blowing through his hair. How I loved Wild Young Dave's laughter at those times! Dave showed me how to suck the sweetness out of the moment, how to fight the darkness that can be so encompassing."

As his mother, I looked forward to our visits. One summer Sunday after church, I stopped by the day room. Aides helped him into my car for a ride to the ice cream store. His face glowered, and repeated growls alarmed me. *Oh, no. He's going into a downer,* I thought. But I kept rubbing his big young man's hand, transmitting my love through touch. He became very peaceful. I brought him back a bowl of heavenly hash and treated myself to a small mocha fudge almond cone.

I knelt down to feed David ice cream in the parking lot of Craig, enjoying his obvious sensual pleasure from eating such good stuff. Then, I transferred him to the wheelchair, tilted him up, and walked him to a shady spot. He and I lay cuddling and talking on the grass. He liked the familiar closeness.

I named his favorite people—Rick, Dad, Miriam, Cathy, David and Esther Gray. He said "school" and "yes" when I mentioned eating pizza with David Gray. Being with people he loved for times of eating and fun registered at some deep level. I kept stroking him, rubbing his head and back. "I love you, Young Dave," I told him. When finally I pulled him up, he kissed my cheek and said "love."

Out on the patio, supper arrived on a tray. I fed him strange strained goulash. I hated to leave him. With a baby tactile playboard in front of him, he looked so humble and vulnerable. He was too weak to initiate much action or to express himself. Patiently, he waited for someone to love him, to take him away from the primal noises of Craig.

I pledged myself to be with Dave as he approached more and more immobility and weakness. I loved him as I did Jon and willed, with God's strength, to be there for him.

Henry Nouwen was right when he wrote of facing the "nothingness" of himself, the false selves, in solitude.[17] In David, who was stripped of everything, all that mattered was love, his humble expression of it, and his ability to receive it. My youngest son was a means of grace to me.

Caring people at Craig and at Batavia worked out a plan that warmed my heart. In September, Young Dave returned to School for the Blind, staying weekdays in the dorm and returning weekends to Sonyea.

The first day back raised questions and concerns. As the bus pulled in at Severne Hall, Dave began to cry. Sobs racked his body. When he refused to get off, they called David Gray. "Hey, Young Dave. You're back! We're going to have a great day!" Uncontrollable bawling continued, even as Gray strapped him in his wheelchair and headed for the dorm. "As he wept, I pushed him all the way down the hall, trailed by the principal, nurse, and psychologist," Gray recalled. "I laid him on the bed and began to talk about the good times."

The gentle voice and strong supporting arm of his friend penetrated grief. "Jon, Jon, Jon," Dave said and pointed to Heaven. Sorrow for his brother's death had supplanted anger. When Gray handed him his bank, full of change, he shook it vigorously. "Money. Pizza!" A trip to Pizza Hut and a wheelchair ride around the school turned the day around. No more tears. It was party time with David Gray.

"Let's go bowling!" he challenged Young Dave. "Your girlfriend Yvonia wants to go with us."

"Yeah, chick!"

After two days of acclimating to school, he was ready. Since the previous Christmas when the two had kissed under the mistletoe, there'd been a friendship. "Let's go!" A sparkle was back in Young Dave's eyes as he felt the big watch around his neck and the lion buckle on his belt.

"Now for the Mexican hat!" Gray planted the sombrero, a party souvenir, firmly on his blond head. As his finger slid around the broad brim, a smile lit up Dave's face. At the bowling alley, a ramp was placed in front of the wheelchair. After a mighty push of the ball, Dave listened for the sound of crashing pins. "A guardian angel must guide it," Gray wagered.

A few more frames and the bowler yawned. "Tired," he said. Strength was limited, but the caregiver was prepared. He unrolled a foam mat in a corner of the alley and tucked Young Dave in for a nap. Yvonia rolled a few more balls, and Gray bowled, too.

The Plantation was a favorite hangout for cool dudes from School for the Blind. It was the era of the twist. When the DJ spun a Chubby Checkers record, Young Dave wanted to dance. Gray backed him against a flat post as those hips gyrated and feet shuffled to the rhythm.

One late afternoon, Rick and Mary, Rick's fiancée, stopped by Hamilton Hall for a visit. "It was one of the happiest times!" Dave Gray remembered. "I loved to see how affectionate Rick was with his younger brother. He crawled right into bed during naptime to shoot the breeze and laugh with Young Dave." Later in the living room, Rick sat in the big chair and entertained young residents with a story of the Wild West. Mary made friends with the girls who reached out to stroke her long hair. Plans were made before they left for David Gray to escort his charge to Rick and Mary's wedding in October.

• • • • • • • • • • • • •

In the Geneseo Baptist Church, I, as mother of the groom, sat tensely waiting in a front pew. With Miriam next to me, I listened for the first chords of the wedding processional. Behind me were David Gray and Wild Young Dave, looking amazingly civilized in a blue sportcoat, white dress shirt, and striped tie. The atmosphere of the church was soaking into his bones. Hands folded and head bowed, he looked angelic. Did I detect a halo above his shining blond hair?

Now Rick, handsome in a grey pinstriped suit and flanked by his father, stepped out front. The familiar strains sent a thrill down my spine. Mary, long hair laced with flowers and arrayed in a simple eyelet dress made by me, was beautiful. Like a magnet, bride and groom were locked in an amazed look of joy. This was their day.

The soloist sang. Chas gave a challenging message. The pastor led Rick through the wedding vows. Young Dave listened intently. "Rick, hi, Rick!" he raised his hand, recognizing his brother's voice.

"Hi, Young Dave," Rick grinned back. Gray slipped him a lifesaver. "Prayer time," he whispered. Obediently, Dave folded his hands, bowed his head, and chomped on the candy.

At the reception, a string band played folk tunes as young and old, square and round, danced. Marigolds, mums, candle-glow, and balloons gave the fellowship hall a party atmosphere. A bounteous buffet of Greek fare nourished family and friends. Aunt Cathy Hicks joyfully reunited with Young Dave. As family showered him with attention, David smiled, knowing he was loved. With David Gray by his side, he was well cared for. "He's tired," Gray told me. "Time to return to Craig."

"Young Dave, have you had a good time at Rick's wedding?" I asked, giving him a hug.

"Yeah, man! Good party!"

TWENTY-EIGHT
TOUGH QUESTIONS

Early June of 1986, I sat out on the screened patio of the Burton Street house, taking inventory of my life. Hanging impatiens, ferns, and ivy created an ambiance of verdant growth. Outside the garden bloomed with new perennials. Zinnias, petunias, geraniums, and marigolds were beginning to spread. The plum tree, lifting graceful limbs, scattered the last of its petals.

Impervious to the beauty, I asked myself tough questions. Who was I at age fifty-seven? Where was I headed as I faced the "golden" years? On the plus side, I felt comfortable with my body. Over the winter I had shed forty pounds. I exercised on the patio in the mornings and then jogged a mile around the block. Ten laps in the pool refreshed me before heading for my job at Centenary. As church growth director, I worked with Pastor Wendell Minnigh to nurture small Bible study groups, recruit and train leaders, and to help newcomers become part of the church family. During our five years together in ministry, the parish was alive and growing.

My thoughts then turned to David. He was, for the most part, content now. Craig Developmental Center provided good care while School for the Blind kept him on campus weekdays. Summer vacation, though, would be a long stretch without his aide and friend, David Gray.

It was time to take a long, hard look at my marriage. I was in the process of making a final decision. Yes, my life had meaning and beauty, but my relationship with Steve was desolate. The old pattern was again emerging—nights away and impenetrable distance when he was home. He worked in his bedroom on the computer while I sat at the kitchen counter with my church projects. I knew he was involved with someone. Jealous, hateful feelings erupted in accusations and demands for change. I disliked the person I was becoming. The grip of destructive dynamics needed to be broken. I yearned to take steps toward wholeness.

One fact was starkly apparent to me. Steve had emotionally abandoned me years ago. I realized it fully during my year of separation in 1974. Nonetheless, I had returned to the old blue house to care for my children. Now, Cathy, Rick, and Miriam were married; Jon was gone; and David was safe at Craig. That left Steve and me at home in a barren relationship. I knew the time had come to end a marriage that was already dead.

This decision produced a whole new crop of terrifying questions. Chas Griffen, our family counselor, worked with me on my fears. How would I make it financially? Deep down, I still loved Steve. Would I be able to let him go? What would a divorce do to the kids? And scariest, my relationship with God? After listening to my dreary litany, Chas observed, "Connie, you're overwhelmed by all the unknowns."

"Yep, I feel as if I'm caught up in a tidal wave of unanswerable questions," I agreed. "Like the other night, I awoke with a start, feeling an impending sense of doom."

"Where was that coming from?"

"A primal fear that God had turned away from me because I was instigating the divorce."

"Keep going…"

"Actually, I was trembling. My teeth chattered. I cried out to God for help." In retelling the incident, I began to cry. Chas handed me the Kleenex box. I wiped my eyes and blew my nose. "Guess what, Chas. The Lord answered me with a Bible verse I'd learned as a child," I continued. "God has not given you the spirit of fear, but of power, and of love and of a sound mind." (2 Timothy 1.7, KJ)

"What did that say to you, Connie?"

"That the power and love of the Holy Spirit are with me. And that you, Chas, can help me with the 'sound mind' part." Several cogent points were established during our counseling session. I needed to be aware of my self-righteous superiority. This stance shut the door on my taking responsibility. My verbal attacks and defensiveness stopped communication in my marriage.

Chas helped me to see an underlying factor in the chasm between Steve and me, the awful loss in the illness and death of our three children. It was unexplored grief in terms of its impact on our marriage.

Our world was crumbling. The house and my presence had been Steve's home base. Now, I was asking him to leave. "Not until October first," he conceded.

"Do you think we could declare a truce?" I asked.

"How?" His face was flushed with anger.

"To look at the split as an act of kindness, setting each other free."

"From what?"

"From your anger toward me and my anger toward you." He looked like a hurt little boy. Part of me wanted to hug him.

"I'll think about it," he grudgingly decided.

The truce was tenuous, especially as we secured lawyers to work out the separation. My way of coping was to go on a "Single Again" weekend. Getting together with my friends—Lee, Pat, and Meredith—also lifted my spirit. We'd often take in a play or concert or hike in the hills. Pat and I were partners in commiseration because her marriage was ending as well. Our laments and diatribes against the male species must have been difficult for the others to endure.

On a spiritual level, I had the support and prayers of the Wednesday night study group, seven of us, including my three friends. Our focus pinpointed a sore subject: forgiveness. Our guidebook, *Love is Letting Go of Fear*, stated:

> *Forgiveness is the key. The unforgiving mind is confused and afraid...It justifies its anger and the correctness of its condemning judgement. The unforgiving mind sees itself as innocent and others as guilty...Forgiveness becomes a process of letting go and overlooking whatever we thought people may have done to us or whatever we have done to them.*[18]

I knew that God was speaking to me about the bitterness forming in my heart. Solitude was calling me to a place away from dissension, stress, and sadness. I was ready for a campout at Stony Brook State Park, this time by myself. But could I survive alone? Thoughts of nocturnal varmints who might snuffle around the screen house for food sent shivers down my spine. Ah, but the waterfalls and piney air! I would go!

With a station wagon full of camping gear, I headed for campsite fifty-three at the end of the road. With the clanking of poles and pounding of stakes, I hoisted up my brand new 10'x14' Hilary tent. It was a ritual bred in my clan throughout generations. For my dad's family, it was an army tent at the summer Bible conference. A month at Sebago Lake in Maine was my family's hangout when I was a teenager, and camping in the Adirondacks with our own kids had been close family times for Steve and me.

In a journal entry dated August 1987, I wrote: "The magic of #53 is that it faces out on a steep wood path down to the brook. On the other side is a winding trail through the pines up a hill to the meadow. No other site is visible. My hammock is slung between two hemlocks. Lying in it, I feel totally comfortable. I sigh in relief as my weary body unwinds in this oasis of peace. Light and shadow play in the treetops. I feel the caress of a gentle breeze and hear the melody of a song sparrow. Already tension is being replaced by gratitude. I can only say, 'Thank you, God.'"

As the sun set, I gathered wood. The sounds of a family talking and laughing brought back memories of other campfires. I pictured Karen at nine as I helped her roast a marshmallow; Rick and Jon, listening raptly to their dad's pirate story; and Miriam's bright face reflecting the blaze while she cuddled baby Cathy. By the fireside, I wrapped myself in a blanket for comfort.

Something rustled in the bushes. What was that creature scrambling up the pine tree? My flashlight revealed a raccoon peering down at me. I locked my food box and cooler in the wagon, lit my Coleman lantern, and zipped up the tent door for the night. Snuggling into my cot, grateful for a thick foam pad, I felt like a small child.

>"*Jesus, tender shepherd hear me,*
>*Bless thy little lamb tonight.*
>*Through the darkness be there with me,*
>*Keep me safe 'til morning light,*" I whispered.

I slept like a log until eight A.M. The early sun dappled my tent with rosy light. I was drawn to the path up the hill. As I walked along the wooded trail, misty rays made sparkles on dewy hemlock boughs. I heard cicadas singing and the plaintive coo of a dove. Returning along the road, I noticed a cluster of wild flowers. Orange pop'ems, tiny blue forget-me-nots, goldenrod, and daisies grew in quiet beauty beside a tinkling stream.

What a little miracle was the way sunlight made a hologram of each leaf! Catching the mist, rainbow colors shimmered, and then, a touch of breeze turned it into diamonds. I marveled that God created such pockets of beauty just for me to enjoy.

In the screen house, morning sun touched my table with warmth. Yellow mums and a flowered tablecloth added splashes of color. I pumped up my Coleman stove, and soon bacon sizzled and coffee perked. Scrambled eggs and toast were delicious. From down below came the music of tumbling falls wafting on a breeze. I was one with God's creation.

Afternoons, I read Tozer's classic, *The Pursuit of God*. The chapter "God As A Person" spoke to me:

> *In the deep of His mighty nature God thinks, wills, enjoys, feels, loves, desires and suffers as any person may. In making Himself known to us, He communicates through the avenues of our minds, wills and emotion in a continuous interchange of love and thought between God and the soul.*"[19]

I was beginning to grasp just the smallest part of the infinite Creator. I was being drawn to see the wonder with inner eyes, and herein lay the path to healing.

On the way home from Stony Brook, I stopped in at Craig to see Dave. He was in bed and hooked to a catheter. Because a urinary track infection made him prone to seizures, they had wheeled him into the big day room. Blaring TV, grinding teeth, and zoo-like noises gave me the urge to get him outside. "Yesterday, Dave was the loudest roarer of them all," an aide reported. "Sometimes; it's his brain backfiring. This time he was letting us know he felt miserable."

"It's such a lovely day. Is there any way I could take him for a walk?" I asked. The aide and I settled him into his wheelchair, catheter and all. On a seventy-five degree afternoon, with wind blowing though our hair, our walk around the grounds refreshed us.

Dave kept trying to tell me something. "H-h-h-h-hat."

I finally understood. "You want your hat?"

"Yes," he answered. I extracted his well-worn Bills' cap and his watch from the wheelchair basket. In his smile, there was a flash of a proud dude as he touched the visor and fingered his old timepiece.

We found a sheltered place by a bench in the sunshine. Young guys played basketball nearby. Dave turned his head to hear their voices. He looked up at the sound of a plane overhead. A car started in the parking lot. "Hear it?" he asked.

I caught a glimpse of the small boy with silken blond hair, alert and listening, enjoying his world. As his head rested on the tray, I laid my cheek on his. Long lashes, half smile, and big hands, both gentle and warm in mine, reminded me of the beautiful person within the damaged body. I thanked God that Dave was aware, peaceful, and happy. I then reluctantly wheeled him back to the day room and its cacophony of sounds.

• • • • • • • • • • • • • • •

Rumors began flying among Craig's staff that a major move was in the making. Restructuring of DDSO (Developmental Disabled Service Organization) would do away with Craig as an institution. Our family gathered in the day room to hear the news. "There's a home, ranch style, being built for your son and eleven others who need special care," the director announced. "Everybody will be placed in a similar residence under construction now in various locations. In three months, we will be completely moved out of here." Dave would have his own room at LaRue at Wayland. Wow! I thought. *This sounds too good to be true.*

On the way home, we took a detour down Charles Street to see for ourselves the new construction. As a contractor, Rick was interested. "This place is built like a fortress," he noted, walking through bare rooms before sheetrocking. "Plywood walls—in case Young Dave gets wild!" Roomy and spacious with a front porch and back patio, we could only imagine what a gracious home this would be for its residents.

After Thanksgiving, invitations to open house at LaRue Intermediate Care Facility came in the mail. Sunday, Steve and I along with Miriam and Rick met on the front veranda. With gray siding and white trim, the rambling ranch boasted two large wings. Christmas lights were already strung along the porch roof. Inside, the long dining room table was festively adorned with meat trays, cookies and punch. "Dave and the others will eat out here?" I asked.

"We're the cooks, learning how to feed a mob!" Jodi, an aide, laughed. Bedrooms were decorated with personal touches. Dave's was bordered with Buffalo Bill helmets and curtains to match. A living room on each wing provided sofas and recliners.

"How do you like the change?" I asked Jodi.

"I love it!" her eyes sparkled with excitement. "What a difference it's made in staff morale! It feels like family!" Dave in his wheelchair was listening and grinning. The party atmosphere and homey surroundings agreed with him. He held a blue stuffed Bills mascot that squeaked. Jodi ruffled his hair and gave him a hug. A memory of Mary Jo and Jon reminded me that God sends an angel to "the least of these." LaRue would be Dave's home, a place of caring and comfort, for the rest of his life.

TWENTY-NINE
THE ROCK AND DOC SHOW

It was actually happening. Steve was in the process of moving his belongings out of the Burton Street house. Breaking up the household had been a gruesome task. So many celebrations around the old dining room table! He was taking all the Castor antiques with him, including the cherry drop-leaf. After two and a half hours of separation negotiations with our lawyers, anger brewed in both of us.

"You know, Connie, the Castor pieces aren't included in my fifty percent," he stated.

"So, you're going to get sixty-five percent while I end up with a measly thirty-five percent!" I accused him. "I'm going back to talk to my lawyer!" I stormed into my room, shaking with indignation.

As I sat at my desk trying to cool down, very clearly an inner voice spoke to me. *Are you going to allow mere possessions to turn your final days together into bitterness?* I was ashamed of my barefaced greed.

"Okay, Steve, let's keep going," I conceded. In each room, we took turns making a choice. The crucial pawn was my grabbing the computer and desk in his bedroom. In exchange, he gave me the living room oriental rug and blue velvet sofa. Secretly, I gloated. My acquisitive nature was still there.

Over the weeks, as he toted away trailer loads of his furniture, the rooms looked bleak. I was detaching myself from the family ranch house and thinking about having Rick build me one of my own. On the rare occasions when Steve was home, I felt acutely uncomfortable. Gone was the veneer of summer friendliness. The truce was over. Morose withdrawal and avoidance took its toll. When would he finally move out?

Toward the end of October, on a blustery fall day, the doorbell rang. It was Dan Stone and Burt Rosenburg from Union Life, leaders of our fall retreat at church. With our extra bedrooms, Steve and I had agreed to invite them to spend Friday and Saturday nights at the Burton Street house. A mop of silver hair complemented Dan's ruddy face. His warm smile and direct blue eyes gave him an air of friendliness. Burt was a lanky young man with long wild curly hair. "Have we got the right house?" he asked. "Looks like somebody's moving out." In the entryway were stacks of boxes and a suitcase.

I burst into tears. "Steve's leaving," I sniffled. "It's happening this weekend." What a way to greet guests!

"Come on, Connie, let's talk about it," Dan suggested. Over a cup of coffee at the kitchen counter, I filled them in on the impending divorce.

Burt offered a prayer. "Lord Jesus, keep both Connie and Steve open to Your presence, even in the midst of pain."

Had God sent two angels at this desolate time? I wondered.

The theme of the retreat was, "Christ In You, the Hope of Glory," the main focus of Union Life Ministries. Cogently, with powerful biblical emphasis, Dan and Burt taught from John's gospel. "You are in me, and I am in you," Jesus revealed to His disciples. "'If anyone loves me, he will obey my teaching. My Father will love him, and we will come to him and make our home with him.'" (John 14.23, NIV)

We broke into small groups to look at the implications of Christ living in each of us believers. "If I could really grasp what this means, I could let go of my resentment and fears," I confessed to my circle of friends. "Steve's packed and ready to leave. It's scary to be totally alone."

"Connie, don't look now, but Steve just arrived," Lee reported. "He's talking with Pastor Minnigh." I turned to see him pass an envelope to Wendell. I later discovered he had given each church leader a letter, enumerating my faults and exonerating himself. It was the cry of a hurting man.

As Steve walked out the door with nary a goodbye, I knew that this was the end. At that moment, my friends' touch communicated a power beyond myself. I knew as they prayed for me that inside me was the Spirit of our Lord who would always be with me.

Saturday night, lying on my bed in the back bedroom, I was wide awake. Outside, I heard the scrape and rustle of dry leaves being blown against the house and along the driveway. It seemed like the loneliest, saddest sound in the whole world. A sense of isolation and fear closed in on me. I thought about waking Dan and Burt who were sleeping next door in Young Dave's old room, but the message of the retreat had penetrated my spirit. Now, the reality of Christ living in me came clearly to mind. He was my companion, my husband, and my Savior. I prayed, "I want You to be the ground of my being, Lord Jesus, the solid rock on which I stand. Only You can fill the lonely void in me. Teach me the reality of union with you and empower me each day to live it, else I perish." I became peaceful as hope, like a candle's flame, flickered in my being.

The next day at the front door, the Union Life messengers said good-bye. "You're going to be fine, Connie," Dan encouraged me. "You'll daily be in my prayers."

"You two were sent from God just when I needed strength," I thanked them.

"Christ in you, the hope of glory!" Burt reminded me.

How long I'd be able to stay in my home was uncertain, but I was determined to make it cozy. A new sofa in the family room and a refinished dining room set filled the empty spaces.

There was one room that drew me like a magnet—the small den. It would make a perfect nursery for my first grandbaby who was due around the first of March. It was going to be a big one—I could tell by the size of Cathy's tummy at Christmas. With Mary and Rick also expecting a baby in July, 1987 would be a fruitful year, an antidote to loss.

Wallpaper in tiny hearts, a border of bunnies, and crisp white curtains trimmed with red ball fringe transformed the den. Stuffed animals and toys fit nicely on the shelves. A secondhand crib painted white looked new with the addition of a handmade bumper and quilt with appliquéd hearts. The nursery was ready, and so was I.

• • • • • • • • • • • • • •

Cathy was almost two weeks overdue. "Mom, I'm going in tomorrow to have labor induced," she told me over the phone. Her voice quavered. "I'm kind of scared. Please pray for me."

"Oh, honey, you can count on me," I promised. The long tedious eighteen hours before Karen had arrived were vivid in my memory. Because this was a good-sized baby for a slender girl, it could be difficult.

The next day at church, my attention wandered as I tried to concentrate on work. *Lord, just give her strength and patience*, I prayed, almost feeling the contractions myself.

Miriam arrived in the afternoon to wait with me for news. By suppertime, I was on edge. "Shall I call the hospital, Mim?"

"Yes! Do it, Mom!"

The nurse in obstetrics was encouraging. "Mrs. Collier is working hard right now. It won't be long." Miriam and I grabbed each other with a yelp of joy.

Twenty minutes later the phone rang. Cathy's voice, a bit hoarse and shaky, announced, "Mom, I'm holding your grandson. Want to speak to Joshua Mark Collier, eight pounds, eight ounces?"

Tears of wonder streamed down my face. "Hi, Josh," I managed to say. A chirp and a squeak came over the phone.

"Mom, come as soon as you can. He's utterly adorable!"

Miriam pulled the phone away. "Congratulations, little sister! I'm proud of you!"

Mark spoke to me, "Connie, it was awesome! I caught my son as soon as he was born and cut the cord."

I assured them both I'd be there in two days. "I'm going to need you, Mom," she acknowledged before we said goodbye.

I wasn't prepared for the surge of elation that made me want to celebrate. Three blue balloons were soon blown up and flashed a message, "It's a BOY!" Exuberant, I drove down to the church council meeting and shot a balloon into the lounge. Laughter and clapping! I tied one to the mailbox and the other to my antenna.

• • • • • • • • • • • • •

I lay resting on the sofa after my five hour drive to Butler, Pennsylvania. While Cathy napped, Joshua, my new grandson, snoozed on my chest. It seemed that nature herself sang a lullaby as wind sighed in the pines outside. Sunshine touched his velvet-capped head. With my fingers, I traced his tiny nose, shell-like ears, and rosebud mouth. Those eyelashes came from Mark. An occasional chirp spoke contentment. The flood of love that filled my being was grammy bliss. As I felt the warmth of his little body, I thanked God for this new life.

On July eighth, I had the privilege of witnessing the birth of Jacob Thomas Castor, six pounds, three ounces. It had been a long labor. Contractions stopped and the midwife, Meg, suggested a pitosin drip to start action. At last, it was almost time. A cap of fine brown hair was showing. "Now push, Mary," Meg encouraged. Rick and I caught our breath in amazement. The little face was so beautiful! "Another push for the shoulder," Meg directed. Gently, she brought out one arm, then the other, and at last the whole tiny body. "It's a boy!" Rick began to weep. I joined him with tears of awe. The baby coughed and turned a lovely pink.

Mary reached out for her son, still attached to the umbilical cord, and helped him latch onto her breast. We laughed when we saw that strong nursing instinct. The gentleness of the birth, the amazing moment of his first breath, what a miracle!

Meanwhile, back at the ranch house on Burton Street, there stood a "For Sale" sign out on the front lawn. A banker and his wife who were interested returned several times. Steve and I accepted their final offer in March of '88 and promptly closed the deal because they wanted to move in by the end of May.

Following the frenzy of packing and leaving Burton Street, a caravan of trucks carried my belongings to a friend's barn for storage. What would I have done without my kids and my church family to help? Anna and Harry Beeman from Centenary graciously provided me a room in their country home for the summer. With the barest essentials, I settled into a small bedroom, a place of peace and simplicity.

It was early spring and the nesting instinct ran like sap in my bones. Rick and I had finally settled on "do-able" plans, a small ranch home with an attached garage.

"Actually 1,350 square feet is spacious," Rick commented.

"If we include a family room in the basement, it will be around 2,000 square feet," I added. "I need room for parties and family gatherings."

"Have you decided where you want to build?" Rick asked. "Come May, Doc and I will be ready to start the job."

"I'll let you know after tomorrow," I replied. "I'm checking out something near the park."

Up the hill to Mossy Bank I drove, stopping at John Olynic's home. A jolly man with a Slavic accent, he greeted me with a hearty handshake. "I tink you'll like the lot," he smiled. "Good view!" He pointed up the road. "It's just up the street from here. See that hedgerow? It's the acre on the other side. Go and take a look."

It was a sparkling clear day. A brisk breeze stirred in the bare limbs of elms and maples. As I walked the acre through a hay field, I sniffed the pure sweet air. Looking out toward the west, I noted a sizeable pond. Reflected sunlight danced on the water. Vistas of hills, woods, and azure skies met my eyes as I gazed northwest. "I'll face the house into this marvelous view," I muttered to myself. "In the morning, sunrise in the east will flood the dining room and my bedroom. In the evening, I'll sit on the porch watching the sunset." I could already picture a blue ranch with white trim and maroon shutters on Mossy Bank.

"The price for the lot is $1,000," John Olynic informed me when I returned to his home.

"Wow!" I thought. I was glad I didn't pay $10,000 for that downtown half acre lot. "I'll take it!" I replied, barely hiding my eagerness. I wrote him a check, and he gave me a receipt written on a scrap of yellow paper. "What about the deed?"

"Oh, I'll talk to my lawyer," he replied nonchalantly.

My entire savings account was wiped out. No matter! I was now a landowner. Pride and sheer exhilaration welled up in me. God was so good!

Rick joined me to stake out the location of the house. "Mom, what a deal!" he exclaimed. "A beautiful view no matter where you look. This will be fun!"

"Rock and Doc's first house!" I laughed.

Around the middle of May, the well driller came with his equipment. The thump, thump, thump of his power-driven drill was music to my ears. After several days, success! "We've found good clear spring water at one hundred twenty feet," he reported.

Next came Vic with the bulldozer and backhoe to dig out the cellar. Would he pay attention to our yellow stakes? Mountains of dirt and rocks piled up in the front yard. Rick arrived to begin work the next day. First thing he did was whip out his tape to measure the rectangular hole. "Blast it!" My son was angry. "Vic cut this corner short! I can't begin until he makes it right!"

"I'll track him down," I promised. Nothing was going to hinder progress on my new house. I found Vic working on a school project nearby. I stood right in front of his bulldozer, frantically waving my arms. Alarmed, he climbed down to face a furious woman. "I'm not paying you until you fix that corner," I scolded. "You're holding up my work crew!" He pondered a moment, rubbing his grizzly chin.

"Okay. I'll get the truck, load 'er up, and come right over."

Next day, the Rock Construction truck pulled in, along with truckloads of gravel and lumber. Rick and his co-worker Dave began what they called "The Rock and Doc Show." Lithe brown bodies sprang into motion as saws buzzed, nailing guns popped, and rock 'n roll radio blared. With a chant of "Heave ho, up we go," cellar walls of treated lumber were raised.

By the first of August, a charcoal roof and blue siding with white trim enclosed the house. Rick or "Rock," Doc, and I, the gofer, sat one noon on a pile of dirt, admiring the beautiful home that had emerged from a hole in the ground. To me, it looked like the Taj Mahal.

"Rock, just look at those graceful arches on the porch!" I exclaimed. "I'm proud of you!"

"Yep, I must say I'm happy with the way it looks," he replied, a pleased smile on his tan face.

"Great job on the siding, Doc," I added.

"We did it together," he said. "Now for the wiring!" Best friends, both intelligent, they loved the challenge of their first house, and they brought zest to the job each day. I kept them supplied with donuts and coffee, and I tracked down anything they needed from our local lumberyard.

Rock and Doc were in their element as the drywall went up. After we primed ceilings and walls, not a seam was visible. At last, the paneled doors and trim were in place with the rich grain of natural pine adding warmth to rooms. Down in the basement, I had spent hours staining and varnishing woodwork. To view the results was deeply satisfying.

My bedroom papered with a flowered stripe under the chair rail and a mini-print above looked inviting. Carpeting throughout created a warm, homey look. Golden oak kitchen cabinets were installed. Finally, Rural Electric hooked us into the transformer.

On Saturday, October 29, my daughter Miriam and three stalwart young men from church hauled truckloads of boxes and furniture up the hill from a storage barn. Other friends brought lunch, sawed wood, and cleaned. That evening, I was suddenly alone in the midst of chaos. An autumn wind howled down the chimney and rattled the Bilco door. I sat up in bed, listening. What was that knocking sound? (the electric heater) The water pump's unfamiliar hum kept me awake. What had possessed a nearly sixty-year-old single woman to build a house in the country? Loneliness and a sense of responsibility felt like a heavy weight.

The turning point was the assistance of Todd, my woodsman friend. With great care, he hooked up my stove to the hole in the chimney. "Let's try 'er out, Connie," he challenged. The navy blue enameled Vigilant radiated comfort and warmth as the first fire merrily crackled. I stretched out on the blue velvet sofa and felt deeply at peace.

After a sound sleep, I awoke the next morning to a comfortable home. I tossed a few logs in the fire and settled in the rocker by the hearth with my Bible, journal, and a steaming cup of tea. My quiet times with God had been few and far between during the crunch of building. I offered a prayer of thanksgiving. "Thank you, Jesus. You provided for me beyond anything I could imagine. Thank You for my very own home. It's You and I together up here on Mossy Bank." Through the archway, I watched as dawn splashed rose and peach clouds. My dining room was flooded with sunshine. I knew inside of me a fresh new morning of my life was beginning.

THIRTY
LOVE PENETRATES MISERY

The cold north wind of winter gripped my ranch on Mossy Bank with its fury. March had indeed arrived like a lion. The force of the blizzard blew snow in horizontal sheets down the driveway, and white drifts were carved on my porch and against the garage door. I was deliciously snowed in, snug in my little home.

The copper teakettle sang its steamy song. I stoked the wood stove with more logs and poured hot water into the teapot. Sipping lemon zinger, I sat back and slowly rocked in the chair by the fireside, looking around my living room. On the old pine dry sink were pictures of my children and grandsons. Brocade drapes from Burton Street fit the bay window perfectly. Potted plants on the sill added greenery and a touch of color and the sofa, fondly named "the blue cloud," looked inviting on the red and blue Oriental rug. Favorite books and my father's masterpiece, the Maine lighthouse, reminded me of my parents' love. How could I be so blessed? I breathed a prayer of thanksgiving for the gift of this home.

In the late afternoon, the wind died down. Blue skies and sunshine created a sparkling world of pristine beauty. In hushed awe, I watched as the sun slowly sank behind the trees. Just above the horizon, the afterglow spun streaks of coral and peach.

Harsh ringing interrupted my reverie. I picked up the phone. "Connie, it's Pat," I heard my friend's voice. "I just want to let you know that Steve called me this afternoon.

"What for?" I asked. Into my tranquil spirit crept a twinge of anxiety.

"He wants me to serve you with divorce papers. I'm the only Notary Public he knew in Bath. How do you feel about that?"

I was caught off guard. I had heard that Steve had been working on a "do-it-yourself" divorce. With the separation agreement securely in place, the rest was fairly simple. Still the finality of the break felt strange. "He's planning to get married, isn't he?" I questioned. Rumors from the children were my source of information.

"He didn't say, but he wants me to give you the papers as soon as possible. It's just a formality," Pat explained. "Then you'll be a free woman!"

The word "free" rang a bell. "Hey, do it, Pat! Can't think of a better person! Let's celebrate with a dinner up here—you, Lee, and me."

In the darkening room, I sat thinking, feeling a potpourri of emotions. I would be free, but free for what? I would soon be turning sixty. Self-pity began to rear its ugly head. Who would take care of me in the twilight years? *After Steve is married, there will be two Mrs. N. S. Castors,* I thought glumly. Suddenly, with clarity, an idea blossomed. Why not go back to my maiden name? Yes, in honor of my godly parents, I would be Constance Ann Jackson again.

Pat served me the papers, and I signed them. The necessary groundwork had been done for an official name change. On Sunday, I made an announcement at church. Later, Pat, Lee, and I sat at the dining room table enjoying a chicken cordon bleu dinner. The stereo played a Rachmaninoff concerto. Candlelight reflected in their faces the warmth of friendship. Lee raised a crystal goblet. "A toast to Constance Ann Jackson! May this be a year full of wonderful new possibilities!" We clinked glasses. Welling up in me was a sense of gratitude for my loving friends and for the heritage of my name.

Just before my sixtieth birthday in May, my inner self felt very shaky. Old anxieties warned me that it was time to listen to my deep hurts and to take a day apart to be in God's presence. Two things were bothering me. I was about to begin my first year of old age. What would it be like to grow frail? I wondered. The second thing was the canker of bitterness within me. My ex-husband of thirty-five years was being married again the next weekend. A few sleepless nights full of fearful, resentful thoughts prompted me to clear May fifth for a day of solitude.

So, that morning with a blaze crackling in the wood stove, I settled on the sofa with my Bible, my journal, my sixty-year-old baby book, and a photo album that Mother had labeled, "This Is Your Life, Connie Castor." As I leafed through the yellowed pages of "Baby's Days and Baby's Ways," I noted a snapshot of my young seminary student father tenderly holding tiny me. Then, there was a picture of twenty mothers and their babies—my first birthday party, "Done in green, yellow, and white," mother wrote. I realized with gratitude how much my parents cherished me as a small child.

The photo album also included snapshots of me as a young mother, all of us camping together in the Adirondacks. There was Karen, holding baby Cathy; Jon and Rick playing with trucks; and Miriam smiling in the hammock with her dad. The sense of loss brought tears. Karen and Jon were no longer here. The marriage had ended in divorce. Yet, I was acutely aware of the love we shared. How blessed I had been to mother these dear ones! The words of Psalm 139.5 brought me comfort: "You, O Lord, both precede and follow me and place Your hand of comfort on my head." (TLB)

I thought of my dad at age eighty-four, just two months before his death, blessing my children and me, his daughter. On Christmas Eve, he had presented each of us with a prayer diary. Haltingly, he spoke, "The Lord Jesus has been the mainstay of my life." He paused to catch his breath. "Through prayer, you will grow to know Him as I have known Him."

As I journaled and remembered and wept that day, I sensed God's hand of blessing on my head, His love interlacing the strands of my life. My heart overflowed with thanksgiving for His grace that redeems tragedy and for my present gifts of tranquility and beauty in my new home atop Mossy Bank. In my weakness, the Holy Spirit had strengthened my inner self.

On the day of Steve's wedding, I was surprised to find myself peaceful. Later, I was genuinely able to wish him and his bride the best. The bitterness was being healed.

• • • • • • • • • • • • • • •

One Sunday afternoon, I went to visit David at LaRue. I found him in bed, curled up in a fetal position. His arms and legs were so thin. I reached in over the heavy padding on the rails to touch him. He recoiled from my hand. His face twisted in misery as he cried out. I sat beside his bed feeling helpless and angry. "Look at you, Davey," I said to myself. "You used to be so bright and active. I hate this terrible disease that has robbed you of everything!" In tears, I asked God, "Lord, how can I relate to my son? He doesn't even know I'm here."

The answer came back clearly, *Get in there with him and love him.*

But I *don't feel like it, the way he's yelling.*

Do it anyway, Jesus spoke to me inwardly. *I'll supply the love.* I took off the padding, lowered the rail, and lay down beside David. I poked his teddy bear under his chin and kept rubbing his back.

"I love you, Young Dave," I said over and over. Such tenderness I felt for my son! The cries became farther apart as his body uncurled. At last, I heard that familiar chuckle as a big grin lit up his face. I learned that love penetrates misery.

The people who were in charge of Dogwood Day Treatment Center in Wayland also knew this. Diane Koffka, occupational therapist, was on hand to work with Dave and other residents who came daily for a special program. With a pixie face, smiling eyes, and a lively sense of humor, she knew how to make him chuckle. At twenty-six, my son was often too weak to keep his head up. I wondered how he could possibly participate in activities. "Come and visit," Diane invited me.

The annual art show was an extra incentive to see Dogwood in action. The day room burst with color and design. All kinds of media—finger-paints, watercolor, clay, and sticks—created an ambiance of fun and joy. "Yes, this is Dave's handprint," Diane explained. "He dipped his palm in paint and out came this amazing flower." Somehow with a little help, it had become an exotic plant.

"I like to get Dave's favorite kinds of finger food," Diane continued. "On good days, he loves to feed himself bits of pizza, chips, and apple."

"You know, Diane, you're an angel sent from God," I told her. "You see my son as a person and what he can still enjoy and do. I tend to focus on his losses."

"Oh, Wild Young Dave's personality is still there," she laughed. "Just the other day, he snatched my sunglasses and started to put them in his mouth. 'Here, have a chip instead,' I wheedled. He chortled as only he can do!"

Now, we were in the classroom for Dave's unit. On the floor was a boxed-in mattress with lambskin pad. "Before naptime, your son lies here while our physical therapist gives him a massage." Diane described the process. "As her strong gentle hands knead arms, legs, and back, he purrs like a kitten. We're trying to keep his body from contracture." I experienced again a sense of awe. God's "angels on earth" were right here at Dogwood.

• • • • • • • • • • • • • • •

It was almost noon on August eighth, David's twenty-seventh birthday. Under the shade of LaRue's front porch, we set up a picnic table and covered it with a red checked cloth. I fired up the grill and called the boys. "Rick and Jake, let's go in and get Young Dave." We found him in the living room, sitting in his wheelchair with his head down on the tray. I ached to see how thin his face was and how flabby his strong arms had become.

"Hi, Uncle Dave," Jake tousled his hair. The response was an irritated growl.

"It's Mom, Davey," I touched his arm. "Happy Birthday!" My son pulled away from me as if in pain.

Rick was sad. "Man, I hate to see him this way! What has he got to look forward to? Just getting worse and…" Tears filled his eyes. Jake was bouncing a ball. Wham! A direct hit! He bounced it off Dave's head. His uncle sat up, rubbed his head, and chuckled. We clapped and laughed. Jake knew the magic key!

The picnic table was crowded. Our family had been growing. Rick and Mary had given me two beautiful granddaughters. Rose was five, and Peachy was three. Miriam had re-married after a divorce. She and Mike had a daughter, Little Liz, who sat in a booster seat.

For the rest of our time together, Dave sat outside on the patio, too weak to raise his head, but aware that his family surrounded him. A smile flickered on and off whenever we knelt down to talk with him.

He couldn't eat much. A little piece of angel cake made him choke. His favorite present was a squishy, squawky duck. Each quack brought a smile. When we sang "Happy Birthday," it was with poignant awareness of the limited time remaining for our boy.

Before I left for home, the nurse in charge asked to talk with me. "Mrs. Castor, we've made an appointment at Strong Memorial Hospital for some tests on your son."

"What kind of tests?" I asked. The twinge of fear hurt.

"Batten Disease is affecting his swallowing." Her face was serious. "It's extremely difficult to get even pureed food down without his choking. Tests would indicate if food is being ingested into his lungs."

"That means the likelihood of aspiration pneumonia," I said, remembering the cause of Jon's death. The knot of dread tightened.

"Yes," Kathy looked troubled. "I suggest you and Mr. Castor consider the possibility of a G-tube." I recoiled. Several residents at LaRue were fed this way by a tube directly from a bag of formula into their stomach.

"I doubt if Dave's father and I could consider this," I demurred.

Later, I called Steve and brought up the subject of a feeding tube for Dave. "Absolutely not," he was adamant. "I don't want to prolong his life unnecessarily." I agreed that artificial means of keeping David alive, when swallowing was shutting down, hampered his time to die. I agreed, that is, until I saw the sonograms, a result of his tests at Strong.

Dr. Frame, LaRue's M.D., explained the pictures. When he choked, food was going into Dave's lungs. It was clear in the sonograms.

"What about his quality of life?" I asked Kathy.

"Not good," she replied. "Without the tube, starvation and bout after bout of pneumonia. With the tube, he would feel the comfort of food in his stomach. His weight would be built up. He's losing rapidly now."

The nurse revealed the deciding factor. David would have to be moved from LaRue to a nursing home. "The State mandates that we give our residents nourishment," she explained.

The idea of moving him appalled me. "This is his home," I thought. "He is loved and cared for here like a member of the family."

· · · · · · · · · · · · · · · ·

Kathy and Dr. Frame had convinced me that physical comfort and staying at LaRue were basic needs for my son. Now, *how can I persuade Steve that a G-tube is best for David*? I wondered.

Steve was angry. "I thought we'd agreed not to prolong his life. Starvation isn't painful, you know."

"Two things convinced me, Steve."

"What were they?"

"One, he'll be plagued with pneumonia. Quality of life will be miserable. The G-tube, on the other hand, would make him comfortable."

"What's the other?"

"I want him to stay at LaRue, his home. Without the G-tube, he'll have to be transferred to a nursing home."

Silence, then a long sigh. "We both want the best for our son," I added.

"You sign for the operation, Connie," he reluctantly agreed. "I don't feel right about it, but I understand where you're coming from." Two hurting parents had come to a very difficult decision.

Two weeks after my son's minor surgery, I sat with Dave in the activity room. His lunch slowly dripped through tubing from an elevated bag. Already there was healthy color in his cheeks and three pounds gained in weight. Staff was relieved. No longer did they struggle to feed a choking resident. All of us knew that the right decision had been made. "I couldn't stand to let him go," Kathy said.

"He's one of our boys, part of the family," Jodi agreed.

"And God's dearly-loved child," I said.

THIRTY-ONE
CROSSING THE THRESHOLD

It was almost Christmas 1994. A frigid December wind whistled down the chimney and whipped greens and red ribbons on the porch. I was taking a moment to relax after frosting a batch of cut-out cookies. Sitting in the rocker and being warmed by the wood stove, I looked out the bay window. In a burst of afternoon sunlight, iced tree limbs glistened. Inside, sunshine illuminated the nativity scene on the dry sink. The Chrismon tree with its gold and white symbols, spoke of Immanuel, God with us.

Just two days from now, I'd hear tramping of many feet on the porch. The front door would burst open when my three children, spouses, and seven grandkids would arrive to celebrate Christmas with me.

The phone rang. Dr. Frame informed me he was calling from the Dansville Hospital. "David's in the emergency room. He's not responding to treatment."

How familiar yet cuttingly wounding was this scenario: tranquility shattered by Batten's encroachment! "What's happening?" I was frightened.

"It's his heart, a very erratic rhythm, sometimes twelve or fifteen seconds between beats. We're thinking of a pacemaker."

"I'm driving right over." My throat felt tight. *Not at Christmas, Lord, please not now*, I pled in prayer as I drove.

In the emergency room, I was shocked to see David's condition. He sat nearly upright on a tilted hospital bed, his face pale with a sallow tinge. During the long pause between heartbeats, there was an eerie silence. Was he gone? Then, with a jerk like a small seizure, his face flushed deep pink as his heart struggled to regain its rhythm. Steve, with his wife Carol, stood watch. "It's just like Jon," Steve recalled, lines of misery etched in his face. "I wonder how long Dave can last this way?"

"What do you as parents think about using an external pacemaker?" Dr. Frame asked.

"Batten Disease is clogging his brainstem, so a device like that wouldn't help." Steve was firm.

"No pacemaker," I agreed. "With his brother, the heart righted itself. Let's wait and see."

Christmas Eve found me sitting beside David's bed in the hospital. For two days, his heart had been faltering, at times only nine beats a minutes. I held his limp hand as he struggled to breathe. "Davey, you're a fighter," I said to my son. "I'm nuts about your feisty spirit, your crooked smile. I like your growling chuckles, even your one and only word. I'm not ready to let you go." Tears blurred my vision. "When I come to see you, the first thing I say is 'I love you.' And you always let me know you love me in return. Remember when right out of the blue you said 'I ove oo om?' It was the best you could do. Oh, Davey, I cherish you!"

It was painful to watch and wait. Dr. Frame offered no hope. One by one, aides and nurses from LaRue came to say goodbye. Jodi sat on the edge of the bed, stroking his hair. "You're still my handsome man, Dave, and you're still a fighter. Don't give up yet." The irregular heartbeat still continued. We were surprised at the sheer tenacity of his hold on life.

It was with a strange sense of isolation that I sat in church on Christmas Eve. I felt as if I were walled in by grief, walking through the dark valley of the shadow of death. Clear lights twinkled in the Chrismon tree. Candles glowed around the church. Each of us held our own flickering light as we sang "Silent Night," but nothing alleviated my sadness.

Mentally, I was still with David by his bedside. *How much he has given me in pure affection!* I thought. *How precious is his smile when I rub his head!* All was stripped away; his essential core, though, was in union with God. Immanuel God with us was the gift of Christmas. I prayed, *You came, Lord Jesus, to heal the brokenhearted and to set at liberty them that are bruised. Please give Davey back to me for just a little while.*

The next morning, I was delighted to find Dave sleeping peacefully, his pulse normal. "The best present in the whole world! Thank you, God." Words were inadequate to express my gratitude.

The doctor was amazed. "This is one strong young man!" he exclaimed as he checked vital signs.

When the tramping clan arrived laden with presents late Christmas Day, I welcomed them with open arms. We celebrated with an enormous sense of relief and appreciation for a life spared. When we gathered around Dave's bed, Jake climbed up beside his sleepy uncle and chucked him under the chin. "Hey, Uncle Dave, wake up! It's Christmas! Here's a present from me!" He squeezed a fuzzy stuffed gorilla that emitted a raucous roar. A big smile lit up my son's face, and his chortle warmed our hearts.

A blessing to me at this time was my work at New York State Office for the Aging (OFA). Back in the fall of 1990, I was awed how my own experience had prepared me for the challenge. Caring for my dad during his last years and for my Batten children had given me understanding and compassion for caregivers. These were the often forgotten people who quietly provided for the needs of frail loved ones.

A Christmas tea found thirteen of us gathered around the table in the family room, sharing lessons we'd learned over the past year. Al, in his late 70's, cared for his wife with Alzheimer's. "I was planning to bring you a batch of my famous peanut butter cookies today," he explained. "She dumped a half a bag of flour in the bowl and a few eggs with shells." We laughed. Al's humor kept us from being bogged down in the tedium. "But the messiest incident was when I noticed a white stream of goo dripping out of the kitchen cupboard. My wife had stored the ice cream in there after our shopping trip." Monthly meetings and occasional seminars on how to cope provided a network of support and education. I was moved by the courage and determination of these special people.

The other facet of my job entailed coordinating the Ombudsman Program. "Ombudsman" refers to someone who will speak up for the needs of others, in this case, the frail elderly. I trained and worked with twelve volunteers. We regularly visited nursing and adult homes, advocating for the residents and their concerns.

The one frustration with my job was my cramped little office upstairs in the old hospital building where OFA rented space. There was hardly room for a caregiver or ombudsman to sit down and talk. Downstairs was a big room piled high with file boxes and old furniture. "You know, Linda, this place would make a spacious Caregivers Resource Center." OFA director Linda Tetor and I peered into the junk-stuffed interior. "Three windows and its own powder room," I added.

"Let's take a look," she decided. We moved into the room and opened the bathroom door. "P-e-e-ew! Smells like the black hole of Calcutta!" She held her nose. We skirted the cast-off desks to the window area. In spite of the stench, Linda had a visionary gleam in her eye. "Can't you just picture this nook for the caregiver library?" she asked.

"A bookcase on each side would fit perfectly," I agreed.

"I'm going to work on it, Connie," she promised.

My boss was a woman of action, so within two months, the work crew had painted the walls and ceilings sparkling white and the floor shiny brown. Even the powder room smelled good.

I spent my day off hanging mauve and blue wallpaper at chair rail height with a matching border. Sheer curtains topped with mauve swags, two area rugs, a bargain conference table, and flowers in the library nook created an airy light-filled gathering place.

Ombudsmen and caregivers dropped by for visits. Support groups and training took place around the table. When OFA funding was in danger of being cut, we met for prayer. At this time of concern for David, camaraderie, humor, and understanding from OFA staff helped keep my morale up.

One Sunday in early spring of 1996, I was disturbed to see a change in my son. "Dave, it's Mom!" I gave him a hug after I wheeled him down the hall in LaRue to the activity room. "How about a smile?" His face was expressionless. He sat rigid and upright, his eyes wide and staring. Chalk white, he was like a statue carved from marble. I felt his forehead. It was cold and clammy.

The nurse took his temperature. "Eighty-nine degrees! I can't believe it." Batten Disease in the brainstem was eroding the inner thermostat. "We're going to warm you up, young man," Kathy promised. "An electric blanket and cap will help."

The next time I saw Dave, he was warm, snugly tucked in bed with a stocking hat on his head. A little smile let me know he enjoyed a backrub. Massaging his arms and legs relaxed him. He was sleeping more and more. Staff included Steve and me in making plans for his final days, so a hospice team came to explain how to make a patient comfortable as death approached. Dr. Frame and Kathy, the nurse, made a promise. "LaRue is David's home. We will care for him here until the very end." We were deeply grateful for the love that made this commitment possible.

While I was at work on Monday, May twentieth, the dreaded call came, "Connie, David's taken a turn for the worse." The nurse's voice was strained. "You'd better come right over." The week before, cardiac irregularity had been a problem, but Sunday evening, a heart rate of sixty beats a minute and his smile had reassured me.

My heart was now in my throat. "You mean...You're saying...he's dying?" I could hardly say the words.

"Yes, blood work indicates that vital organs are shutting down."

"I'll be right there," I wept at my desk uncontrollably. The shroud of impending loss was heavy.

Neysa, an ombudsman friend, had come for an appointment. She gently put an arm around my shoulder. "Is it David?" she asked.

"Yes...he's...very bad..."

"Is it time for him to be with Jesus?"

"Yes." To be with Jesus! Her words gave me hope for his true destination.

"I'll pray for you." My friend offered Dave to the Father. "Thank you, Lord Jesus, that You are holding him in your strong arms and have prepared a place for him. Thank you that soon David will have that new body You promised him, Lord. May Connie be aware of Your presence as she sits by his side. Give them both Your peace that passes understanding. In Jesus' name, Amen."

I entered David's bedroom with fear and trembling. What would I find? Was he still alive? The bed was placed in the middle of the room with chairs surrounding it. Miriam and Rick were there, and Carol and Steve kept vigil. Craig's chaplain joined the circle. I bent over the still form, all my senses drinking in the essence of David Mark Castor.

His blond hair was shining clean. I noted the slow pulse in his temple. Eyes were slightly open, glazed by unconsciousness. Breaths were rapid and shallow. The body was not thin like Jon's because the feeding tube had kept him nourished. Those big young man's hands were warm. I kissed his cheek, soft and sweet smelling.

Strangely, there was an aura of peace around my dying child. Murmured greetings welcomed me into the circle of love. We joined the chaplain in the powerful words of the twenty-third Psalm: "Yea, though I walk through the valley of the shadow of death, I will fear no evil, for Thou art with me. Thy rod and Thy staff, they comfort me… and I will dwell in the house of the Lord forever." (Psalm 23.4, 6b KJ)

We shared memories. "I like his fighting spirit," Rick recalled. "He faced Batten Disease and roared."

"Yet in the darkness, he found the light of Jesus," I said. "I'll never forget the day he realized God would give him a new body."

"I'll always remember our hike in Alaska when Dave heard the Dama sheep breathing," Miriam was crying.

"I'm thinking about camping with my son, sitting by the fireside, roasting marshmallows, and telling stories," Steve recalled. We wept, and we laughed as we sat by his bedside.

Tuesday, I watched as LaRue staff, one by one, came in to express their love. "I'm going to miss you, David," Jodi whispered. His face was pallid, and his breathing became more rapid. I believed I was ready to let him go.

On Wednesday, I found his Bible tapes and listened to 1 Corinthians 15.43: "The bodies we have now embarrass us for they become sick and die. Yes, they are weak dying bodies now, but when we live again, they will be full of strength." (TLB) Breathing was labored now for Dave, and circulation was slow. His fingers and toes were turning blue. Still that slow throbbing pulse in his temple was precious. How could I express what he meant to me? I spoke softly, my eyes streaming with tears. "Thank you, Davey. Thank you for being the one pure loving person that I could hold and kiss and tell you 'I love you.' You battled demons of anger and fear to come into this deep peace. You're just about to cross over the threshold into the light of Jesus. Oh, I will miss you, my baby, my son." I realized that even the flickering life in each shallow breath was dear to me.

Around six o'clock that evening, I was returning to Dave's room after a light supper with the staff. The door was partly shut, so I reached to open it. "Don't come in, Connie. Please wait." The nurse's voice was urgent. I waited outside trembling.

"He's passed on," the young male nurse wiped away tears. "You may come in now." Dave's eyes were closed: his mouth was open; and his cheeks were still warm. But his body was empty; the essence of Davey was gone. I laid my head on his chest and wept great wrenching sobs of a bereft mother.

A siren sounded outside. The ambulance had already come to take the body to Strong Memorial Hospital to garner brain tissue for research. "Wait for his dad to see him," I pled.

"Steve's on his way," the nurse said. I gave my son one last hug and headed for Rick's house nearby on the outskirts of Dansville. As I drove, I wept, crying out, "My son, my son." I felt a terrible sense of incompleteness. A piece of myself had been torn out of me. Quietly, insistently, an inner voice spoke to me amidst the storm of grief.

You do know where he is, don't you?

"Show me, Lord." The mists of earthbound mourning parted. I saw David straight and tall, walking into the light. The heavenly camera zoomed closer to his smiling face. Every detail of his countenance radiated joy. Eyes were vivid blue, dancing with joy. Skin, vibrant with health. His Castor ears were pink and his blond hair a nimbus of light.

He turned to me, saying, "This is who I am, Mom. I got my new body."

The tears stopped. The vision was immediate and real. In my croaky voice, I praised God by singing "Amazing Grace":

"Yea when this flesh and heart shall fail,
And mortal life shall cease,
I shall possess within the veil,
A life of joy and peace."[20]

Gratitude poured out of me in the form of prayer. "Wow, Lord! Thank you, thank you! You're holding my son right now. You've given him his deepest desire. Behold, You make all things new."

Rick met me at the door. One look at my blotchy tear-stained face disclosed the truth. "Dave is gone, isn't he?"

"Yes, Rick, into the presence of Christ."

"You're peaceful, Mom."

"I had a glimpse of him as he is now." With tears of thanksgiving and awe, I shared the vision with Rick. Inside Mary and the children were getting ready to leave for Jake's spring choral program. She gave me a hug. Rick called the family together. "Let's join hands in a circle. Gram has something to share with us."

"Young Dave is with Jesus now," I told them. A strange joy welled up within me, the feeling of coming to the end of a long, hard race. "He died around six o'clock this evening. But the real eternal part of him is where?"

"In Heaven," Jake spoke up. "He's brand new!"

Rick offered a prayer. "My brother is with You, Jesus." His voice broke. "Karen and Jon are welcoming him. Thank you for giving him the heavenly body he longed for. Thank you for giving each of us Your life. In Your name, Jesus, Amen."

Jake took my hand and pulled me outside to the bubbling creek that flowed through the back yard. Late afternoon sun silvered evergreen tree-tops. A robin's chirp and sparrow's song melded with the melody of the brook. "Grammy, I miss him already." Tears filled his trusting eyes. "Tonight, I'm gonna sing for Uncle Dave."

"I'll be there, listening," I promised.

Young high voices soothed my spirit and reinforced peace deep within my being. Jake flashed a smile in my direction as the third grade grouped to sing "Like an Eagle."

> *"And now is the time, now and farewell,*
> *And as we part, you taught me well,*
> *You gave me strength, you showed the way…*
> *Like an eagle, I will race above the stars,*
> *I will fly to places yet unseen,*
> *Go beyond my wildest dream,*
> *Know that you are watching over me."*

"Davey," I whispered a prayer. "Did God send me to this place to hear these words? Are you watching over me right now?"

Yes. Affirmation from another realm settled into my soul. I know that beyond Dave's dreams, beyond the rising sun, an angel had lifted his frail body into the very hand of God. What a celebration in Heaven for Wild Young Dave as Karen and Jon embraced their brother!

• • • • • • • • • • • • • •

Two days after David's death, the family sat huddled around tables pushed together at Wayland Country Kitchen to plan his memorial service. "Young Dave was a fighter!" Rick spoke emphatically, emotion in his words.

"Yep, I think he knew he had Batten Disease right from the first eye exam," Miriam added. "He didn't take it lying down."

"I remember his comfort in knowing he'd have a new body," I recalled. "How Dave enjoyed listening to Bible tapes!"

"But he loved a good party," Rick continued. "Let's make this memorial service a real celebration of who Young Dave really was!"

"Yes!" we agreed wholeheartedly. Ideas began to flow.

Steve and Carol suggested, "Our friend Kristine has sung beside Dave's bedside. 'We Need The Time To Say Goodbye' is beautiful." Rick would write and lead the call to worship. Several offered to share memories, so gradually, the pieces came together in a colorful mosaic of David's personality.

Miriam created an invitation to send to family and friends. A simple verse expressed our hope: *"Yet when the walls of flesh grows weak, / In such an hour it well may be / Through mists and darkness, light will break, / And each anointed sense will see."*[21]

On Sunday afternoon June 2, 1996, Centenary United Methodist Church was full. On the altar were two photographs: Davey at four, blond and bright-eyed, and at twenty-seven, still grinning. A blue urn held his ashes. Spring flowers and a white candle spoke of eternal life. Jon's banner declared, "Nothing Can Separate Us."

Rick called us to worship: "We remember Dave's smile."

"And his 'never-give-up' spirit," we responded.

"David inspired us with his persistence," Rick continued.

"We remember the gentle clasp of his hands." I began to cry.

"Thank you, God, for the life of Young Dave, our brother, our son, our friend."

All of us joined in, "We rejoice that he is free in the light of Your presence."

Ah, the singing! "Christ the Lord Is Risen Today" raised the rafters. Cathy had the privilege of reading Dave's favorite scriptures, and I shared what his life meant to me. Miriam's description of time with her brother in Alaska painted a powerful word picture. Then, Rick had us laughing with party memories.

For his earthbound family, Steve expressed our feelings in words of remembrance. "Already we miss him, more than words can say…We grieve for ourselves, but we cannot really grieve for him. We can only give thanks for his courage in facing the unfaceable, his steady loyalty to each member of the family, and his indefinable innocence and purity. His life was a gift to all of us who knew him.

"For David, the long night is over; the dawn has come, bright and beautiful. His tongue can once again speak and sing his love and joy."

After the service, I was caught up in what Emily Dickenson calls "the bustle after death"—hugs, shared memories, and eating together in the fellowship hall.

On Mossy Bank, the memorial garden, newly planted, was shadowed while the sun slid behind blue hills. At the end of a very long day, family stood with me as my sister Miriam spoke the ancient words of committal. I looked around, noting Karen's marker flanked by an urn and a sculpted girl with a kitten. I glanced at Jon's garden. His figurine depicted a young boy with a puppy. And then I faced David's section with its marker newly placed. A lamb beside a cherub reminded me of the core of my son. Stripped of sight, speech, and intelligence—his loving spirit had remained intact. Now, he was gone, another child absent from the family.

How could this be? Desolation swept over me. Visits with Davey had met a primal need. I was a young mother again, cradling her baby. The memory clashed with the cold reality of his ashes held in my hands. I bowed in grief, hardly able to speak. "Never ever did I think that three of my children would die." Miriam held me as the enormity of the loss gripped me. My soul wept with generations of bereft mothers:

"A voice is heard in Ramah,
weeping and great mourning,
Rachel weeping for her children
and refusing to be comforted,
because they are no more." (Matthew 2.18, NIV)

As we sang "Amazing Grace," I placed Dave's urn under the rose bush.

All summer long the memorial garden was an oasis where I could remember the children. Peace slowly seeped into my soul as I sat on the bench, breathing in the beauty. Zinnias bobbed cheerfully in the breeze as bright blooms contrasted against spikes of blue salvia.

One quiet morning, as early sun made dewy diamonds on deep-hued flowers, I caught my breath in wonder. Here was holy ground. A touch of heaven, the garden spoke to me of eternal life, and this was just a fore-taste. *My children are embraced by God's love in a place too beautiful for words*, I thought. *Thank you, thank you, Lord.*

PART IV

LIFE AFTER LOSS

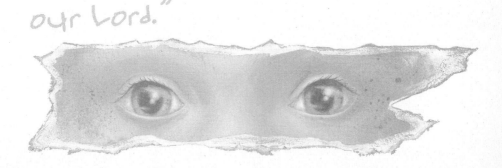

THIRTY-TWO
MIRIAM

It had been nearly four years since David's death. What impact did the loss of three siblings have on Miriam, Rick, and Cathy, the survivors? How had living with Batten Disease shaped their lives—and mine too? It was a Pandora's box that I was afraid to open, yet I knew there was much to learn from my three adult children.

When I'd packed for our spring vacation at Litchfield Beach, South Carolina, I included a small tape recorder, hoping for an interview with my two daughters. Now was my chance with Miriam since Cathy had taken the children swimming.

Eyes clouded, Miriam handed me the manuscript. "Wow, that was tough, Ma, reading Dave's story," she sighed. "It stirred up memories. Let's go ahead and get it over with!" In the master bedroom, my oldest daughter sat propped up by pillows on a king-sized bed. In her forties, she looked vulnerable with tilted nose, wet eyelashes, and tousled blond hair.

Outside the surf broke rhythmically along the beach. Cry of seagulls and a salty breeze swept in through an open window. Sunlight on the ocean painted a scene of tranquility.

Inside, uneasiness hung between my oldest daughter and me. What murky waters would be stirred by my questions? Apart from my perspective, each of my adult children had uniquely experienced the lives and deaths of their siblings. I switched on the tape as Miriam began:

"My heart feels heavy just to look at the lives of my loved ones, especially Dave's. There is also lingering pain from the separation and divorce, but mostly I see goodness. I'm thankful for my mother who helped shape my belief that bitterness is not an answer to anything, and I admire my risk-taking, fun-loving father who encouraged family adventures in the places he took us. Savoring life to the fullest in spite of Batten Disease is what I learned from Dad.

But there is a dark side. I recall in those early childhood memories that I didn't do well with Karen. Sometimes, I hated to go out and play with her. Not wanting to be seen, I'd watch her out the window, all by herself. I'd feel sad.

As a seven-year-old, I shared with my best friend the secret of Karen's impending death. I felt so guilty for telling that I thought I might go straight to Hell. In my struggle with guilt, I made a serious attempt to work it through with Bible reading.

Sometimes, I felt mean toward Karen. My feelings of anger turned inward. Since I couldn't blame God or be perfect, there were hateful emotions inside toward who knows what. Yet I knew I was my mother's right-hand person, a role I both loved and hated. I'd come up with little chores my sister could do, like peeling carrots in the kitchen, and I'd play along with her 'Miss Manners' thing. She kept reminding us to say 'please' and 'thank you. '

Living with Batten siblings definitely impacted my faith. As a young adult, I experienced a different side of God, an impersonal hands-off Creator who is expressed in nature and in the goodness I saw in others. I didn't believe in a God who pulls strings or who was in charge of people's lives. Now, my belief is less Judeo-Christian, so that I won't have to blame God for losing my brothers and sister. Still, I respect the redeeming theme in my family's faith, so going to church has meaning for me.

The burden of being a survivor has been heavy upon me. My parents expected me to excel. I'm the lucky one to live. I owed my dead sister in a way that made me want to achieve. Could I ever get my parents' approval?

We [unaffected] children were raised with serious inner neglect. I felt like an after-thought, growing up feeling very alone. There was one adult who nurtured me as a person. My third grade teacher, Miss Young, chose me as a student to play tennis with her and have dinner. More caring people are needed to reach out like this.

I felt left out of the family—not cherished. It's a huge hurt that you don't ever get over, but when I cracked, my parents were there for me. Maybe, I was born with a depressive personality. I hate feeling sorry for myself.

There is pain but also valuable lessons learned. My love for God's creation was healing when I took a year off from college to learn landscaping and horticulture in New Hampshire. After hearing of the stress with David and Jon, I came home. I then finished a degree in elementary and special education.

While Jon was in the infirmary in Geneseo, I worked on a course project making screw things and items to sort. He taught me not to focus on limitations but to build on what's there.

Dave responded to my love and concern when Joey, my husband, and I lived in Geneseo. My brother usually spent one night a week with us. Joey felt a closeness to him, building a tree fort and hoisting up a woodstove. Later, we put together an Indian sweathouse, complete with fire and rocks. I can still smell the eucalyptus leaves burning.

"Caring for Jon and Dave helped prepare me for being a mother. When Liz and I go to church, I feel my daughter's little fingers just as I did my brother's. She loves trips—the animals, sights, and sounds. Sometimes, I feel David's spirit is right there. Liz has a sensitive understanding of handicapped kids. Next to her in school is an ADD [Attention Deficit Disorder] student whom she likes to help. She knows people's brains aren't all the same.

Ultimately, I've learned to truly appreciate my physical being because it's important to me to maintain my health. I'm learning to accept limitations in life and make the best of it. I have my flaws just as real as my Batten siblings. They weren't crushed by their reality, and neither will I be stunted by what life's dealt me. Grab each day and savor the moment!"

• • • • • • • • • • • • • •

Miriam enjoys country living in a gracious old farmhouse near Geneseo with her husband Mike and daughter Liz. Life abounds on the farm with a donkey, a horse, Alex the dog, cats, and a few heifers. Flowers, cropping up in nooks and crannies, brighten the front porch. Mim is an elementary special education teacher for children with learning disabilities.

THIRTY-THREE
RICK

May 7, 2000, had been an evening of celebration. From the kitchen, Mary carried in an angel food cake, resplendent in swirls of Cool Whip and topped with ripe red strawberries. Seven glowing candles, one for each decade, reminded me that time was precious. As "Happy Birthday to You" rang out, each face around the table was kindled with inner light. "We love you, Gram!" Yes, I was grateful for the gift of three grandchildren, Jake, Rose, and Peachy Castor. Affection came naturally, nurtured by loving parents.

Now, I shut my bedroom door and turned to Rick who was comfortably sprawled out on my big four poster. "Are you ready for this?" I asked, handing him the tape recorder.

"Mim warned me your questions were tough," Rick replied, "but I'm willing to help." My son, at forty-one, was physically fit from his work outdoors building houses and from weekly tennis matches. Blond hair, alert blue eyes, and a ready chuckle, Rick's rugged good looks warmed my mother's heart. He settled back in the pillows and relaxed.

"No snoozing!" I ordered. "The tape is running." Rick then shared:

"After extreme adversity, our family tried to see the good in things. Since I was spared, I am full of gratitude for my sight. Growing up with siblings dying around me, I adopted the role of class clown. Humor is important. You've gotta keep laughing. There is so much great about life that I naturally identify with the positive.

I don't put energy into worrying about things I can't control. I refuse to get uptight over trivial happenings that go wrong. I know what it's like to suffer great loss. I've always been the peacemaker by making people happy. Humor is a big part of my philosophy. Especially at work, I try to be aware of how people feel and cheer them up.

Life was difficult for me during those teenage years. I sometimes felt embarrassed to have a blind brother, afraid that if I took him out he'd have a seizure in the wrong place. In Elba, I didn't want him with me at the Onion Festival. Back then, I didn't like constrictions on my schedule.

Skiing was different, though. I liked skiing with Jon. He was tough. When he took a bad spill, he'd yell, 'Ooo, Ow, Ooo, Ow!' and get over it. I didn't worry. I learned from J.P.'s persistence and loyalty. He was stubborn. 'You don't try, you do!' was his motto. His courage in wrestling and his appreciation for life meant a lot to me.

Gerald, his big black roommate, was one of my favorite people. He had a huge place in his heart for his weaker friend. At two hundred fifty pounds, Gerald looked like a professional football player. He'd roll around the floor with J.P. and teach him moves. Occasionally, the three of us would imbibe a few beers like normal rebellious teenagers.

When Jon gave me one hundred dollars monthly support while I was at Highland Christian Mission in New Guinea, I had a new understanding of his generosity and commitment to me. Returning home, I had a real desire to spend time with Jon. Even though conversation was limited, we could always communicate in his room at the infirmary.

Dave was more of a rock and roller. As the disease developed, he was tormented by what he could see of his future. He wanted to be free like his brother Rick. Dave and I shared party times at Joey and Mim's apartment, rebellious teenage acts (our secret) that made him feel normal.

I respect my brother for coming to terms with the disease. No matter how bleak and angry he was, he took time to listen to the Bible tapes. Because he made an effort to open himself, the power of the Holy Spirit was able to reach him.

Overwhelming sadness was prevalent for me throughout the rest of his life. When we first discovered Dave had Batten Disease, I was heartbroken. I felt such a loss of potential. Quite a physical specimen my brother was! Sometimes, I wonder what it would be like to have Dave working beside me, helping me build an addition.

As for my own faith, there was never a time when I shook my fist at God. Seeing how the Lord can work in even the direst circumstances has strengthened my relationship with Him.

There's a memory that dates all the way back to when I was eight and Karen had died. The empty bed. The finality of death. At each loss, that memory returned. I couldn't sniff my sister or Jon or Dave anymore.

I like the way our family handled death—the sharing of memories around Dave's bed; cremation instead of an open casket; and being with people who cared beforehand. I loved the informality of the memorial service.

With Young Dave, I experienced emotional burnout. I didn't allow myself to get too close as he came toward the end. At that time, I concentrated on fathering my own children. Mary and I have a good solid relationship. My family is a source of satisfaction and joy for me. I'm very thankful for their health, though I don't know what's around the bend.

I'm in the process of putting a huge addition on our house which is situated beside a beautiful bubbling creek. Fifteen hundred extra feet will tie the upstairs of the barn into the rest of the place. I can let a project consume me. Rose came down early one Sunday morning and saw me taping drywall like mad. 'Dad, are you going to church?' she asked.

I hesitated.

'Do you think you should go to church? Well, I want you to go to church.' Her final statement settled the matter.

'Rose, I'm going to church,' I replied, definitely influenced by my daughter. The kids are a grounding force for me. I understand God's love now that I have children. Jesus compares His love to the Father's for the Son. He would never throw us out.

But there is still unresolved grief, so hurtful that I push it away. The Batten conference in Orlando in 1996 made me come face-to-face with it. The workshops helped me deal with the awful losses. Dr. Dick, my counselor, once said to me, 'You would be a completely different person if one of your brothers had survived.' Oh, how I wish one of them had!

Each one of us survivors has our own weird, debilitating, secret ways to escape the pain. An overwhelming wave of grief sits right over our shoulders. We never know when it will break. I just think that we all carry the weight of half our family being obliterated. Yes, there's eternal life in Christ, but there's the ugliness of seeing three we love wiped out by this disease. How it affects us is more significant than we realize. It continues to come out with time.

Living in the shadow of Batten Disease makes being a dad more valuable. When I ski with Jake, I see him jump into the woods to take a leak and jump out again. I see him ski the bumps and tackle a black diamond slope. Memories and present blessings mingle—of my courageous dead brothers and of my daring lively son."

• • • • • • • • • • • • • • • •

Rick has been a self-employed builder for sixteen years. He and Mary enjoy their spacious home, surrounded by woods, and are active in the local United Methodist Church.

THIRTY-FOUR
CATHY

"So, Cathy! I can't believe this interview is actually going to happen!" I teased. I'd been ready to pounce for nearly a year with recorder and notebook in hand.

"Not now, Mom. I can't handle your questions," Cathy would put me off. On July 2, 2001, my youngest daughter, looking slightly irritated, admitted defeat. "Now that your book is ready to be published, I'll cooperate." She leaned back against the pillows on my bed and sighed. "Just take it easy on me, Mom."

A swoop of blond hair shadowed her eyes. Golden tan from gardening and swimming, Cathy in bib shorts looked years younger than her age of thirty-nine. I knew feelings were near the surface. "You're a professional artist, Cathy," I had chosen a safe topic. "How did that all come to be?" Cathy's face softened as she looked back. The tape was running. She took a crunchy bite of the long knobby carrot she was holding and began talking:

"God gave me a wonderful gift. Mom encouraged art lessons in Elba where I discovered I was an expert copier. My sculptured clay dog was really good.

I remember sitting at the kitchen table with my sister Mim as she taught me how to do calligraphy. In Blue Mountain style, I painted watercolor scenes with a calligraphied poem or saying. During the separation in 1974, art was a way of getting out my feelings. I made a friendship book, expressing my emotions through painting and verse, for my best friend, Mary Ellen.

Receiving a fractür* for a wedding present sent my life in a new direction. Folk art in watercolor along with calligraphy...Wow! I fell right into

* Note: When the Germans came to Pennsylvania, fractür was a beautiful way for them to record important family events, such as births, baptisms, and weddings. Today the art is reviving, using traditional Pennsylvania German designs and colors. Fractür still celebrates family history.

it! It was a big thing to create fractürs and see it become my vocation. Such a great way to express my love with gifts of fractürs to Mom and Dad in memory of Karen, Jon, and David."

(Now, Cathy was looking at the framed originals.)

"I painted Karen's with touches of lavender. Jon's has tiny pictures of a fort with a gangplank drawn in the corner. I have memories of being trapped in there. In another corner is 'Amazing Grace' with musical notes. Jon used to bellow, 'Who saved a wretch like you!' I see Gerald's black face and, in the last corner, a Bible. Reading the Bible to J.P. made an impression on me. It brought out a tender Christian spirit in both of us. A huge comfort it was to hear those verses in John 14.2: 'In my Father's house are many rooms. I am going to prepare a place for you.' (NIV)

From Jon, I learned how to smile in the face of adversity. I liked his strength. He was stubborn and spunky. I learned to forgive myself and lean on others when I'd rather not. There are certain things about Jon I'll never forget like the feel of his thick brown hair and the smell of his skin. He let us in to take care of him, to smooch him, to touch him, and to love him.

It was a huge blow when Jon went to the infirmary—like a horrible letting go. I wanted to be there, to visit him. It was a new part of our relationship, just to love him without the responsibility. Singing and playing ball—we were close. Because of caring for my brother, I feel compassion for the handicapped. I have seen the other side of life and know what a gift health is.

On Dave's fractür, I painted in the corners a Buffalo Bills helmet, a grizzly bear, a cross with a lamb, and a cap with musical notes. We've still got the Bills blanket in my son Chris' room, but my memories of David go back to when he was a small guy in Webster. Sometimes, I dressed him up as my little sister. A spoiled brat at times, he'd have temper tantrums. His big blue eyes and soft blond hair made him look innocent, kind of angelic. I enjoyed doing artistic stuff with him at Agawam. When he could still see, we went exploring.

That year of separation in Webster, all my innocence disappeared. My security came tumbling down when I learned about the hurt between Mom and Dad and the reality of Jon's and Dave's disease. One thing I discovered, though, was that God is real. I got into the habit of reading my Bible.

I needed strength beyond myself because things felt haphazard at home. I was lonely in a big family, aware of lostness. I wished I could count on being read to, but mostly, this only happened when I was sick. In the big huge Elba house, I felt lost like I did on the inside!

As the mother of three kids, I have had to take an honest look at what shaped me. I needed to stop blaming myself for everything. What didn't I have control over? What was missing? How was I mothered? Fathered?

Through counseling, I began to understand that my mother was only able to do so much. And my dad? He was gone a lot. I didn't like that I was allowed to hang out with kids who were smoking and shoplifting at a very young age. It was not because I wanted to be bad. I know I had a decent heart, but I wanted a thrill, a way of escape. There was not enough direction given at home.

A bigger factor than Batten's in our family was my parents not being a strong loving unit. This was more of a force than three sick siblings in shaping me. My counselor asked, 'What would you like to give to the little girl inside of you?'

I answered, 'Two parents who really loved each other.' Out of that good things flow. It's a core of protection for the children.

Knowing that my siblings were dying shook up my insides. I didn't know what I could count on. Would my mother get cancer and die? I was fearful of losing her. Even with my own children, there's a lingering dread that they won't make it into adulthood.

As for my personal faith, my biggest question was, 'Why does God allow innocent kids to suffer?' Especially for Dave, it was the worst kind of pain he could go through. His inner torment was sheer anguish. If that's the way God shapes us for Heaven, I just didn't understand.

I wonder about horrible suffering being part of the Christian walk. Is this what we need to come to Him? If God loves His babies, His creation, it seems like a sick goodness. I would never want my own children to suffer, so why does God allow it for His children?

It's hard for me to trust God. I associated goodness with suffering, and I ran from it. Going His way felt too hard for me. One foot in the Christian arena is fine, but I wanted to keep control. The high road looked like a road of pain. My mother's journey is a picture of what I'm afraid of.

With my brothers, I could see the difference trust in God made in their lives. Jon surely could see with eyes of faith. With David, I had glimmers of how hard it was for him. When he listened to those Bible tapes, I could see the difference—the peace.

Counseling has helped me face the loss of my Batten siblings—just pouring out grief for each kid. Lots of tears for Karen, even though I didn't know her as well. To hear that the family gathered around David's bed as he was dying, and I wasn't there. It broke my heart. I was too wrapped up in my own problems.

Thinking back, I was always feeling guilty about something. Maybe, I was born guilty. I carried the weight of each kid like some sort of burden. When people ask me how many children are in my birth family, do I say three or six? There's a story to tell, and I don't always want to tell it.

Joni Eareckson Tada has helped me look beyond this life to a glimpse of heaven. My faith is in process. I respect Joni's vision and my mother's, and I have hope in what God has for us.

Counseling has also helped me understand the pieces in the puzzle of my life: three siblings who died of Batten Disease; a mother and dad who were not a loving unit; and three of us siblings who are still hurting. What's the way to wholeness?

It's breaking the cycle of looking for comfort and peace through escape. It's coming to acceptance of the way it was. I'll never have a healthy background. I'll never get rid of the person I was. In counseling, I've traveled through the grief process. I'm longing for birth into freedom and acceptance. I'm on a journey with the Lord God. I give myself over to God constantly. I'm trying not to feel guilty for failure along the way. I'm slowly coming to realize that God is not looking at me the way I look at myself. Jesus died for me; He loves me. I see myself wrapped in a blanket of forgiveness. These facts are the foundation I am slowly building upon. In reality, this is who I am.

What my life will turn into is totally God's thing. I want to live as a forgiven person, not in bondage to the past. So, it's a real basic relationship. It's not a big devotional life. I can't do it, but I have a real on-going conversation with the Lord. It's kind of self-centered, a rebuilding of my inner self so that I can care for other people. There's sadness that I can't give more spiritually to my kids right now. If you don't have it, you can't give it. I hope as I get stronger I'll have more to offer them.

My deepest desire is that I will not be afraid of God. I want to experience God with me. I'm still tentative about being a Christian. I don't want to be some cookie cutter Christian that I see as phony. I want to find Him on my own and have a genuine relationship with Christ, and I'd like to see evidence of His working in the lives of the people I love.

What's good about my life is that there's a spirit of total love and acceptance from my mother. And vice versa. This closeness is uncommon, a great gift to both of us. It evolved in my adulthood after the birth of Josh. I began to understand what it means to be a mother.

There's another joy in my life—the gift of creativity. Through my gardens, hand-hooked rugs, and fractürs, I see a reflection of God. In our one-hundred-seventy-year-old house, things are beat-up and used. Oldness says family and warmth—people have been here. There's Castor history in the antiques. The hand-crafted atmosphere speaks 'Welcome.' I love having my work around. It's a place of hospitality. Taking time to be close to people is really worth it.

Mark, my husband, has put a whole lot into making our home what it is. He's dependable, loyal, handsome, and fun. There's stability in his conservative Christian faith. We are always able to talk spiritually, and we really like being together.

Joy and fear are part of being parents to our kids, praying they'll turn out fine. They are a huge gift—Josh, Chris, and Caitlyn. I just look at them and am amazed I'm a mother when part of me sometimes feels that I'm still a little kid. I look at each individual child and love him and her to pieces."

• • • • • • • • • • • • • •

Cathy lives with her family in Pennsylvania in an old brick farmhouse with a porch and barn and surrounded by maple trees. There are flowers on the patio, fresh veggies in the garden, and kids bouncing on the trampoline. The Country Scribe sign hangs in front of the fractür house, formerly the garage that Mark remodeled.

THIRTY-FIVE
CONNIE

It began as an urge to escape. Around the first of August 2001, I had been sitting in my office, writing a list of "must do's"—organize a small group picnic, a membership prep class, recruit new Sunday School teachers, and on and on. Coming at me from all directions was an attack of the "shoulds." On staff at Centenary United Methodist Church as assistant to the pastor, I felt my stomach clenching and my heart pounding. Ten loose ends dangled on my list. Who was I to tackle such a challenge?

Turning to Mark's gospel, I found a word from Jesus spoken to his disciples under stress. "Then because so many people were coming and going that they did not even have a chance to eat, He said to them, 'Come with Me by yourselves to a quiet place and get some rest.'" (Mark 6.37, NIV)

That one sentence gave me a glimpse beyond the urgent to still waters and a crackling campfire. Oh, yes! It was time for my annual retreat to one of my favorite campgrounds.

As I packed for Cowanesque two weeks later, each piece of equipment fit snugly into the back of my Escort wagon—even the portapotty! "I love getting ready," I thought as I stuffed a bulging dufflebag of bedding into the last pocket of space.

Later, during the middle of the night, fingers of doubt pried at my spirit. *What are you doing, Connie Jackson? You're seventy-one years old and going off by yourself. Won't you be afraid?*

My gut contracted. The prying fingers reached deeper. *You know you'll have to deal with the hurts your children expressed in their interviews. You were right in the middle. Are you ready?*

A low blow, but it was the truth. I cried out to God, "Oh, Lord, I can't do this alone!"

"Come with Me to a quiet place and get some rest," I re-read Jesus' words in Mark 6. Peace settled over me. My Friend would be going with me, and He had included "rest" in the invitation.

By water's edge the next morning, I unfolded the big Eureka tent. With every clank of poles and pounding of stakes into the rocky ground, I felt in my bones the heritage of camping. Thoughts came of my father, a little boy at Stoney Point, Long Island conference grounds in an army tent with his family and Mama and me lugging down from the attic piles of gear which Papa packed in a trailer. I recalled Steve and me as young parents at Racquette Lake in the Adirondacks, setting up my folks' old Hedroom tent for our brood. Now, here I was, carrying on the tradition, solo. "Okay, Lord. It's You and me—thank you for this beautiful campsite."

The evening supper smelled delicious. String beans boiled in the old camp pot, and the skillet with half a handle sizzled with home fries and chicken. In the screenhouse, light shimmered, reflecting from the lake. With a hiss from the Coleman stove and a cozy table setting, I felt at home.

That night I wrote in my journal: "Right now, I'm sitting close to a snapping campfire, breathing in the aroma of wood smoke. The lantern warms my face as I sit at the picnic table and write. I hear waves musically lapping along the shore and the cry of a hawk taking its last dive for fish. Over the hills, a bright moon rises, painting a path of silver on the lake— my soul is at peace."

In the middle of the night, my aging bladder and something scratching in the screenhouse roused me from sleep. Probably a skunk, the nocturnal scavenger of Cowanesque. "Just leave it be, and there'll be no trouble," the campstore lady had warned me. As I sat on the portapotty looking out my screened door, a fish leaped high and then smacked the water. Ripples in a widening circle glistened in moonlight. An owl's "whoo, whoo" and cicadas' chorus filled the air.

Wide awake, I plumped my pillows, leaned back in my comfortable cot and beamed a flashlight on my Bible, Psalm 63.6-8:

> "On my bed I remember you,
> I think of you through the watches of the night.
> Because you are my help,

I *sing in the shadow of your wings.*
My soul clings to you;
your right hand upholds me."(NIV)

The moon was partially hidden by a small cloud edged in light. Beauty broke over my spirit. *How can this be, God? Your artistry just for me!* I felt at one with the ancient psalmist. Praise rose from my innermost being as gratitude brought tears of joy.

The next morning as I settled down to write at the card table in my tent, distant rumbling signaled an impending storm. I zipped closed the windows and covered the camp kitchen with tarps. Suddenly, a loud clap of thunder and swoosh of wind left me vulnerable. Rain pelted against the canvas roof. Lightning streaked across a leaden sky. I donned a slicker, grabbed my writing pad, and in a lull between flashes, dashed for the car. Once safely inside, I watched the fury of the storm.

Out of scudding mists and angry waves, I heard the putt-putt of a motorboat. At the helm was a dad who'd been fishing with his boys. He safely docked and then gathered his sons close. Later, when skies were clearing, I heard Brad, the oldest exclaim, "Wow, Dad! I thought we were goners! That storm was scary!"

A picture came to mind of my struggling children. Batten Disease was like a tidal wave, battering all of us. Add to that a disintegrating marriage. Each of us was thrown out of the assumed safe haven of a healthy family. But who was there to protect Miriam, Rick, and Cathy?

Barbara Rosof, in *The Worst Loss*, explains it well: "When a child dies, parents and siblings are stricken at once with the same grief. Although the fantasy is that they will cling to each other and comfort each other, what happens is often sadly different."

Rosof continues from a bereft mother's viewpoint: "Elaine…sees herself alone on a tiny life raft. She can see her husband and her children, each on their own rafts, battered by the same storm. But she is so close to sinking herself that she must focus all her energy on staying afloat…Parents are so overwhelmed by their own grief that they cannot comfort their children or help them grieve. In such situations the surviving children suffer a second loss. Not only has a sibling died, but they have lost their own connection with their parents."[22]

Several of my children spoke in their interviews of feeling lost, left out, lonely, and without direction. Enormous interior questions, particularly for Miriam and Cathy, remained unanswered. Guilt, anger, and grief burrowed underground only to emerge later.

Hardest for me to face was the yearning the little girls felt for consistent reading-aloud time. To snuggle close to Mom or Dad and to hear a familiar story—it's such a simple bond of comfort, but it was pushed aside without much thought.

Yes, Batten Disease complicated mothering. I recall how acute my grief was at the time of diagnosis and how, to stay afloat, I withdrew from family and friends. In desperation, I turned to God. But what about my healthy children who were silently struggling with dark feelings? Who was there to help them vent their emotions?

I remember when I was nine my brother's best friend Lloyd was killed after jumping off a moving railroad car. I walked with my mother into the family's living room where he lay surrounded by flowers in a white coffin. I gazed in shock at the still pale form. Mama hugged Mrs. Swanson. Hushed weeping and murmured words of sympathy clashed with the lively funny kid Lloyd had been. I wanted to scream, "It's not true. You're just sleeping. Wake up, you daredevil!"

"Where is he, Mama?" I asked on the way home.

"In Heaven, honey. He's with Jesus."

For the first time, I understood that I was not immortal. A kid could die.

Up the stairs to the third floor of the parsonage, I trudged to my attic room. Mother tucked me in, and we prayed "Jesus Tender Shepherd" together. I lay shivering in the dark, afraid that I might die, too. For weeks, I tried to stay awake to fight off death if it came to get me in my lonely room. Never once did I tell my parents how scared I was. Eventually, I asked to move in with Marti, whose snoring assured me that she was still breathing.

Oh, how I wish I had been aware of my own children's silent struggles and that I had gently opened the door to listen and care! A beautiful gift to me now is my daughters' forgiveness. I know God forgives me, too.

• • • • • • • • • • • • • • • •

On the third morning of my camping excursion, acorns and hickory nuts bouncing on the roof served as an alarm clock. Two squirrels chattered gleefully as they pelted my tent. Outside, early sun slanted soft rays across a misty lake. Silently, a lone kayak cut through still water, young arms paddling in perfect cadence.

I pulled on grubby denim shorts and headed for the woods. Fragrance of new mown grass along the path, diamonds sparkling on wet pine branches, a cardinal's whistle, and the squawk of a surprised blue heron flapping its big wings—all sang the Creator's praise: "This is my Father's world. All nature sings while 'round me rings the music of the spheres."[23]

Today would be for reading. Settling into a lounge chair on a pebbled beach, I opened Philip Yancey's book *Reaching for the Invisible God* that I had borrowed from my pastor. Out fluttered a note: "Dear Connie, may He who began a good work in you complete it until the day of Jesus Christ…Have a spirit-renewing time apart and listen to the Lord—Jeff." I could almost hear him blessing my get-away.

What did Yancey have to say about suffering? Succinctly he stated, "The world is good, the world is fallen, the world can be redeemed."[24] Into the warp and woof of life's texture is woven sickness, misery, greed, and hatred. My family's slice of pain was Batten Dsease. That's the "fallen" element, not what God originally intended.

Ah, but the world is also interlaced with strands of love. Always behind the scenes God works for the good of those who are open to His grace. With bodies and minds decimated by Batten Disease, Karen, Jon, and David still held onto their faith that Jesus loved them. He sent earth angels who worked with their potential to the very end.

As I was completing this final chapter, I asked myself a question: "Connie, why did you write this book? At times you wanted to quit. How come you stuck with it?" Why? Because I wanted to recount the ways God's grace has redeemed tragedy. To see and share the big picture in hopes that my children, all six of them, will make a difference in the lives of others.

Reading and thinking as I sat by the lakeside that day, I was grateful for the means of grace that had guided me along the way. Four A.M. quiet times, early morning walks, scripture, prayer, worship, meaningful work, inspired authors, small group fellowship, and caring friends—all had brought me close to the Source. C. S. Lewis explains it well: "If you want to get warm you must stand near the fire; if you want to get wet you get into the water. If you want joy, power, peace, eternal life, you must get close, or even into the thing that has them...If you are close to it, the spray will wet you; if you are not, you will remain dry."[25]

That evening, I rested in the lounge chair, soaking in the afterglow of sunset. A tentacle of fear briefly diverted my attention. *Remember the list*, it asked. *The one with ten dangling 'shoulds'?*

"Be gone!" I commanded. "Right now, there's the sunset." The lake mirrored bright peach and mauve clouds. The flipping fish jumped high for a moth. Wood smoke drifted down from a neighboring campsite. I breathed a prayer of thanks.

The next morning, I awoke from a dream with an unusual sense of well-being. Vividly, the details came back to mind. I was meandering along a wooded path, trying to get my bearings. Where was I headed? I felt like a lost child.

As I walked, I sensed Someone directly behind me. Coming from this person was an aura of tender strength and unconditional acceptance. Its essence blanketed me with peace. With a sense of relief, I leaned back and allowed myself to be carried.

Beckoned by a ringing church bell in the midst of the forest, we came to a small brown chapel. The Presence set me down, gently took my hand, and we walked into the sanctuary. On the altar was a luminous white cross, surrounded by flickering candles.

It was holy ground.

Dare I turn to look up into the face of the One beside me? Yes! I was irresistibly drawn to those piercing eyes. I remember no other features but those eyes sparkling with joy and compassion, eyes that said, "I love you just the way you are. I've been with you all the time."

Even so, come, Lord Jesus.

FACTS ABOUT BATTEN DISEASE

Batten Disease was first described in 1826, more than 170 years ago, by a British pediatrician. Its scientific name is neuronal ceroid lipofuscinosis, and it is one of the more common neurodegenerative diseases.

There are four major forms of Batten Disease, defined by age of onset and severity of symptoms. (See chart below.)

TYPE	AGE OF ONSET	SYMPTOMS	LIFE EXPECTANCY
Infantile (Santavouri-Haltia)	6 mos. - 2 years	Seizures, blindness, and rapid mental and physical decline	5 - 10 years
Late infantile (Jansky-Bielschowsky)	2 - 4 years	Same	8 - 12 years
Juvenile (Batten-Spielmeyer-Vogt)	5 - 10 years	Blindness, seizures, dementia, ataxia, spasticity, loss of motor skills	Late teens - early 20s
Adult	Usually before 40	No blindness. Milder, slower mental and physical decline	Varies

Batten Disease is rarely diagnosed immediately. It is often mistaken for epilepsy, mental retardation, even schizophrenia in adults. An ophthalmologist can observe pathological changes in the retina. This often provides one of the first diagnostic clues. Often it begins with deteriorating vision and seizures, personality and behavior changes, and always progresses through mental and physical deterioration to death.

Batten Disease is an inherited disease. It often strikes more than one person in a family that carries the mutated/defective gene. A person must have two such defective genes (one from each parent) in order to develop Batten Disease. A person with only one such gene will not develop the disease but is a carrier. If two such carriers have children together, there is a 25% chance that both will pass the mutated gene on to a child, who, therefore, would develop the disease.

Carrier testing is available for some forms of Batten Disease. Siblings of children with Batten Disease, their partners, and others may wish to participate in this testing when planning their families.

THE ORGANIZATION

The Batten Disease Support and Research Association (BDSRA) is an international non-profit organization created to provide information and support, as well as to further research to fight and eventually eliminate Batten Disease. It is the only support organization in Canada, the United States, and Australia specific to Batten Disease.

Individual and corporate contributions provide the funding for BDSRA's family-centered support and research programs.

THE RESEARCH

The major questions remain unanswered. However, research is ongoing worldwide. BDSRA provides research support in three ways:

1. seed money funding for research projects,
2. family participation in research by providing information and biological samples,
3. participation in the National Batten Disease Registry.

Researchers continue their search to isolate the exact genetic defect in Batten Disease. Potential treatments may then be developed.

Facts about Batten Disease used by permission.
A portion of the proceeds from the sale of this book will be donated to
the Batten Disease Support and Research Association.
For more information, contact:
Batten Disease Support and Research Association (BDSRA)
120 Humphries Drive, Suite 2
Reynoldsburg, OH 43063
Phone 1-800-448-4570
World Wide Web: http://www.bdsra.org (Provided by Virtual City Visions)
E mail: bdsra1@bdsra.org

NOTES

1.   Roz Rinker, *Prayer Conversing with God* (Grand Rapids, MI: Zondervan, 1959).

2.   Agnes Sanford, *The Healing Light* (New York: Ballantine Books, 1947) 19.

3.   Ibid, 27.

4.   Katherine Kuhlman, I *Believe in Miracles* (Parasmus, New Jersey: Prentice-Hall, Inc., 1963).

5.   Sanford, *The Healing Light*, 25.

6.   Catherine Marshall, *Beyond Ourselves* (New York: Avon Books, 1968) 46.

7.   Ibid, 46.

8.   Christina Rosseti, "In the Bleak Midwinter" *The Methodist Hymnal* (Nashville, Tennessee: The United Methodist Publishing House, 1966).

9.   *Living Light: Daily Light in Today's Language* (Wheaton, IL: Tyndale House Publishers, 1973).

10. Merlin R. Carothers, *The Power in Praise* (Escondido, CA: Merlin R. Carothers, 1980).

11. The Who, *Rock Opera Tommy* (New York: Music Theatre International, 1996), audiocassette.

12. Ibid.

13. Joseph Mohr, "Silent Night, Holy Night" *The Methodist Hymnal*, 1966.

14. Ibid.

15. C.S. Lewis, *The Business of Heaven* (San Diego, California: Harcourt Brace and Company, 1984).

16. Emily Dickinson, *The Collected Poems of Emily Dickinson* (New York: Barnes and Noble Books, 1993) 226.

17. Henri J.M. Nouwen, *Out of Solitude* (Notre Dame, Indiana: Ave Maria Press, 1974) 22.

18. Gerald Jampolsky, *Love is Letting Go of Fear* (Berkeley, CA: Celestial Arts, 1979).

19. A.W. Tozer, *Pursuit of God* (Camp Hill, PA: Christian Publications, Inc., 1948) 13–14.

20. John Newton, "Amazing Grace" *The Methodist Hymnal*, 1966.

21. Ernest Christopher Dowson, "Extreme Unction" eds. Frank Kermode and John Hollander, Vol. 2 of *Oxford Anthology of English Literature* (New York: Oxford University Press, 1973).

22. Barbara Rosof, *The Worst Loss: How Families Heal from the Death of a Child* (New York: Henry Holt and Co., LLC, 1994) 35–36.

23. Maltbie D. Babcock, "This is My Father's World" *The Methodist Hymnal*, 1966.

24. Philip Yancey, *Reaching for the Invisible God* (Grand Rapids, MI: Zondervan Publishing House, 2000) 285.

25. C.S. Lewis, *Mere Christianity* (New York: The Macmillan Company, 1952) 153. *Mere Christianity* by C.S. Lewis copyright © C.S. Lewis Pte. Ltd. 1942, 1943, 1944, 1952. Extract reprinted by permission.